Jim Lee's Chinese Cookbook

Jim Lee's

HARPER & ROW, PUBLISHERS

NEW YORK, EVANSTON, AND LONDON

1817

Chinese
Cookbook

Illustrated by Isabella Lee

Contents

Foreword   vii

ONE: ESSENTIALS OF CHINESE COOKING

1   Planning a Chinese Meal   3

2   Cooking the Chinese Way—Methods and Utensils   7

3   Your Chinese Larder   23

4   Organizing Your Cooking   37

TWO: RECIPES

5   How to Use These Recipes   49

6   Vegetables   53

7   Pork   83

8   Beef   117

9   Chicken   143

10   Duck   181

11   Seafood   193

12   Soups in the Chinese Manner   251

13   Rice and Rice Dishes   267

14   Noodles and Noodle Dishes   287

15   Jim's A-Shame-to-Throw-Away Pages   317

     Appendix: Sources for Mail-Order Chinese Foodstuffs   329

     Index   331

Foreword

LIKE most authors who have never written a book before, I was sincerely overwhelmed with the great message I was to give the world. I began by thinking in lofty terms such as "The Philosophy and Art of Chinese Cuisine," or "The Effect of Chinese Cooking on Human History." The more I wrote the more sacred the subject became until finally my eyes shone with the gleam and fervor of El Greco's saint's in his painting "St. Francis in Ecstasy."

After much soul searching, and the deflating realization that I have no competence as a philosopher, sociologist, or historian, I decided on a much more modest aim. That aim is merely to be your guide in your kitchen when you need some help while you experiment with Chinese cooking. There is a standing joke between one of our friends and me. Whenever she is stuck with a cooking problem, she calls me on the phone and begins with the greeting "Mother, . . ." I can't give her all the answers. None of us mothers can. But I have been able to give her enough answers to make her a pretty good Chinese cook.

There are different ways of teaching cooking. One can give very specific instructions in each recipe, and have many recipes.

Then a student may just follow directions. The other approach is to use the old Chinese method, in which the mother taught her child by telling him *why* she did such and such. The Chinese bride did not have a cookbook to follow. The latter method is the one I intend to use in this cookbook. I believe a cookbook's basic function is to instruct and inform, and not be a mere compendium of recipes. It is my hope that if this book is successful the reader will understand how to cook Chinese food, not merely learn some new recipes.

Most of the recipes in this book are Cantonese, because I am too. Other regions of China produced fine cuisines also, and I've experimented with recipes from those areas. Invariably I am drawn back to Cantonese cooking, and I am now convinced it is not because of any native bias. Historically most Chinese gourmets agree that Cantonese cooking is the best. I remember reciting as a child in Chinese school a lesson in geography which began, "Chung Kwok yau saap butt shaang" (中國有十八省) ("China has eighteen provinces"). Then after the name of each province was given the attribute for which it was famous. Presumably if one was rich enough he could travel all the eighteen provinces of China and get the best of everything. One province had the best silk clothes because the mulberry leaves grew better there than anywhere else, so the silkworms produced the best cocoons. Another province produced the most beautiful women, so one should go there to marry. One province had the best scenery; and so on. At last, when one was old, he should go to the province which grew a species of tree that was fragrant and water-resistant for a vehicle to be used to travel to his ancestors. Ah-h-h, but if one *really* wants to eat well— Sik joy Kwong Chau! "Eat in Canton Province." (食在廣州)

Writing a cookbook is hard work, I discovered. Unlike a novel, where the writer's flight of fancy is enough to carry a reader into joyful realms, a recipe has to be tested and retested many times. So, in addition to writer's cramp, I now have dishpan hands.

But I should not give the impression that I labored alone. It is not possible in the present stage of human development to be completely independent of others. I owe many great debts.

For me, there are two kinds of debts a person can incur. One kind is the material one, which can be seen and touched. It may be as small as a cup of sugar, or as large an amount of money as you can borrow. This has to be paid as soon as possible, so that your own good self-image and personal dignity will not be crushed by it.

The other kind of debt is a spiritual one. It is the one that spurs man to be better than he is, and somehow drives him to go beyond the call of need and duty. One should wear this kind of debt as a suit of shining armor. It can never be fully repaid, but you wish that it could be, with such compounded interest that it would be beyond the wealth of Midas.

I used to envy people who say, "I don't owe anyone anything!" Now I only feel great pity for those people because they've cut themselves off from the world and human society. How lonely they must be! As I worked on this book, there were wonderful debts to humanity, past and present, which spurred me and moved my hands to share with you the contents herein.

The list of those who helped to make this book possible is a long one. All are people who out of friendship and love spent precious hours typing, proofreading, kitchen testing, and correcting my recipes as well as my grammar. The following is a partial list of that valiant, loyal group, who think of friendship as something very special:

Bea Wardlow; Anna and her husband, Dr. Wong Y. Wai; my sister Betty; Professor Désiré Kauffmann; George Hornby: Elaine Klein; Herman Woo; Nita and Alex Minewski; Herma Briffault; Ed and Eileen Lawrence; Ida Schuman; Tanya Jacobi; and a man who writes to me regularly, and always signs his letters: "Your father, Gow S. Lee."

Then there are the following who went beyond the call of duty, on whom I would bestow a Nobel Prize if I could:

Mr. Lee Lum, who, out of love and debt to the same sources of humanity which we both value, spent some of his precious days off from an arduous job as head chef of my favorite Chinese restaurant to give me lessons and guidance even at the sacrifice of rare moments of leisure with his wife and two lovely daughters.

My wife, Isabella, who would rather do anything than cook. It was she who first made it possible (nay, imperative!) for me to learn cooking. She gladly tasted and evaluated each recipe I tried—and often the same one several times in one night. It was she who bore most of the weight in the creation of this book, and she has had to go on a strict diet ever since.

Lil Kaplan, whose wit is as fast as her typing, and whose compassion and strength I drew upon when mine flagged. It was she who did most of the typing and correction of this manuscript.

Genevieve Young, my editor, whom I loved and hated alternately for using her terrible swift editor's pen, which welded this book into a coherent whole.

I have not the words to express adequately my feeling to the above personages, so I must borrow from Shakespeare's *Henry V:* "We few, we happy few, we band of brothers [and sisters]" —to them my love and thanks.

JIM LEE

New York
July, 1968

PART ONE

Essentials
of Chinese Cooking

For instructions on how to use the recipes, see page 49.

The symbol † means that substitutions and variations are suggested at the end of the recipe.

Planning a Chinese Meal

I T has been said that a nation's cuisine is an expression of its culture, and reflects economic and social forces which shaped that culture. This is certainly true of Chinese cooking. The Chinese family puts all its food in one or several common dishes in the middle of the table, and each person just reaches over and picks up what he wants with his chopsticks. This simple act speaks of the poverty that has afflicted China through most of its four-thousand-year history as a nation. Its poverty made individual portions impractical since they are a luxury that the great majority of people could not afford. The greatness of a society is often revealed by how it handles adversity. The Chinese society used its poverty to weld a closer family life, where things are shared, and self-discipline is taught even at the dining table. At a meal, no one would think of taking more than his share, no matter how hungry he was, nor would he pick the choicest morsel for himself.

A Chinese meal may also tell us something about the Chinese character, and even some of its philosophy. The Chinese are great lovers of variety, and the food we cook often reflects this love of variety. When a family becomes affluent, or on special

3

occasions such as birthdays and holidays, the family does not simply make more of the same dish; instead, we increase the number of dishes. Essentially, variety is increased, not just quantity.

Variety in a Chinese meal means more than just different dishes. It also means a variety of contrast in taste, texture, and even size, shape, and color. There are five flavors which our taste buds can readily distinguish: salty, sweet, sour, acrid, and bitter. The Chinese call these the "five fragrances." Whenever possible, a good cook tries to include all these tastes in a meal. The Westerner may wonder why anyone would want to eat something that is bitter. Yet my father's favorite vegetable is the Chinese bitter melon. It is really bitter, too. It is something one has to actively learn to like, and some of our American friends have acquired a taste for it. As for texture, a Chinese gourmet would frown upon dishes where everything is soft and tender. This is why ingredients with diverse textures are always incorporated into a Chinese dish, and those items are put into the cooking pot at different times, so their inherent textures are kept to contrast with each other.

This idea of contrast is very dear to the Chinese. It applies not only to food, but to everything they do. There is even a symbol in the Chinese philosophy to describe and venerate this idea, which is called "Yin and Yang." The pictorial representa-

tion is a circle gracefully divided exactly in the middle by a swirling curve. One half of the circle is white, the other half black. This symbol tells us that life is a contrast between opposing forces (light and darkness); it is in constant motion as the swirl suggests. The circle denotes that although life is made of opposing forces there still are harmony and wholeness, because a circle has no beginning or ending.

Now we can begin to understand why Chinese cooking developed into what it is. It should also suggest principles for us to follow in preparing a Chinese meal. The cardinal point to remember is that there should be variety. If you plan several dishes use one of pork, one of beef, one of fowl or seafood. You should avoid making two beef dishes cooked by the same method (for example, stir-fried), even if the vegetables and other ingredients used in their preparation are different.

A good cook considers marketing to be one of the most important steps in the preparation of a meal. Be flexible enough to change your menu if need be. Don't spend hours chasing around, hunting for a special item for your dinner.

Take advantage of the seasonal vegetables that come to market, such as asparagus in the spring and certain squashes in the early fall that are wonderful. Most other vegetables— string beans, peas, peppers, tomatoes—are available all year. However, there is a seasonal time for *good* tomatoes, such as in the summer and fall when you can get those succulent, tart tomatoes rather than the hothouse ones available in the winter or spring.

There are a few other things we should know in planning a Chinese meal. Cooked rice is a central item in any meal. When we were all new to America, my father went to a big American banquet. I eagerly awaited his return to hear of his great adventure. He described every detail for me and said the food was very good. "But," he added, "the trouble with American food is that you soon get hungry after eating it." Thereupon, he went to the kitchen and ate some leftover Chinese food we had had for dinner. How many times I've heard the same sad tale about Chinese food from American friends! I have analyzed this mystery and have come to a fairly simple answer. Both complainants are right. Neither one ate the other's "filler" foods. My father did not eat the bread and potatoes; my American friends ate hardly any rice with their meal. Consequently, both were hungry shortly after eating. Rice is the mainstay of a Chinese meal, and most Chinese will eat one or two large bowls of it with each meal.

The individual recipes in this book are conceived for two fairly good eaters. As for how much to cook for how many people, the best bet is to plan your meals in a flexible manner. For four people, make a minimum of two dishes plus rice. Try out a recipe on your family and friends to see if you have made too much or too little. You will cook the right amount next time in the light of your own experience. For every addition of two people, add one more dish to your menu and increase the amount of dry rice by another cup.

Each person's capacity differs, and you must judge for yourself the needs of your family and friends. If you invited your friends the Meeses and the Manns over to dinner, they may not have the same food requirements, quantitatively. Thus, "The best laid schemes [for] Mice and Men gang aft a-gley." This has happened to me, and may happen to you. In such cases, learn to snatch victory from defeat with a clever exit line. It may sharpen your repartee as well as your cooking skills!

2

Cooking the Chinese Way—

Methods and Utensils

CHINESE COOKING METHODS

If you stop to think about it, there are only three basic ways
by which food can be cooked: in water, in oil, or by itself—as
in roasting or baking. Nevertheless, the Chinese have managed
to elaborate and combine these three fundamental processes
into a great array of cooking methods. Here I shall stop to describe the ones that are most commonly used, and the ones on
which the recipes in this book are based. In each case I shall
give the name of the process in English, then the Chinese term,
both phonetically and in Chinese characters.

Stir-Frying (*Chow*) 炒

This method is uniquely Chinese. It consists of frying sliced
or chopped pieces of food in a wok or pan with a small amount
of hot oil in it over an intense flame. The food is stirred and
turned constantly until all the surfaces are browned. Then
a little sherry or another alcoholic beverage is added to the food,

7

and the wok or pan is quickly covered for a minute or so to let the flavor of the liquor permeate the food. Then the sauce is added to make the gravy and complete the cooking process.

Sautéing (*Poh Yau*) 泡油

This is very similar to Western sautéing. More oil is used (a cup or more) than in the chow method. The oil is heated only to a medium-low temperature, so the food will cook gently until it is just barely done. Then it is usually removed and added to ingredients cooked by other methods such as "stir-frying." The remaining oil is saved for future use.

Deep Frying (*Jah Yau*) 炸油

Most readers are already familiar with deep frying. In Chinese cooking, the method does not vary from its Western counterpart, although the food preparation may be different. Essentially, a large quantity of oil is brought to a high temperature; the food is cooked in the oil until it is golden brown; then it is removed and drained on absorbent paper.

Dishes cooked by any of the three above methods should be served as soon as they come off the stove; after this "moment of truth," they will lose some of their appeal. If left standing, they continue to cook from retained heat and the vegetables in particular may become overcooked and watery. If left together under such conditions, the individual ingredients tend to merge with each other and lose their own identity. Each ingredient was put in to play a certain role, and the dish is at its best when everything harmonizes to make a whole while each ingredient still retains its own character. Once that quality is lost, it cannot be recaptured.

Fortunately, not all Chinese cooking requires split-second timing. The following methods are more leisurely.

Simmering (*Loh May*) 鹵味

The Chinese characters for this method of cooking suggest only "salted flavor," but it is more than that. It is very similar to Western-style simmering. Generally it is a slow cooking process, in which the meats are cooked fast at first by being placed in boiling water for a few minutes to cook the outer layers and to remove any foreign tastes that may be present. Then the water is discarded and the meats are rinsed in cold water. The meats have been cleansed and the pure flavor has now been sealed in by the cooked outer layer. Then various sauces are added with a little liquid, all is brought to a high boil, after which the heat is turned down very low. The food is then allowed to cook for a long time to allow the sauce to penetrate and the food to get very tender.

Steaming (*Ching Ngaau*) 蒸餚

Food cooked by this method is placed in an open dish, which is in turn put into a vessel containing about an inch of water. The vessel is then covered and the water brought to a boil. The food in the dish is cooked by the steam which circulates over and around it. A wok makes an excellent steaming vessel, but a steamer can easily be improvised from the pots you have on hand. Essentially, you need a pot that is large enough to hold the bowl in which the food to be cooked is placed, and a well-fitting cover which will keep the steam within the pot. You must also have some kind of rack—an inverted cup, bowl, or cake rack will usually do—which will hold the dish above the water. (It is risky to put the bowl or dish of food directly in the water, since the water may overflow into the food when it is boiling vigorously.) I should emphasize that a double boiler will not do as a steamer, since in this method of cooking the steam must come into direct contact with the food and cook it by its moist heat.

Besides being delectable, steamed dishes are a great convenience, since they can be cooked in advance, then kept warm in the steamer over a low flame until ready to serve. It is almost impossible to overcook a steamed dish, and most leftovers can be resteamed without any detectable loss of flavor.

The methods mentioned above are the major ones the Chinese use in cooking. They are subject to variations as the cook sees fit. If you have mastered these methods, chances are you will experiment further and discover the less frequently used methods briefly noted below.

Red Searing (*Tung Shiu*) 紅燒

This method is very similar to the sautéing, or poh yau method. The meat, fowl, or seafood is breaded, with egg and flour and water. Then it is fried in oil over medium heat until golden brown. It is then added to other ingredients as described in "Poh Yau." This method is used whenever a breaded golden crust is desired, as in sweet and sour dishes.

Red Cooking (*T'ung Woh*) 紅窩

Red cooking is similar to stewing except that a much larger amount of liquid is used. The liquid with its seasonings (a major item of which is soy sauce, which gives the food its "red" look) is brought to a boil. The meat or fowl is then put in, and the heat immediately turned down very low, so that the liquid will not boil again. After a long, slow simmering the meat is tender and juicy.

Food Cooked in Rice (*Guk May*) 焗味

This can only be described, since there is no equivalent word for it in English to my knowledge. There is a whole category of food that is cooked right with the rice, then removed and cut up separately and eaten with the rice. A prime example is the Chinese sausage. When cooked this way the flavor of the sausage seeps into the rice and seasons it with great delicacy. Foods which may be prepared in this way include Chinese bacon, spiced duck, and other cured meats.

Barbecuing and Roasting (*Foh, Shiu, Guk*)   火 ,燒 ,焗

I have made no attempt to list these cooking methods in order of importance or deliciousness. This last category of cooking is so well liked and justly famous in Chinese cooking that it could well be first on the list.

In Chinese cooking the three methods included here, called "foh," "shiu," and "guk" respectively, mean fire, sear, and bake. They all describe a method of dry-heat cooking which we call barbecuing or roasting. A barbecued duck will be called a "foh app" yet a barbecued pig is known as "shiu ge," when both were cooked in the same stove. Why the distinction I cannot tell. Let's leave these weighty problems to philosophers!

A WORD ABOUT YOUR STOVE

If we could equip an ideal kitchen for Chinese cooking, we would start with a gas line at least 1½ inches in diameter. Then we would hook a gas unit onto it as large as that used in a gas furnace to heat a house. The reason is very simple. A most important requirement in some forms of Chinese cooking is fast, intense heat which can be stopped immediately when not needed. Since the equipment described is not practical, the next best thing is a regular gas stove. What if you have an electric stove instead of gas? Can Chinese cooking be done successfully on it? The answer is yes, but you will have to modify some of the cooking techniques when you use the stir-fry method. The transfer of heat from an electric stove to the pot is by direct contact; the more efficient the heat distribution, and the hotter the pot, the more successful will be your cooking. In the case of electric stoves, the Chinese wok described below cannot be used successfully, since the wok's bottom is semispherical and offers only a very small area of contact with the heating unit. Use a flat-bottomed pot instead. Since the heating coil retains heat a long time even after the current is shut off, you need to remove the pot from the coil and put it on an unheated surface so that the cooked food within will not get overcooked.

One other modification may be needed. Electric stoves do not have the same speed of heat recovery as gas stoves. If food is dropped into hot oil, its temperature will drop. A gas unit will bring the temperature back to the desired degree faster than the electric one. You can overcome this drawback by cooking a smaller amount on the electric stove, or else by partially pre-cooking some of the ingredients by blanching, as suggested on page 64.

For all other methods of Chinese cooking, the electric stove can be used successfully without modification of method.

If you possess some of the popular electric cooking appliances, such as electric frying pans, electric deep fryers, or rotisseries, they can be of extra help in many types of Chinese cooking. For example, all the deep-fried items can be cooked in your electric deep fryer, poh yau or sautéing may be done in your electric skillet, and barbecued pork or spareribs can be cooked in your rotisserie. Other uses will suggest themselves, as you gain confidence and experience.

An outdoor barbecue stove is also useful, and you will find several recipes in this book which can be cooked over charcoal. Your favorite but familiar fare may taste better done with a Chinese flair!

COOKING UTENSILS FOR CHINESE FOOD

It should be emphasized at once that you really need not add a single item to your kitchen for Chinese cooking, assuming that your kitchen is fairly well equipped for everyday use. All you need at the outset is an understanding of the different Chinese cooking methods, so that you can select the proper pot for each process. I mentioned earlier that intense heat was needed for the method called "chow" or stir-frying. For this type of cooking, select thin cooking vessels, so that they can heat up quickly. Use heavy pots for cooking rice, or for red cooking or braising, since in this case we want the heat to be retained. In the steaming method, the only points of importance are that the pot be large enough to hold the dish to be steamed, and that it have a tight-fitting cover.

As your skill and devotion to Chinese cooking increase, you may want to add to your cooking equipment the several items listed below, perhaps one at a time. You will find that these special utensils will be a great help. Good equipment does not make the expert, but experts work better with good equipment. The best equipment you can buy for Chinese cooking is inexpensive by American standards; the cost of all the items listed below may not exceed $20 to $25. You will find a list of stores on page 329 where these items may be bought directly or by mail.

The Wok

This most distinctive and useful piece of equipment is a semispherical frying pan that the Chinese have used from time immemorial. It has not been changed, nor can it be improved. It is made of thin iron and sits over a gas burner with a rim or collar to hold it steady. Woks come in different sizes, with covers to match. The ideal sizes for a beginner would be 14, 16, or 18 inches in diameter. They take up a lot of room on top of a stove, so if you plan on using two simultaneously, get the smaller size. Be sure to buy a cover and a rim collar at the same time you purchase the wok. A wok is ideally suited to Chinese cooking, since it heats up fast, and when the heat is turned off it does not retain the heat to overcook the food within

it. It can be used for practically all the methods of cooking which the Chinese use. It is useful for deep-fat frying and poaching. It serves as an excellent steamer if a round cake rack is placed in it to elevate the dish from the water and the cover is used to contain the steam.

Like a new car, a wok can be had with optional equipment. But unlike a car, where the optionals may cost hundreds of dollars, the two items made for the wok may cost you $2-$3 together, depending on size. One is called a "wok chon"; the other is called a "wok hok." The chon is shaped like a pancake turner but has a tiny rim on three edges to hold the gravy as you scoop up the food. The bottom of the chon is gently curved to conform to the shape of the wok. A hok is a ladle-like utensil, which is used to scoop up the food from the wok or to put in or take out soups and liquids while cooking. These two utensils are used like extensions of a chef's arms. The chon is held in one hand and the hok in the other. During stir-frying they are kept in constant motion to stir and turn the food in the wok to keep it from burning, and to make sure that each piece is cooked evenly on all its surfaces.

A few other utensils deserve a brief mention. Many of these are not Chinese utensils, but items to be found in any house-wares department, and you may already have some of them.

Barbecue Tongs

These are very handy for putting in or taking out deep-fried items such as shrimps or chicken. They should be as long and large as possible so that food can be handled easily.

Deep-Frying Thermometer

The secret of good deep frying lies in the exact control of the temperature of the oil. This is why I suggest that every kitchen should have a deep-frying thermometer. There are other ways to tell how hot the oil is without using a thermometer, but they are more troublesome and less accurate.

There is not much leeway in deep frying. If you inspect your thermometer you'll notice that the deep-frying range is very narrow. Anything under 350° F. is too low for deep frying, and if you go even slightly above 400° F. the oil will vaporize and turn dark. All you have, then, is 50° between too low and too high.

There is another very important factor in successful deep-frying. It is the recovery rate of the heat of your oil. I mentioned earlier that when you bring the oil to the proper temperature, and then put the food in to fry, the temperature of the oil goes back down. How long does it take for the heat from your stove to raise the temperature back to where you want it? And how many degrees does the food you put in lower the oil temperature? If the oil gets below 350° F. for any length of time, your food may get soggy and oily. A thermometer will help you keep tabs on your oil temperature at all times. It will tell you when to raise or lower the heat in your stove, and when to increase or decrease the amount of food you are adding to the oil.

How to Judge Cooking Temperatures

While we are on the subject of temperatures, a few more notes may be helpful here. How can you judge the temperature of the oil without a thermometer? How can you tell the temperature when frying with a wok or frying pan when there is only a little oil used?

If you are deep frying and do not have a thermometer, the easiest way to tell when your oil is ready is to drop a small piece of vegetable or meat into the oil. If the item you put in starts to sizzle, and "swims" around the pan while it floats on the surface, the oil is hot enough. If the item sinks, the temperature is too low. If the oil gets smoky and darkens, and the item put into it becomes browned too quickly, the oil is too hot.

Judging the temperature in a wok while stir-frying becomes easy after a little experience. When the wok or pan is heated hot and dry, and a small amount of oil (up to ¼ cup) is put in, the oil immediately becomes hot enough for frying. If the oil starts to smoke, it is too hot. Turn heat down immediately. You can also use the vegetable piece to test the temperature in a wok for stir-frying. Moderate temperature in the wok can be determined if a small piece of garlic or ginger dropped in will not sputter and swim around too wildly. Of course even a very hot wok or pan will lose its high temperature as soon as a large quantity of food is placed in it to cook.

Generally, heat the wok hot and dry over high heat for about a minute. Then add the oil and coat much of the pan inside with the oil. Turn heat down immediately to medium. Then put in the ginger and garlic to brown when those ingredients are called for in a recipe. When garlic and ginger become golden brown, turn heat up to high and add the other ingredients while stirring.

Lower temperature must be used when you don't want the items fried to be browned, as in sautéing (poh yau), page 8. The food put into the oil should barely bubble, and no smoke should be visible.

Knives and Cleavers

The knives found in the average kitchen are a pet peeve of mine. A good sharp knife is one of the most important tools to have in a kitchen. Yet practically all the knives I have found in friends' homes are a menace and barely usable. I've spent more money buying friends good knives instead of wine or other dinner gifts. But, by the next time I called on them, those knives that I had tenderly whetted to a razor's edge had become almost as dull as the ones they replaced. I once caught my father-in-law using one of my favorite knives for hacking a piece of firewood!

The most dangerous tools in the kitchen are dull knives. Such knives make you use such force in cutting that a slight slip may give you a deep, jagged cut. On the other hand, cutting with a sharp, clean knife is safe, efficient, and pleasurable.

A brief discussion of the types of steel used in knifemaking may be useful at this point. There are literally hundreds of types of steel put out by the steel industry. The characteristics of a particular type of steel are determined by the addition or subtraction of other ingredients used in its manufacture. For our purposes, we need only speak of two types of steel: stainless steel and carbon steel. There are a hundred varieties of these two types, but we need only know why one is superior to the other in cutting performance.

A knife made of a hard steel will hold a keen cutting edge better and longer than a knife made of a softer steel. Carbon steel is much harder than stainless steel. In order to give stainless steel its rust-proof quality, chrome is added to the iron in manufacturing. As a metal, chrome is much softer than iron, and the finished product combining these two metals has lost some of the original hardness of steel.

A choice has to be made. It is very attractive to have a knife that always looks shiny, doesn't stain and doesn't rust. But a knife's major function is to cut, so choose knives made of carbon steel. They will serve you better, and do not demand a great deal of extra care.

Chinese Cleavers

These are wonderful knives to have for any type of cooking. They come in different sizes and weights, but all are shaped exactly the same. A pair of medium-weight Chinese cleavers come as close to being universal cutting tools in a kitchen as I can imagine. Used together, one in each hand, they can be used to chop meats or vegetables, fine or coarse as you wish. Alone they can be used for slicing, trimming, or chopping through softer bones and shells. The broad flat surfaces are an aid in transferring the ingredients from the cutting board to the pot. These cleavers can be bought only in Chinese grocery stores or hardware stores.

Boning Knife

This type of knife you may have seen in a butcher shop. It is rather small and thin. The blade is about 5 inches long, and is pointed, curved, and narrow. With its wooden handle, it is about 10 inches long. The function of this knife is suggested by its name: it removes bones from meat or fowl.

Carving Knife

In Chinese cooking, carving is seldom necessary, since all foods are already cut into bite size. I include this knife here because I assume you will do other types of cooking. If you have an electric carving knife, there is no need for you to get another non-electric one.

French Knife

This may be substituted for a Chinese cleaver, if you do not have, or do not care to get one. A French knife is a triangular pointed knife that many chefs use for slicing and cutting.

The question will now enter your mind where you should buy these knives. In almost every city, there are cutlery stores which cater to the "trade." These stores supply knives to chefs, restaurants, and butcher shops. (On request, these cutlery stores will shape and sharpen your knives by a professional grinder before you ever use them. Have a honing stone to keep your knives sharp, and occasionally, when there are nicks or the shape has worn down, send them back to the store and have them reshaped and sharpened again.)

Care and Maintenance of Knives

It is much easier to keep your knives sharp and rust-free than to neglect them and then try to restore them to their former condition. Rust is the result of water on iron (oxidation). Dry your knives and keep them dry after each use, and rust cannot form.

All knives will lose keenness after repeated use. The sharpness can be restored by the use of a honing stone, which is a rectangle of compressed abrasive material. These honing stones are manufactured by Norton Abrasives Co., Carborundum Co., and others, and are available at all hardware stores. The proper size and type for the home would be one that is about 1" x 2" x 6", and has two different surfaces bonded to each other into one stone. One face is coarse, and the other side is made of a finer abrasive. The coarse face is to be used when your knife is quite dull, or has fine nicks on the cutting edge, because the coarse abrasive will remove the steel faster and with less effort. The fine surface is to be used when your knives are in good condition, and you merely want to maintain their keenness.

To use the honing stone, place it on a nonslippery surface (such as a wooden cutting board) and place a few drops of household machine oil or water on the stone. Then hold the knife almost flat against the stone, so that the knife edge comes into direct contact with it. Gently rub the knife against the stone three or four times on one side; turn the knife over and repeat the process. For safety use both hands when sharpening knives. One hand holds the handle while the other is placed on the flat of the knife.

Storing Knives for Safety and Sharpness

How you store your knives when they are not in use will also determine their condition and safety. Never just throw them into any drawer with other things. It is a dangerous practice, and if the edges of the knives rub against each other, it will dull them very quickly.

The best way to store your knives is, after drying them thoroughly first, to stick them into slots as they do in butcher shops. If that is not possible in your kitchen, reserve one shallow drawer exclusively for knives. Have a spot for each particular knife, and always return it to its assigned place. You can easily make a scabbard for each of your knives by using folded pieces of cardboard, gluing or taping them together. This will add to safety and maintain the knives' keenness.

Steamed Dish Retriever

The only problem a steamed dish presents is how to grapple the hot dish out of the boiling water when it is cooked without spilling it or burning yourself. I recently discovered a clever little gadget that is a great aid in this. It is called a "shuenk kup"; in Chinese 餸鋏 . It is a three-pronged tool which automatically adjusts itself to the size of your dish.

The last time I priced this utensil in New York, its cost ranged from $1.50 to $2, and it is widely available. When you are ready to order some other items from a store listed in the back of this book, you might trace the Chinese characters representing this utensil and ask if it is in stock.

Cutting Board or Chopping Block

It is a surprise to me how many American kitchens do not have this essential piece of equipment. All Chinese kitchens have them. The Chinese just saw off a disk of wood from a tree trunk and use it as a chopping block. Here, we can get chopping blocks that are better looking and more efficient. Usually they are made of laminated hardwood, fastened together with long bolts or glued together. They come in different sizes and thicknesses and can be bought in all hardware stores, housewares sections of department stores, or restaurant and luncheonette supply houses. It is impossible to prepare food efficiently without one of them.

Your Chinese Larder

I SAID earlier that human taste buds can detect only five distinct variations—salty, sweet, sour, acrid, and bitter. But actually taste is not limited only to one's tongue; the nose plays a part too. There are a great many spices and condiments used almost universally to enhance aroma and flavor; it is the way in which they are combined and used that gives each cuisine its individuality. This is true of Chinese cooking, which makes use of such common ingredients as salt, garlic, and onions, and spices such as anise and cinnamon, in its dishes. In addition, the Chinese have evolved some unique sauces and seasonings.

In this chapter you will find two lists of the ingredients most often called for in the recipes given in this book. The first list consists of everyday items you may already have on your shelves, or which are available in any market. The second is a basic list of specialized Chinese ingredients. Although you may be able to cook "Chinese style" with the first list alone, you must have a minimum of the spices and sauces on the second list to get an authentic Chinese flavor into your food. The items you must have are marked with asterisks; the unstarred items are nice to have but not absolutely essential. At any rate, the entire list is very short, and even if you buy everything on it the cost will be modest.

You will find a list of stores where these items may be bought (either directly or by mail) at the back of the book (page 329). In the list of Chinese ingredients I have again given the name of the ingredient in English, followed by its phonetic transcription and the Chinese characters. Copy or trace the Chinese characters when you are ordering since there may be several English names, varying in accuracy, for each item, as well as phonetic variations. I have tried to indicate the minimum quantity to order in each case. Since all the items listed will keep almost indefinitely, you need not worry too much about waste if you find you have too much on hand. I have also included suggestions about storage wherever I felt it was needed.

INGREDIENTS OBTAINABLE IN ANY MARKET

Long-Grain Rice

To most Chinese, the "staff of life" is rice, and no meal is complete without it. There are many varieties of rice, but the most desirable type for an everyday meal is the long-grain type such as the Carolina brand. Allow one cup of dry rice for every two people in your dinner plan. One cup of dry rice will make almost two cups of cooked rice.

Cooking Oil

The ideal oil for cooking is one that is bland and light, so that its taste will not intrude upon the flavor of the food cooked in it. Most edible vegetable oils meet this requirement. Olive oil is the only one I know which is not suitable for Chinese cooking since it has a very distinctive taste of its own and is rather heavy.

My own preference is peanut oil because I think it has a more delicate flavor. Experiment by buying small bottles of several kinds of oil, such as peanut, corn, and others, and see which you prefer. They are all acceptable for Chinese cooking. In the recipes, I will just say "vegetable oil." The quantity indicated is the same for any type of oil you may choose.

Many people hesitate to deep fry because after the oil has been used its disposal may be a problem. To discard it is wasteful. Properly stored, the same oil may be used many times before discarding. If the oil is heated to the proper temperature before the food is put in, it will not retain the flavor of foods cooked in it. Heating oil to correct temperature is important for other reasons. Overheating vaporizes the oil, and makes it thick and dark in color. Underheating will make the food oily and soggy. Strain used oil after it has cooled into a wide-mouthed jar or container which can be covered tightly. Make sure the storage container is dry, because oil mixed with water will spatter when heated. Oil need not be refrigerated. Discard when it becomes thick and dark after repeated use.

Always heat the wok or pan dry and hot before adding the oil, and spread the oil evenly over its cooking surface. This will prevent spattering and help keep foods from sticking to the cooking utensil.

Monosodium Glutamate

Monosodium glutamate is a white powder which looks like granulated sugar. It has been widely accepted as a flavor aid in cooking by restaurants, food processors, and home cooks alike. It is almost impossible not to have eaten a bit of it during an average day.

Monosodium glutamate has an interesting history. It was first made by the Chinese and Japanese by evaporating liquids from cooked shrimps and fish. Then the Japanese synthesized it from soybeans. The United States then started manufacturing it on a large scale, and is now the biggest producer of it in the world.

The best-known brand available in grocery stores is called "Ac'cent." That name has become synonymous with monosodium glutamate even though many other brands are on the market.

What does this magic powder do to foods? No one seems to be certain, scientifically. But for cooks the effect it has on food, in bringing out the flavor, is unquestioned. It does not give its taste to the food, but seems to blend with and enhance every kind of food—even vegetables and fruits. You may have noticed that many canned foods have listed on their labels that a certain amount of this product was used in their processing. Most recipes here include a small amount of monosodium glutamate.

Garlic

Without garlic, many Chinese dishes would lose their character. Use fresh garlic whenever possible. A head of garlic is composed of separate sections or cloves, which vary in size.

When a recipe calls for a clove of garlic, the size should be about the size of the first segment of your little finger. Add or subtract to make its equivalent.

An easy way to peel and mince a clove of garlic is to place it on your cutting board and flatten it with the side of a heavy knife or cleaver. The skin can then be easily removed, and the garlic will now be flat and receptive to your knife for mincing without skittering around. Minced garlic gets burned easily when fried, so the oil should not be too hot while browning it, and speed and care should be used. Some cooks prefer to fry garlic in clove form first, so that the oil will be infused with the aroma, then discard the garlic before going on with the cooking. Both methods are acceptable. Garlic juice added to hot oil will spatter, so do not use it for stir-fried dishes.

Cooking Wine

Alcohol is used by almost all peoples, even by some of those with very primitive social development. Rice whiskey is used for cooking in China, but since we are an adaptable people, we use other alcoholic beverages in this country because they are cheaper or more available. The most commonly used is sherry wine.

You need not buy the most expensive imported sherry; domestic sherry is very good for the purpose. It makes very little difference whether the sherry is dry or sweet. Most (but not all) of the alcohol will evaporate, but the flavor of the wine will linger to exert its mellowing influence on the food, as wine can with a convivial company of people. Use it judiciously; too much can overpower the food, as overdrinking can overpower our senses.

Sugar

Plain granulated white sugar is most frequently used in Chinese cooking. In some recipes, dark brown sugar is used to vary the taste subtly when more than one sweet dish is served at a meal. When sugar is used in nonsweet dishes, its function is to blend and harmonize the various ingredients. Do not worry when a recipe calls for the use of some sugar. The dish will not be sweet.

Vinegar

For cooking, use plain white vinegar. It gives a tart sourness to delight our taste buds and act as one of the "five fragrances" the Chinese enjoy. For dipping, or as dressing for food that may be oily, such as Lo Mein (noodles fried with oil), the preferred vinegar to use is wine vinegar. It is closest to the mild vinegar used in China.

Canned Chicken Broth

Using canned chicken broth can be a great convenience and time saver. It is easily stored on the shelf, and the flavor of it blends easily with anything without overpowering the other flavors. You should be able to find one or more brands of plain chicken broth on your supermarket shelves. This broth can be used as a base for many Chinese soup recipes unless a great quantity is needed, in which case you may want to make your own soup stock. Recipes for such stock are given in this book, page 253.

The most frequent use of canned chicken broth is in making sauces and gravies, since it adds to the flavor of your food, rather than diluting the flavor as plain water might. The unused portion of an opened can may be transferred to another container and refrigerated for future use. It will keep for a week or more without losing its flavor or becoming spoiled.

Scallions

Fresh scallions are called green onions in many parts of this country; they have the grace and zest of the onion without some of the onion's less desirable characteristics. In Chinese cooking, always use all the green ends of the scallion as well

as its white tip. Scallions are not only cooked into many Chinese dishes, but are also frequently chopped up and used raw as a garnish.

Cornstarch

Cornstarch is the most commonly used thickening agent for sauces, gravies, and soups in Chinese cooking. Liquids thickened with cornstarch remain translucent, and it is easier to use than flour. Cornstarch has greater thickening powers than flour, and only about half as much is needed to achieve the same consistency.

When mixing dry cornstarch, put the amount required in a cup and add a little cool water to it. Mix well so that no lumps are present, then add to the other ingredients of the gravy mixture. When mixed with liquids cornstarch will settle to the bottom. Be sure to stir the gravy mixture thoroughly before adding to wok or pan.

Other Ingredients

The following ingredients on your shelves or locally available are also used in Chinese cooking. When called for in a recipe, each one's function will be self-explanatory or a brief discussion will be included:

Salt	*Honey*
Pepper (white and black)	*Leeks*
Star anise seeds	*Onions*
Chili sauce	*Tabasco*
Ketchup	

SPECIAL CHINESE INGREDIENTS

*Soy Sauce (*She Yau*) 豉油

Of all the Chinese spices and sauces, the most distinctive and irreplaceable is soy sauce. Soy sauce comes in two types—light and dark. Brewing good soy sauce is an art in China; there used to be special stores which sold only soy sauces, to which connoisseurs came to choose their soy sauce as one would select a wine. Japanese soy sauces, such as the Kikkoman brand, are also excellent if Chinese soy sauces are not available. Do not use American soy sauces if you can avoid it since they are chemically made and only a poor approximation of the real thing. Authentic soy sauces are brewed from fermented soy beans, parched wheat, salt, and water.

Both light and dark soy sauces should be kept in a well-equipped kitchen since they are akin but not exactly alike. The light soy has a more delicate flavor and is generally used for dipping, seafoods, or soups, whereas the dark soy sauce is used for dishes which should have a darker gravy. Unless light or dark soy sauce is specified in a recipe, either one may be used. Soy sauce is inexpensive and keeps indefinitely. Buy a large bottle (28 ounces) of each type.

Experiment with soy sauce in your own cooking: you will find it adds an unexpected new dimension to the most familiar food. But both soy sauces are salty, so whenever you use it go lightly with the salt.

*Fresh Ginger Root (*Saang Geung*) 生薑

Fresh ginger and garlic are a combination which give the Chinese flavor to dishes. Garlic has been covered in the preceding list, since it is available anywhere. It is mentioned here

* Asterisks indicate essential ingredients.

because Chinese cooks speak of "ginger and garlic" in one breath, as though they were inseparable.

Fresh ginger is a most distinctive seasoning. Although we can make some substitutions, nothing really takes the place of it. Fortunately, fresh ginger can be kept for months if it is stored properly. If you are far from a place which sells it, you need only send for it or go to buy it two or three times a year.

If you do not expect to keep ginger longer than two or three weeks, you can keep it in the butter compartment or similar spot in your refrigerator. Don't store in the vegetable bin or crisper because the moisture there makes ginger moldy.

The best method for keeping fresh ginger is to have a crock with a cover, filled with moist sand. (Not wet sand because too much water will rot the ginger.) Bury the ginger in the sand and cover. Store in a cool place. Sprinkle a few drops of water on the sand occasionally to keep it moist. I have seen my father keep ginger fresh for a year with this system. The ginger actually grows sprouts under these conditions. Break off an irregular section of it as needed and leave the rest in the sand.

Fresh ginger is available in all Chinese groceries, and may be bought by mail from the stores listed in the back of the book (page 329). It may also be purchased in most Spanish stores, if your locality has a Cuban or Puerto Rican population. They call ginger "jengibre" and it is used by them to brew ginger tea. Ginger preserved in a thin syrup can be bought by

the jar or can in fancy-food departments of large department stores or supermarkets. While preserved ginger is not as good as the fresh, it will do in a pinch. Use the same quantity as fresh ginger in the recipes. Dried powdered ginger is not a satisfactory substitute.

Since very little ginger is used in cooking, when you order fresh ginger a quarter to a half pound will be enough for months of use.

*Oyster Sauce (*Ho Yau*) 蠔油

While oyster sauce, which is made from extracts of real oysters plus other ingredients, is not as essential as soy to Chinese cooking, it is highly valued by the Chinese. Used in place of soy sauce in many recipes it changes a dish into one with a different, more subtle flavor. It is also used for a dip. Plain boiled foods dipped in it are delicious.

This sauce comes in bottles or cans and the consistency is heavy and thick. It is rather expensive but it goes a long way. Buy a small bottle first. Then, if you like it, buy the 5-pound cans; they are more economical. Transfer from can to bottle for easier handling. Refrigerate.

Five Fragrances Powder (*Mm Heung Foon*) 五香粉

This seasoning is a combination of spices, the two principal ones being star anise and dried ginger, which have been further soaked in the liquid of other spices, then ground into a fine powder. This powdered spice is added to barbecued or roast meats, or is mixed into sauces and marinades. Use judiciously; ½ to 1 teaspoon usually is sufficient.

Five Fragrances Spices (*Saam Lei, But Kok*)   三理，八角

The Chinese translation of this spice is interesting: "Saam lei, but kok" literally means "three governing principles and eight corners" (anise seeds are octagonal). This combination uses the same spices as its cousin, the five fragrances powder above, but the spices are not ground. It is used in stewed dishes made with beef, pork, and chicken. Every five fragrances recipe must have this spice. When called for, usually a tablespoon of the spice, tied in a piece of cheesecloth, is enough. The spice bag is then placed in the liquid to be cooked with the meats. It is removed and discarded when the dish is done.

NOTE: Do not use either form of this spice for fish or other seafood, because they are too delicate in flavor to withstand this rather insistent spice. When buying, 50 cents' worth of each form is sufficient. They are both nice to have on hand, but not absolutely necessary, since you can approximate the flavor by using anise seeds, fresh ginger, and whatever spices you may like. In a way, it is like a curry powder, which is also a combination of spices whose lesser ingredients can be varied to the maker's taste.

Dried Chinese Mushrooms (*Tung Koo*)   冬菇

All mushrooms are known as "koo." The "tung" translates as "winter." There are several types of dried mushrooms used in Chinese cooking, but this type is most commonly used. Always soak them in a little water an hour or so before using. Save the water and use it as part of the stock. Dried European mushrooms make a good substitute for the Chinese variety, and canned button mushrooms will also do. The price of tung koo is about $1.50 per quarter-pound package. Since the mushrooms are dry, these packages hold a lot, and one package is all you need to buy at a time.

*Salted Cured Soybeans (*Dau She*) 豆豉

These beans have been cured with salt and sliced ginger and dried in the sun. This is a very distinctive spice. Some American diners complain that food in Chinese restaurants is not as good when they go alone as when they are accompanied by a Chinese friend. The explanation may lie in the chef's deliberate failure to use this ingredient in the food, since chefs have learned that some Americans do not care for this flavor. On the other hand, no Chinese kitchen is complete without it. I've included dau she in some recipes, but it can be left out if you don't like the taste. Dau she comes now in 1-pound plastic bags, and only costs about 50 cents a pound.

Sesame Oil (*Gee Mah Yau*) 芝麻油

Most of us are familiar with sesame seeds, since they are frequently used in pastry making. They have a sweet, nutty flavor, and, being very tiny, they can be spread over a wide area without having to be crushed, thereby lending their flavor evenly. The Chinese also use sesame seeds extensively in their cakes and cookies.

Sesame oil is made from the seeds, and has the same agreeable qualities. The oil has a decided flavor, so a few drops are all that is necessary in a recipe. It has another great virtue besides its flavor; it can mask fishy tastes, without destroying the seafood flavor. Every fish or seafood recipe is improved with its use.

Sesame oil may be bought in Japanese or Near Eastern groceries, as well as in the Chinese stores listed in the Appendix. Buy only small bottles of sesame oil; it lasts a long time.

*Sweet Bean Sauce (*Hoi Sin Deung*) 海鮮醬

"Hoi sin" translates literally into "sea fresh" and "deung" means a "paste," but generally it means seafood sauce. It is a sweet bean sauce used in cooking and on the table like ketchup when some fish or seafood is served. Also, this sauce is used in some marinades, as for barbecued spareribs. It comes in pound cans. Transfer unused sauce to a jar; there is no need to refrigerate it. It keeps for months.

Yellow Bean Sauce (*Yuen Shaai She Deung*) 原晒豉醬

This is a fermented bean paste made from yellow beans. It is more delicate and less salty than the dau she, or black soybeans which have been salted and cured. It comes in a can and is very inexpensive (about 35 cents). A little of this bean sauce goes a long way; usually only a tablespoon or two is all that is needed in a recipe. Once the can has been opened, transfer the sauce to a covered jar. It does not have to be refrigerated, and will keep indefinitely. This sauce is used principally as a seasoning for roast ducks or chickens, where it is mixed with other spices and then put into the cavities to season the fowl.

Preserved Cucumber (*Cha Kwa*) 菜瓜

This vegetable, also called a Chinese sweet cucumber, belongs to the cucumber family, but is not the cucumber we know. It is sold in pound cans, and is a very useful addition to dishes requiring a touch of sweetness and crispness. Sweet pickled gherkins, available at any grocery, are a good substitute.

The following items deserve a brief mention. They are in no way essential to the recipes here, but are often used by the Chinese:

Plum Sauce (*So Mooi Tseung*) 蘇梅醬

A favorite sauce with Americans, made of plums, sugar, and spices. It is used mainly as a dip for fatty roast meats, such as duck. It comes in pound cans. (Some Americans call this "duck sauce.")

Bamboo Shoots (*Chuk Sun*) 竹筍

These are the sprouts of bamboo canes, which are very tender yet crunchy. Drain and discard liquid, as it has no taste. They are packed several pieces or halves to a can. Buy 2 small cans to start.

Water Chestnuts (*Ma Tai*) 馬蹄

Water chestnuts are misnamed, since they are not nuts but rather a root vegetable. Small, sweet, and very crisp, they blend with most foods and are widely used in Chinese cooking. Leaving them out of a recipe will not affect the taste of a dish, but their inclusion always improves it. They come whole or sliced in pound cans. If you live within reach of a Chinese grocery, you can also buy them fresh.

Bean Curd (*Dau Foo*) 荳腐

There are a few items that are hard to categorize. Bean curd is one of them. It is made from dried beans which have been ground up and jelled. Once it is made, it becomes a fresh perishable product that must be refrigerated and eaten in a short while (3 or 4 days). Bean curd is made into cakes about 4 inches square and about 1 inch thick. In appearance it is moist and white and spongy. It must be bought from a Chinese grocery and it cannot be shipped by mail, because of its perishable nature. The process of making it is so involved that it cannot be done at home.

If you live in a city where you can buy bean curd, it is one of the nice Chinese vegetables (mineral? animal?) to try. It is cheap, versatile, and nutritious. It can be fried, steamed, or boiled, and with each different cooking process, and with the different things it is cooked with, delightful differences develop.

4

Organizing Your Cooking

BE YOUR OWN "DOP MAH"

In Chinese cooking, preparation is the most important and time-consuming part of the job. The more efficient and organized you are in the preparation of the ingredients, the faster and easier it will be for you to cook Chinese food. If everything is well planned and prepared ahead of time, the actual cooking of several quite elegant dishes for a large dinner party may not take more than half an hour. However, do not be misled into thinking that the cooking time plus another hour or two will suffice for all the work you will have to do. Generally speaking, for every minute of cooking time you will need at least five to ten times that amount for proper preparation.

The two key men in a Chinese restaurant are the chef and a man called the "dop mah." Literally translated, "dop mah" means "pick horse." He is the man who determines what and how much of each item goes into every dish you order, then hands it to the cooks. This man is as highly skilled as the head chef, and must know what goes into every recipe, how much, and in what order.

As each order is called into the kitchen, this man, with light-ning speed and not a single wasted motion, will go to the refrigerator with a platter, pick out all the raw or semicooked ingredients which have been prepared beforehand, and arrange them in a logical sequence, so that the cook can almost auto-matically put into the wok what should go in first. The amazing speed with which you get your food in a Chinese restaurant, where each individual dish is cooked separately, is only possible because of efficient, logical planning and organization.

We can with great profit take a lesson from the dop mah. Everything should be prepared and ready before you turn on a single burner of your stove. First, all the ingredients and seasonings should be soaked, cut up, or mixed together as directed in the recipe, then put on plates or a platter. My own system when cooking several dishes is to use a single large platter for each dish, arranging the items clockwise in the order they are to be put into the pot, with any liquid ingredients in a small bowl in the center. If these preparations have been made well before cooking time, the platter can then simply be covered and stored in the refrigerator until needed.

This systematic approach is particularly important in cooking stir-fried or "chow" dishes, where each ingredient should be put into the pan in the proper sequence and cooked just so long and no more. Since the total cooking time is brief, you will not have time to stop to cut up or mix ingredients together at that point. However, you will find that the usefulness of a system-atic approach, with everything prepared in advance, is not limited to stir-frying. It will save you time and energy in the long run no matter what method a dish is cooked by.

CUTTING

Whenever possible, the Chinese chef will try to achieve "har-mony of cut." He will cut all the ingredients used in a particular recipe the same way, so that if the major ingredient is to be shredded, so will all the lesser ingredients. The Chinese love of contrast does not apply here.

The method of cut is so important to Chinese cooking that a dish using exactly the same ingredients and cooked by the

same method may be listed several times on a menu, as if they were different dishes. For instance, a chicken and vegetable dish may be listed five times, as chicken and vegetable *k'au, luk, ting, p'in, sz.* These five Chinese terms refer to the five basic ways food can be cut. (Chopped meats or seafood can also be served another way, formed into cakes or balls and called "p'eng.")

All meats should be cut across the fiber, to make them tender, if they are to be used as slices. (See also page 117.) On some cuts such as flank steak, the fibers are very distinct and it can readily be seen which way these fibers run. In other cuts of meat, the fibers may run in several directions, because there are several muscles within that cut of meat. In this case, use a sharp knife and separate each differently grained piece along its natural contours, then slice each piece. In still other cuts of meat, the fibers may not be visible at all. If this is so then it does not matter in which direction you cut the meat as it will be tender anyway. If you are dicing meat, you need not look for the fiber or "grain." It is cut so small that the long tough fibers will be rendered tender. In cutting meat chunks, with or without the bones, the types of meat chosen for the purpose are tender cuts to begin with, and no special attention has to be paid to the direction in which the fibers run.

Meat that is partially frozen will slice more easily than the fresh kind, because it is not as limp and slippery. Cut the fresh meats into strips, following the direction of the fibers, about the length and width of the slices you wish, then stick the strips into your freezer just long enough for the meat to firm, but not be frozen through. You may now slice the meat into the desired thickness with ease.

Inevitably (as though you didn't know!) I will have to drag in the Chinese saying "A picture is worth a thousand words." There can be no more appropriate occasion to use this saying than when giving instructions on how to cut ingredients, since cutting is the most important part of the advance preparation.

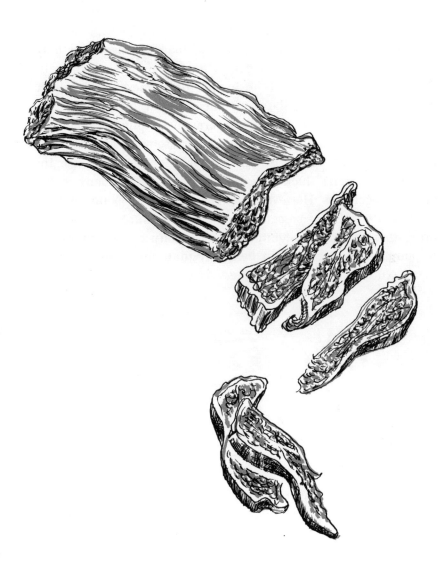

I shall hold my verbal description to essentials, and hope that the accompanying illustrations will save thousands of words.

The instructions given below apply to both vegetables and meats; usually the cut of the meat determines how the vegetables will be cut.

Chunks or Ball-Shaped Cut (*K'au*) 球

In this method of cutting, pieces of meat or vegetables may be irregular in size, about ¾- to 1-inch chunks. The "ball-shaped" explanation is only to justify the Chinese word, which means "ball." It would be impractical to cut ingredients into balls. Chunks or cubes are more accurate descriptions. Of course, in many instances the pieces may not resemble anything like a chunk or cube. Pieces of chicken taken off the bone, for instance, just aren't thick enough, and neither are many stalks of leafy vegetables. However, that is a very minor point, as long as they are cut into something resembling chunks or cubes. I bring this up at the beginning not to confuse you but rather to point up the leeway and flexibility that can be exercised in many phases of Chinese cooking.

Chunks, with Bones (*Luk*) 碌

This is similar to the k'au cut, except that the bones in the meat or fowl are not removed, but are left in the cut pieces. The vegetables are cut exactly the same as in the k'au method.

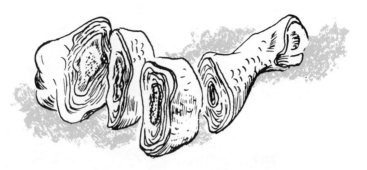

Most Westerners do not appreciate biting into a bone in a piece of meat, but the Chinese believe that leaving the bones in makes the meat juicier and more flavorful. Seldom will you use this type of cut in your own cooking, but it is a good thing to know, because you will find this cut mentioned in many Chinese restaurant menus, and you may want to avoid dishes with bones in them when you eat out.

Dicing (*Ting*) 丁

Dicing needs no special explanation. The pieces are cut small, into about ¼-inch cubes. Frequently a ting dish may be made with green peas, which are the same size.

Slicing (*P'in*) 片

In this method, the ingredients are sliced thin, about ⅛ inch in thickness, and flat. The width and length should be about ¾ by 1¼ inches respectively. Where I use the words "domino cut," use this slicing method, but increase the thickness to ¼ inch.

Shredding (*Sz*) 絲

Sz originally meant "silk." Because silk is made of fine thread, anything fine and long can be compared to it. This cut, when used in the context of cooking, means fine shreds, about ⅛ inch by ⅛ inch, and from 1 to 3 inches long.

Chopping (P'eng) 餅

Chopping is too familiar for you to need details. You may prefer to use a grinder or have the meat ground by your butcher. Be sure to grind it as coarse as possible. Vegetables are never chopped in Chinese cooking by themselves. If vegetables are included in a recipe using this cut, they are either shredded or diced separately and cooked with the meat. However, some vegetables used mainly for their flavor, such as onions, scallions, or salted and spiced vegetables, are sometimes chopped with and mixed into the meat.

PART TWO

Recipes

5

How to Use These Recipes

My aim is to make this book come as close as it can to my actually being in your kitchen. I have tried to anticipate the questions you will have about what to avoid and what to expect, and to answer them in each recipe. I shall also include any suggestions I may have on what could be done to vary the dish, and possible substitutions for certain ingredients. Though some ingredients are irreplaceable, many ingredients can be substituted for others in a Chinese recipe without losing the character or quality of a dish. In the recipes those ingredients for which there are satisfactory substitutes are indicated with a symbol (†), and the substitute will be given under "Substitutions and Variations."

As to the recipes themselves, I have tried to group under one heading the ingredients which go into the pot at the same time. In general, the groupings are as follows:

I   PRINCIPAL INGREDIENTS

Meats, fowl, seafood used in a recipe, quantity and method of cut.

The fresh vegetables used—how much and how they should be cut.

II   SECONDARY INGREDIENTS

This group includes canned or dried ingredients used in a recipe. How to cut them, whether they have to be pre-soaked, or other instructions are indicated.

This also includes fresh seasoning items, such as ginger, garlic, scallions, leeks, onions, hot peppers, parsley, and all other fresh herbs used in a recipe, except garnish items.

III   SEASONING

All the dry seasoning and thickening agents used in a recipe, such as sugar, cornstarch, salted cured soybeans, ground pepper, monosodium glutamate, curry powder, etc., are included in this group.

All the liquid or paste items, such as soy sauce, hoi sin sauce, oyster sauce, ketchup, and water, juice, or stock, are included here.

All the items in Group III can usually be mixed together and put aside for the final gravy.

IV   FOR THE WOK OR PAN

Vegetable or peanut oil; sesame oil; wine, whiskey, or gin; and salt belong in this group of ingredients. When they are listed, have them ready near the stove. The oils are always put in after you've heated the wok or pan hot and dry. Then salt is added before anything from the other groups is put in to cook.

The alcoholic beverage is put in after the other ingredients are partly cooked. Right after it has been added, a cover is placed over the food for a minute or two to let the alcohol permeate all the items.

Garnish items are listed at the end.

Some Points to Remember

These points are made elsewhere in the book, sometimes more than once. But they are important enough to be worth restating here:

1. Except where otherwise specified, each of the following recipes will satisfy two fairly hearty eaters. If you are serving more than two, add a new dish for every two additional people, rather than increasing the quantity of the same dish. Thus, plan on two dishes, plus rice, for four people; three dishes plus rice for six, and so on.

2. One of the hazards of deep-frying in oil is the spattering that is likely to occur. These spatters are caused by the liquids in the food coming into contact with the hot oil. Minimize the risk of getting painful burns by drying the food as thoroughly as possible with paper towels and using long tongs to put it into the fat. Where possible, fry over medium heat. Partially cover the pan so that the cover acts as a shield. Do not put the cover on tightly; otherwise the moisture trapped in the pan will make the food soggy instead of crisp and brown. A colander inverted over the pan makes a good shield.

From Easy to Complex

There are all sorts of proverbs and quotations throughout human history advising us to learn step by step, the easy first, then the more difficult. The most familiar perhaps is "Learn to walk before you run," and a more poetic one may be the Chinese proverb "A journey of a thousand miles starts with the first step."

The recipes are arranged in this book so that the first ones in each group are quite simple to make, with lots of substitutions possible if you do not yet have all the ingredients stocked for Chinese cooking. The other recipes will become increasingly more complex, but it is hoped that your skills will have improved to the point where they will be no more difficult for you than the very first one.

A certain amount of self-assurance is necessary in every human endeavor. I am reminded of the story of a man who asked another, after a violin concert by Heifetz, if he could play the violin. "I don't know," replied the other. "I've never tried!" It is amazing how often confidence makes the difference between success and failure. This is very true of learning to cook. The Chinese use the words 大家 ("taai ga") to mean "everybody." But, literally translated, "taai ga" means "big family." Now nearly one quarter of mankind, or 700,000,000 people (give or take a few million), are cooking and eating Chinese food. You can too. Welcome to our "big family"!

6

Vegetables

I OFTEN amuse myself by making up aphorisms, such as "Life is like a fountain" (because it's all wet?) or "Love is like a rubber band" (but don't stretch it too far!). If I may coin another, "Vegetables are like lovely women." Please do not think that I am making an invidious comparison. I love them both! They are alike in their reaction to the treatment they receive; both should be handled with loving care and especially should not be "overdone."

Connoisseurs (of food) believe that the Chinese treatment of vegetables is the best in the world, because their crispness, color, flavor, and individual characteristics are retained. There is, as well, a great deal of scientific evidence to prove that a greater amount of minerals and vitamins is retained when vegetables are cooked Chinese style.

Man is carnivorous, and will eat meat in preference to vegetables if both are equally available. Watch a child eat his dinner; usually he will eat up all the meat and leave the vegetables. In this country mothers often have to bribe or threaten to get their children to eat vegetables, or resort to outright lies about our cartoon folk hero Popeye, who loves spinach.

This kind of problem hardly ever occurred in China, where meat was a luxury to be enjoyed regularly by only a few wealthy families. I had a great-uncle who was a poor farmer. Whenever I used to visit him as a child, he would invite me to share his meager meal, and I always accepted. The meal inevitably was rice and vegetables, which he grew. Only twice a year did he have a little meat—on his birthday and on New Year's Day. I remembered those meatless meals with fondness. It may have been the food, or my love for that kindly old gentleman, or a combination of both.

The Chinese very seldom cook vegetables alone, unadorned, as we do here in the West. Meatless they may be, but almost always the vegetables are stir-fried in a little oil, with a touch of soy sauce, mixed with a little foo yue (a cheeselike fermented bean curd) or shrimp paste. If one was lucky enough, a little meat would be added to the vegetables.

The stir-fry method for cooking vegetables also had the virtue of economy; it conserved fuel, which in itself was a luxury, since firewood had to be gathered and straw was available only after the harvest. Too, the vegetables had to be subjected to intense heat in order to destroy ever-present microbes. It is exalting to think that the Chinese, under these difficult conditions, not only surmounted the obstacles, but made the food delicious besides!

Just as there are endless paeans to women, I can go on and on about the virtues of vegetables. I shall reserve them for other parts of this book when a recipe calls for a particular vegetable and further details are relevant. The reader will find many additional recipes using vegetables in conjunction with meat, fowl, or seafood further on in this book. The recipes in this chapter use vegetables as the major or "star" ingredient. Learning to cook vegetables correctly is an art in itself, and once you've mastered this skill, you are well on your "journey of a thousand miles" toward pleasurable Chinese cooking.

SPECIAL CHINESE VEGETABLES

Most of the vegetables you find in your local supermarket or vegetable stands are eminently suited for Chinese cooking. The Chinese families who do not live in large metropolitan centers where there are Chinese stores must rely on American vegetables, as you do, for their meals, and they eat very well. Fortunately, most food items are international in character and equally at home in any kitchen. (This is not to say that there are no special vegetables in the Chinese diet. We shall discuss them a little later on.) If this were a book on horticulture we could trace the intermingling and origin of the many vegetables that are common to the East and the West. What was at one time exclusively owned by the one is now available equally to the other. For example, celery cabbage at one time had a Chinese citizenship but now almost every large American market carries it, usually as a salad vegetable. The tomato was only recently introduced to China, and I never saw one there until I was nine years old. Now, it is in extensive use in the Chinese kitchen. To mention just a few others that know no national bounds we can include lettuce, cucumbers, string beans, broccoli, mushrooms, white radishes, spinach, and watercress.

The special vegetables you may have seen in a Chinese store are grown and used by the Chinese and Japanese people. Since these are available only in their stores, they are out of reach of readers who do not happen to live near such stores. They can be bought by mail, but if the distance is long, or delivery is delayed, the special goodness of these fresh vegetables is lost.

Even though you can cook without special Chinese vegetables, do see for yourself what they are like if you get an opportunity to visit a Chinese grocery store. Going into a Chinese grocery store is an experience not to be missed. It's like visiting in the heart of China. If you contemplate a trip to a large city where

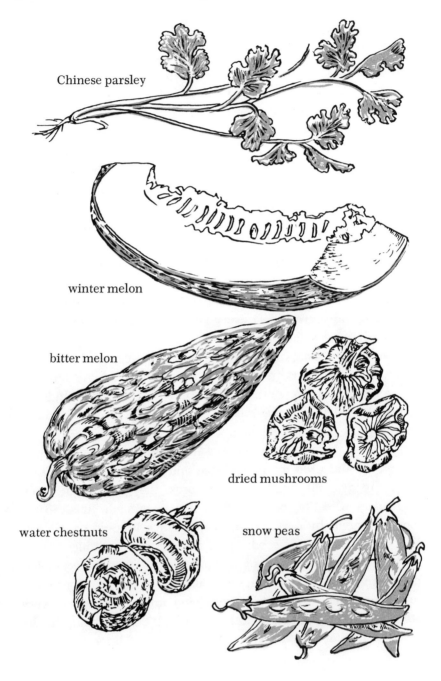

Chinese parsley

winter melon

bitter melon

dried mushrooms

water chestnuts

snow peas

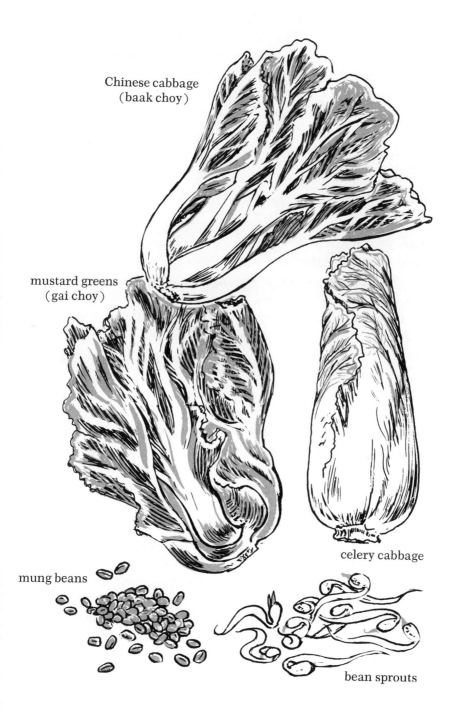

Chinese cabbage
(baak choy)

mustard greens
(gai choy)

celery cabbage

mung beans

bean sprouts

there are Chinese stores, by all means go into Chinatown just before your trip home by whatever means of transportation. There you can buy the fresh foods for your Chinese cooking that otherwise might not be available to you.

Here is more specific information on some of the vegetables which are more or less special to Chinese cooking. I shall use the same system in listing them as in some other sections, with English, phonetic transcription, and Chinese characters in each heading.

Celery Cabbage (*Lung Nga Paak*) 龍芽白

The Chinese gave this common vegetable a very celestial name. Literally it is "white teeth of the dragon." It is a tightly formed head vegetable, snow white in color except for the tip of each broad leaf, which is slightly yellow or light green. Unlike a real cabbage or celery in looks and taste, it is more a cross between the two. Since the heads vary in size and weight, the amount to use will be given in the recipes. Buy a large or small head as you wish, since this vegetable will keep a long time refrigerated.

Chinese Cabbage (*Baak Choy*) 白菜

The most distinctive of Chinese vegetables is baak choy, literally translated "white vegetables." Only the stems of this leafy plant are white; the broad leaves are green. Although used extensively by the Chinese, it is not essential if it is not available in your locality. A good substitute for it is celery cabbage.

The same comments apply to this as for celery cabbage. However, it will not keep as long as celery cabbage because this is a leafy vegetable. Buy only as much of it as you can anticipate using in a week. The specific amount to use will be given in each recipe.

Baak choy hearts are the inner stalks of the baak choy bunch, as celery hearts are to a bunch of celery. The hearts are more delicate and tender than the outer stalks.

Chinese Mustard Greens (*Gai Choy*) 芥菜

This is a cousin to baak choy; it is also a leafy vegetable, but its stems are green. It has almost exactly the same taste as the Western mustard greens, which make a good substitute for it. You will find a recipe on page 261 using this vegetable for a delicious soup.

Snow Peas (*Suet Dau*) 雪荳

Snow peas are much like fresh peas in their pods, which they are, except the pod is tender and crisp and is eaten unshelled. Frozen snow peas are now available in supermarkets. It should be noted that fresh snow peas are superior to the frozen. Of late, this delicacy has been popularly used as a salad green. If they are refrigerated, fresh snow peas will keep for over two weeks. One half pound to 1 pound is plenty to buy at one time. A handful is usually enough to dress up most stir-fry recipes. It invariably is a welcome addition to a dish, since its bright green color, crispness, and sweet, delicate taste please almost all palates. Great care should be used not to overcook this vegetable, or its virtues are lost. It should be cooked no more than a minute.

Chinese Winter Melon (*Tung Kwa*) 冬瓜

The Chinese winter melon is delicious when used in soups, but you can hardly tell the difference between it and the white meat (next to the rind) of the watermelon when it is cooked. There is a recipe in the soup section of this book using watermelon rind as a substitute. I love recipes that serve two purposes; this one makes a delicious soup and gets rid of the messy remainder of a used watermelon.

A more detailed description and accompanying recipe for this melon can be found on page 258.

Winter melon can only be bought fresh. It does not come in cans.

Bean Sprouts (*Nga Choy*) 芽菜

Most people are already familiar with bean sprouts. They were perhaps the first truly Chinese vegetable introduced by the Chinese restaurants to Westerners, in chop suey and chow mein dishes.

The unsprouted beans are called "mung beans" in English; their Chinese name is 綠荳 ("lok dau"—literally, "green beans"). Mung beans are small in size, about like BB shots used by children in their air rifles. Mung beans may be ordered from the stores listed on page 329. They are sold by the pound, are very inexpensive, and will last indefinitely if kept tightly sealed in a jar.

Bean sprouts may be found canned on most supermarket shelves, under such trade names as La Choy. The canned variety cannot compare with the fresh. Bean sprouts can be easily grown at home. You may find this to be a fascinating hobby, especially if you have small children in the house, and they can watch the bean sprouts grow. Many Western fairy tales are of Chinese origin, such as "Cinderella." I believe "Jack and the Beanstalk" may have come from China too. To this day, Chinese children cultivate bean sprouts, not only for food, but as a hobby. I recall that there were contests in my village among the children to see who grew the best sprouts, which they shaped and arranged to resemble miniature gardens. It's amazing how fast bean sprouts grow. The beans will start to sprout in one day, and reach succulent maturity about two inches long in three to four days.

How to Grow Bean Sprouts

Success in growing your bean-sprout crop is almost automatic if you will follow a few simple rules. The beans should be soaked overnight or for about eight hours in lukewarm water. After the soaking period, rinse the beans a few times in cool water.

I found that disposable heavy-gauge aluminum cake or baking pans are excellent as containers in which to sprout the beans. Containers from frozen TV dinners will serve the same purpose. Use a nail or other pointed tool to punch holes at random in the pan bottom so water will drain easily.

Line the pan bottom with a double layer of cheesecloth or clean white material (such as a torn-up old bed sheet). Scatter the beans close together evenly over the cloth. Cover with another double layer of material. (The double layers retain the moisture better than a single layer.) Place the container in the sink and pour several cups of lukewarm water over the cloth until it is wet through. The excess water will drain out from the holes. (Only the cloth should be wet; the beans should not be soaking in water while growing.)

Now you've planted your garden! The next step is to put it into some sort of tray so water will not drip all over the place. The broiling pan and rack in your oven will suit the purpose admirably—if you are not planning to use it for several days. In fact, the oven is a wonderful storage place for your bean-sprout crop while it is growing. Naturally, you must remove the bean sprouts from the oven if you bake or broil, and only put them back after the oven has completely cooled. A closet or pantry or any unused place you may have which is not in direct sunlight will serve equally well.

Water your garden at four- to six-hour intervals with several cups of cool water. (Discard excess water in pan from previous watering.) There is no 4 A.M. feeding on a bean sprout's growing schedule! Sleep well.

Your bean sprouts will be ready to harvest in three to four days, depending on temperature and other conditions. Before using the sprouts in a recipe, rinse several times in cool water. The loosened green husks must be removed and discarded. This may be the only tedious job in growing your own bean sprouts. However, most of the husks will float loose by themselves, and since the husks are edible, if you miss a few they will not in any way alter the goodness of your cooking.

The amount of dry mung beans you use will vary according to your need and the size of your aluminum pan. Use several pans if you need a large quantity of bean sprouts. Every ½ cup of the beans will yield about 1 pound of sprouts.

Chinese Parsley (*Yuen Sai*) 芫茜

This fragrant herb is generally used as a garnish. When used in a dish, it is always optional. It must be used fresh, since it cannot be frozen or dried. You may have used coriander seeds in your cooking. Chinese parsley is leaf coriander, and can be bought not only in Chinese grocery stores but also in Italian markets (where it is called *cilantro*) and in Puerto Rican groceries (*culantro*).

In Chinese groceries fresh Chinese parsley is sold with the roots left on and some of the soil still clinging to them. If you wrap the roots tightly in wax paper and tie it, the parsley will keep for a long time. I've kept Chinese parsley fresh this way

two or three weeks in the vegetable crisper. There should be no water on the parsley or in the bottom of the crisper, or it may rot during storage.

If you cultivate a little herb garden, you may want to include Chinese parsley in it. The seeds may be bought from large distributors of vegetable and flower seeds. You will find it listed as coriander seeds, and growing instructions are available on the package or from the distributor.

I buy my coriander seeds from a Chinese specialty store in New York's Chinatown, but they do not make mail-order sales. The owner, a venerable Chinese gentleman, told me that he did send some Chinese parsley seeds by mail to an American friend in Detroit once. His friend planted the seeds along the edge of his beautiful lawn. Spring, summer, and fall passed, and not a single leaf of parsley appeared. The next spring the friend gave him a frantic telephone call: "My beautiful bent grass lawn has now been replaced with unbendable Chinese parsley!" I don't know what advice this Chinese sorcerer gave his apprentice. The end of the story was drowned out by his laughter.

Other Chinese Vegetables

Most other special Chinese vegetables are available in cans. They include items such as water chestnuts, bamboo shoots, and even bitter melon.

The list can go on, but I think the above has given you a clear idea about Chinese vegetables and their possible "stand-ins." You might even experiment and discover uses and substitutions of your own.

Storage of Vegetables

How long vegetables will keep depends on the particular vegetable, and how fresh it was when you bought it. You probably already know a lot about the storage life expectancy and the best methods of keeping vegetables fresh, but here is one tip which you might not have heard: vegetables will keep better if they are not washed until you are ready to use them. This applies to all leafy vegetables or beans, for American cooking as well as for Chinese. There seems to be a natural protective coating that will preserve the freshness of a vegetable. You can, however, cut the vegetable several days in advance so long as you don't wash it. Once it is washed the natural protection is gone, and the extra moisture tends to rot or discolor the cut surfaces.

Blanching

A very useful procedure to use when cooking Chinese dishes is to blanch or parboil the vegetables ahead of time. This will save precious minutes in the cooking process, where time is of the essence. If you are cooking several dishes for a dinner, it is almost imperative to blanch vegetables, since the cooking time saved also frees your burner or burners faster for cooking one dish after the other, and your many-splendored dishes will come out together closer on cue.

Another advantage of blanching is that your vegetables will come out crisper and less watery. Many home stoves (especially electric ones) are not equal to the task of good Chinese cooking, which requires that vegetables should be cooked in intense heat in the shortest time possible. Slow cooking tends to extract the juices and make vegetables soggy and limp. By blanching the vegetables, you can overcome most of the stove's inadequacy.

Blanching is a very simple process to learn. Essentially it is a "half-cooking" process, in which the ingredients are cleaned and precut, then put into boiling water briefly. When the food is partially cooked (don't let the water boil again when the food has been put in), it is quickly removed and placed in a pan of cold water. Stir the ingredients in the cold water to cool them evenly and fast. Remove from the water, drain and put aside until ready to use.

The exact amount of water (enough to cover the vegetables) and size of pot to use will have to be left to your own good judgment, since I cannot foresee the amount of food you may be blanching. You may have wondered why I used "ingredients" and "food" in place of just the word "vegetables." This blanching process is also sometimes used for meats and seafood to seal in the natural juices or to remove foreign tastes; instructions will be given for that as necessary in the recipes.

In using this process for blanching vegetables, add two tablespoons of vegetable oil to the water. The oil helps to preserve the greenness of the vegetables.

Sautéed Spinach 鶏油菠菜

GAI YAU BOH CHOY

Chicken fat can be used to dress up a variety of vegetables. Next time you cook a chicken, save the excess fat, usually found near the cavity, and freeze it for use in this recipe. About ½ cup of raw chicken fat is all that is needed.

Use fresh spinach, not the frozen kind. Time and effort will be saved if you buy spinach that has been trimmed and washed and packed in plastic bags. It comes in either 12-ounce or 1-pound bags. The weight difference is so slight that the recipe need not be altered to conform to the weights. If you prefer unprocessed spinach, buy 1 pound. Trim and wash thoroughly to remove sand. Drain dry before cooking.

I   1   *bag (or 1 pound) fresh spinach†*

II   1   *clove garlic, minced*

III   1   *teaspoon sugar*
       ½   *teaspoon monosodium glutamate*

IV   ½   *cup unrendered chicken fat*
       ⅛   *teaspoon salt*
       2   *tablespoons sherry*

Heat wok or pan hot and dry. Add the raw (unrendered) chicken fat and turn heat to medium. Stir frequently until the oil has been extracted and only a residue is left, which you may discard. Add the salt.

Add the minced garlic; cook until golden brown. Add the

spinach; turn up heat to high. Stir-fry for 1 minute. Sprinkle the sugar and monosodium glutamate over the spinach. Stir well and add the sherry. Quickly cover the wok or pan and cook 1 minute longer.

Serve with rice, or use the spinach as a vegetable dish with American meals.

SUBSTITUTIONS AND VARIATIONS

Any leafy vegetable such as mustard greens, kale, or turnip greens may be used instead of spinach. Double the cooking time for these greens, since they take more time to cook than the spinach.

Fried Sweet and Sour Cabbage 甜酸椰菜

TIM SEUN YEH CHOY

I have often been impressed with the similarities between many foods used by very diverse societies and people. In a way, it is not too surprising because there are only so many methods by which food can be cooked. I took a friend to have a Chinese tea lunch one day. Her mother is very good at Jewish cooking. Each time a new delicacy came out that was, to me, distinctively Chinese, she would exclaim, "My mother makes something quite similar to this!" I realized, then, that what she said was true. Won ton is quite similar to kreplach, which is quite similar to ravioli.

This cabbage dish has many international cousins. I have had sweet-and-sour cabbage in German and Viennese cooking, as well as Middle Eastern cuisine. I cannot argue that this was a Chinese invention. If the Russians claim they invented it, for all I know it could be true.

I   1   *medium-size head of cabbage (about 1½ pounds)*

III   2   *tablespoons brown sugar*
       ½   *teaspoon monosodium glutamate*

3   tablespoons *dark soy sauce*
2   tablespoons *vinegar*
2   tablespoons *water*

I V   3   tablespoons *vegetable oil*
½   teaspoon *salt*
¾   cup *sherry*

Remove first layer of tough leaves from cabbage and discard. Cut the cabbage head into quarters, remove the hard stems from each and discard. Cut the cabbage quarters crosswise from top to bottom into ½-inch strips.

Combine all the ingredients in Group III and put aside.

Heat wok or pan hot and dry. Add the oil. Then add the salt. Put in the cut cabbage and cook over high heat for 1 minute, stirring constantly. Then add the mixture from Group III while stirring. Cover and cook 1 minute more. Remove cover and add the sherry. Stir to mix well. Turn off heat and serve.

This could be a main meatless dish, if it is served with rice or noodles. The gravy, which is not thickened, goes well with both. When used as a side dish, it could perk up rather bland foods like boiled beef or chicken.

If you like your food hot and pungent, the addition of half a teaspoon of Tabasco to the gravy will do it.

Pickled Sweet and Sour Vegetables   甜酸菜

TIM SEUN CHOY

These pickled vegetables can be used by themselves as a side dish or as a garnish to a main dish. However, you will find them most useful as an ingredient in sweet and sour sauces (see, for example, Sweet and Sour Pork on page 109) where the crisp, colorful vegetables lend color and contrast to the meat. While fresh vegetables can be used in the sauce, these pickled vegetables will taste better, since their flavor will be more than skin deep.

They also make an excellent side dish, or a light dessert after a heavy meal.

This recipe can be made at your leisure, and will keep in the refrigerator for over a year.

I 1 *medium head of cauliflower*
  2 *medium green peppers*
  4 *carrots*
  1 *bunch white radishes†*
  2 *hot chili peppers*
  3 *quarts water for blanching*

III 2 *cups sugar†*
  2 *cups white vinegar*
  1 *teaspoon salt*
  1 *cup water*

Wash all the vegetables and cut into bite size, about the size and shape of a French-fried potato. In fact, a curlicue cutter such as is used for cutting French-fried potatoes is an excellent tool for this purpose. The cauliflower should just be broken off in flowerets from the head. If those pieces are too large, cut into smaller pieces. Discard the stems.

Place the 3 quarts of water in a saucepan and bring to a vigorous boil. Add all the cut vegetables to the boiling water and turn off the heat at once. Let vegetables stay in the water for 2 minutes. Drain off water and spread out the vegetables to dry on a platter. When vegetables are cooled, pack the pieces at random tightly into a glass jar or plastic container.

Put all the ingredients in Group III in a saucepan, mix, and bring to a boil. Remove from stove to cool. Pour this marinating liquid over the vegetables until they are completely covered. Cap the container or jar and store in refrigerator. Let stand for at least 1 week before using.

SUBSTITUTIONS AND VARIATIONS

If white radishes are not available, substitute 3 bunches red radishes. The Chinese white radishes do not come in bunches, since they are much larger, weighing up to 3 pounds. If you can obtain Chinese radishes, use 1 about a pound in weight. The skin should be removed.

Saccharin or liquid sweetener may be used instead of sugar, and not only for weight watchers; some cooks actually prefer it to sugar. Both are equally good.

Using the same marinade and the same procedure, peaches can be pickled for a dessert to be served after Chinese meals. The peaches should be firm and not too ripe; otherwise they would not have the crispness which is desirable.

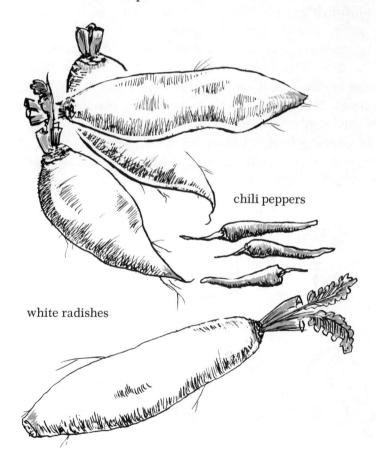

chili peppers

white radishes

Jade-Green Broccoli 炒芥蘭

CHOW GAI LAAN

Broccoli, when cooked to perfection, is really a very delicate vegetable. Once overcooked, as in most Western recipes, this vegetable becomes heavy and strong in flavor. Broccoli literally tells you when it is being overcooked, because the change in color is very pronounced. When done properly, broccoli turns a beautiful jade green. When overcooked, its color is a dull yellowish green, and its texture becomes mushy.

In selecting a bunch of broccoli, look for a bright purplish green color. The stalks should be smooth with not too many leaves on the stems, or marks of where the leaves have been removed. The flowerets should be tightly bunched and should not shed easily when brushed against your hand.

In cleaning broccoli, break off the flowerets from the side of each main stem. The flowerets may be split in halves or quarters, depending on size. Discard all the leaves. Cut off and discard about an inch of each main stem, and, using a paring knife,

cut from the end into the tough outer skin and peel it off between your thumb and the knife blade. This peeling process can be used for all vegetables with stems (see illustration).

Wash the broccoli flowerets and stems in cold water. Drain, and cut the main stems on a slant into ⅛-inch slices.

I   1   *bunch (about 2 pounds) broccoli, sliced, washed, drained, and dried*

II   1   *clove garlic, minced*

III 1   *teaspoon sugar*
     1   *teaspoon monosodium glutamate*
     1   *tablespoon cornstarch*
     2   *tablespoons soy sauce†*
     ½   *cup water or chicken stock*

IV ¼   *cup vegetable oil*
     ⅛   *teaspoon salt*
     2   *tablespoons sherry*

Mix together ingredients in Group III and put aside.

Heat wok or pan hot and dry. Add the oil, then the salt. Turn heat to medium and add the garlic. When garlic is golden brown, add the broccoli. Turn heat up and stir-fry for 2 minutes. Add the sherry and cover wok or pan quickly. Cook covered 2 minutes longer. Lift cover and add the mixture from Group III while stirring. When gravy has thickened, remove broccoli and gravy from pan and serve.

SUBSTITUTIONS AND VARIATIONS

The soy sauce may be eliminated, or oyster sauce used in its place for a different flavor. Use 3 tablespoons oyster sauce. If no soy or oyster sauce is used, increase the amount of salt slightly.

Minced cooked ham, crisp bacon bits, or dried beef may be added as a garnish for extra flavor. Two or 3 tablespoons of any one is sufficient.

Stir-Fried String Beans   炒荳仔

CHOW DAU TSAI

String beans are very easy to prepare. The Chinese beans
look different because they are long and slender—two or three
times as long as their American cousins. I can hardly detect
any differences in taste, however, so I always use the cheaper
and more available American kind. String beans are also called
green beans.

Fresh string beans are available all year round. If you have
a choice, select the smallest beans, since they are younger and
more tender. The color should be a deep green, and the beans
should snap in half easily and cleanly, which is a mark of
freshness. There are yellow string beans, too, and they may be
used in place of the green variety.

Cut or break off the tips from both ends of beans. The
"string" is the fine threadlike fiber that runs the length of the
back, which will be removed with the tips. Some young beans
don't even have any strings. Break beans in half if they are too
long. Rinse in cold water and drain. Dry beans thoroughly
before use, since any water on them will cause the oil to spatter.

I	1	*pound string beans*
II	1	*clove garlic, minced*
	2	*slices fresh ginger, shredded†*
III	1	*teaspoon sugar*
	1	*tablespoon cornstarch*
	1	*teaspoon monosodium glutamate*
	2	*tablespoons soy sauce*
	½	*cup chicken stock or water*
IV	¼	*cup vegetable oil*
	⅛	*teaspoon salt*
	2	*tablespoons sherry*

Mix together ingredients in Group III and put aside.

Heat wok or pan hot and dry. Add the oil. Add the salt. Turn heat down to medium. Put in the garlic and ginger and stir-fry till golden brown. Add the string beans and turn heat to high. Stir-fry until the beans change to a deeper green color. Add the sherry and cook covered 2 minutes. Remove cover, add the seasoning mixture, and stir-fry till gravy has thickened. Remove from pan and serve with rice, or as a vegetable dish with American meals.

SUBSTITUTIONS AND VARIATIONS

The ginger is optional. If it is not used, a dash of Tabasco or a touch of ground pepper will give the beans more zing.

A cup of shredded ham or roast pork added just before the seasoning mixture is put in will give you a different recipe to enjoy.

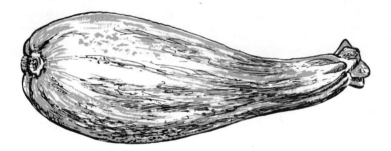

Tender-Fried Zucchini   炒瓜

CHOW KWA

I 'am getting a tremendous education on things to file and forget in the process of writing this book! Is zucchini a squash, or is it a gourd? It seems that both come from the same family of plants and it really does not make any difference except to a botanist. If I may draw my own definition for the purpose of cooking, a squash is more tender and the skin is thin and edible, while a gourd has a tough inedible shell and its meat is stringier and requires longer cooking.

It's strange to note that the Chinese do not make distinctions between a gourd and a squash. The Chinese language is so exact (and so difficult!). As an example, for the English word "uncle" there are three different words which must be used properly to identify the uncle who is (1) a father's older brother "Ah Baak" (2) the father's younger brother "Ah Sook" and (3) a mother's brother "Ah Kau." This complexity also goes for aunts, cousins, and a myriad of other things. Yet the Chinese call melons, squashes, and gourds by one name only. If you ask the question "What is a zucchini?" and find no answer among your literate guests, tell them smugly that it is a "kwa."

This recipe is not limited to zucchini. Any young tender squash may be used. If the skin of the squash is so tender that it punctures when pressed with a fingernail, it need not be peeled. Otherwise peel it as thin as you can with a sharp paring knife or vegetable peeler. Cut each squash into several lengths (depending on how long a particular squash is) of about 1½ inches. Then slice into domino shapes.

Seeds need not be discarded in young squash.

After the onion has been peeled, cut it in half lengthwise. Then cut into ¼-inch slices. The onion layers will separate themselves on being cooked.

I   2-3   *zucchini (about 1 pound), sliced into pieces the size of a domino*
      1   *medium-size onion, sliced*

II   2   *cloves garlic, minced*

III 1   *tablespoon sugar*
      1   *tablespoon cornstarch*
      2   *teaspoons salted cured soybeans, rinsed and crushed†*
      1   *teaspoon monosodium glutamate*

1   *tablespoon soy sauce*
½   *cup chicken stock or water*

I V   2   *tablespoons vegetable oil*

Mix together ingredients in Group III and put aside.

Heat wok or pan until hot and dry. Add the oil. Turn heat down to medium. Add garlic and fry till golden brown. Add the zucchini and onions; turn heat up to high and stir-fry for 2 minutes. Cover and cook 2 minutes longer. Lift cover and add the sauce mixture from Group III, and stir until gravy thickens. Turn off heat and replace cover for 2 minutes to let the flavor permeate the vegetables. Serve at leisure with rice or as a side dish.

SUBSTITUTIONS AND VARIATIONS

The salted soybeans (see page 34) are optional. When they are used, be sure to rinse in cold water and eliminate salt from the recipe. When these beans are not used, add ⅛ teaspoon salt.

Stir-Fried Bean Sprouts   炒芽菜

CHOW NGAR CHOY

To make this simple delicious dish, you must use fresh bean sprouts. Although canned bean sprouts are widely available, they do not have the taste and texture of the fresh kind. If you are not near a source where fresh bean sprouts can be bought, growing your own crop is easy, fun, and inexpensive. See instructions on page 60.

When preparing bean sprouts for cooking, place them in a sinkful of cool water. Swirl them around with your hands a few times to loosen the green bean husks that may be clinging to the sprouts. Pick out the husks and discard. Drain and dry well.

I 1½ *pounds fresh bean sprouts*

II 1 *clove garlic, minced*

2 *slices fresh ginger, shredded*

3 *scallions, cut into 1½-inch lengths, including green ends†*

2 *small sweet gherkins, shredded†*

III 1 *teaspoon sugar*

½ *teaspoon ground white pepper*

1 *teaspoon monosodium glutamate*

3 *tablespoons soy sauce*

½ *cup chicken stock or water*

IV ¼ *cup vegetable oil*

⅛ *teaspoon salt*

2 *tablespoons sherry*

Mix together ingredients in Group III and put aside.

Heat wok or pan hot and dry. Add the oil, then the salt. Turn heat to medium and add the garlic and ginger. Fry till golden brown. Add the bean sprouts, scallions, and gherkins, turn heat up high and stir-fry for 2 minutes. Add the sherry, quickly cover the pan, and cook 2 minutes more. Remove cover and add the sauce mixture from Group III while stirring. When sauce is well mixed with the vegetables, turn off heat and serve.

SUBSTITUTIONS AND VARIATIONS

When using scallions for Chinese cooking, always include the green ends unless specifically instructed not to. If the diameter of the scallions is too thick, split with knife in halves or quarters lengthwise before cutting into 1½-inch pieces.

The sweet gherkins are to lend a tart contrast to the bland bean sprouts. Pickled or candied fruits and rinds may be used to achieve the same results. Use sparingly.

The Chinese version of sweet gherkins is called "cha kwa," and they go particularly well with bean sprouts and some steamed dishes. Since cha kwa will keep for months in a jar without refrigeration, you may want to add this item to your larder.

Creamed Chinese Cabbage 白汁菜

BAAK CHUP CHOY

In Chinese cooking, dairy products are seldom used. I was reared in Canton, and never had a glass of fresh milk until I came to the United States at the age of nine. The first encounter I had with a piece of mild American cheese was almost disastrous. It was at a church picnic during the first summer I was in this country, and I was handed two slices of bread, between which was a sheet of yellowish material. I took one bite into it and had to make a Samuel Johnson decision, at that tender age. (I came by Samuel Johnson much later in life: Boswell recorded an episode in which Johnson spat out a mouthful of hot food at an elegant banquet table and said, "A fool would have swallowed it!") I swallowed it. But the rest of the sandwich I managed to hide in a bush. I honestly thought that what I had eaten was food spoiled by the summer heat. I've since learned to love cheese, but it was not easy.

The reason for the lack of dairy foods in the Chinese diet is understandable. There were no grazing lands in China to support herds of cattle, since every square inch of land was

used to grow crops to feed the hungry millions. In the northern parts of China, the nomads did have herds of goats and horses, and therefore had milk. Genghis Khan's army was able to fight so well and travel so far because each soldier was able to carry a disk of mare's cheese with him in his battles, which freed him from the field kitchen. Perhaps the Chinese never adopted the food habits of the Mongols because they were thought of as barbarians.

But Chinese are a very adaptable people. They now do use a limited amount of milk or cream in their kitchens, as in a few creamed recipes like the one which follows.

I	¾	*pound Chinese cabbage (baak choy), washed and sliced (see page 44)†*
II	1	*small can deviled Smithfield ham†*
	1	*clove garlic, minced*
III	1	*teaspoon sugar*
	⅛	*teaspoon ground pepper*
	1	*tablespoon cornstarch*
	1	*teaspoon monosodium glutamate*
	2	*tablespoons light soy sauce†*
	½	*cup chicken stock or water*
IV	2	*tablespoons vegetable oil*
	⅛	*teaspoon salt*
	¼	*cup heavy cream*

Mix together ingredients in Group III and put aside.

Heat wok or pan hot and dry. Add the oil, then the salt. Turn heat down to medium. Add the garlic and fry till golden brown. Add the baak choy; turn heat up to high and stir-fry for 2 minutes. While stirring, add the sauce mixture from Group III. Cover and cook for 2 minutes more. Remove cover and mix in the deviled ham.

Turn heat to low and slowly stir in the heavy cream. Turn off heat and serve.

SUBSTITUTIONS AND VARIATIONS

Celery cabbage makes an excellent substitute for Chinese cabbage if that is not available. The Smithfield ham adds a distinctive flavor. This type of ham is closest to the real Chinese ham and has been chopped before packing, so no more cutting is necessary. However, its use is optional. Light soy sauce is used here, so that gravy will remain whiter. If you have only dark soy sauce, use only 1 tablespoon of it.

Stir-Fried Tomatoes 炒番茄

CHOW FAAN K'E

Tomatoes, in season, are a wonderful treat prepared in almost any way. Out of season, or not ripened as they should be, it is not worth the effort to eat them, since they are flat tasting and pulpy. Try this recipe only when you have good tomatoes worthy of your skill and labor. Good tomatoes should be ripe, juicy, tart, and firm.

I   6   *medium-size tomatoes, cut into 4 or 6 segments each*
   2   *medium onions, cut into segments with layers separated*

II   2   *cloves garlic, minced*
   2   *slices fresh ginger, shredded*

III   1   *teaspoon sugar*
   1   *tablespoon cornstarch*
   1   *teaspoon monosodium glutamate*
   2   *tablespoons soy sauce*
   1¼   *cups chicken stock or water*
   1   *tablespoon salted cured soybeans, rinsed and crushed†*

IV   3   *tablespoons vegetable oil*
   2   *tablespoons sherry*

Mix together ingredients in Group III and put aside.

Heat wok or pan hot and dry. Add the oil. Turn heat down to medium and add the garlic and ginger; stir-fry till golden brown. Add the onions and stir-fry until yellow and translucent. Turn up heat and add the sauce mixture from Group III. Stir until gravy has thickened. Add the tomatoes and stir gently until they are well mixed with the gravy (about ½ minute). Pour in the sherry. Cover at once and turn off heat. Let the food stand in the pot covered for 2 minutes to blend the different flavors. Remove from pan and serve at once.

SUBSTITUTIONS AND VARIATIONS

The salted soybeans are optional. If not used, add ⅛ teaspoon salt. See page 34.

Elegant Stir-Fried Vegetables 炒大會菜

CHOW DAI WEY CHOY

Chinese vegetable dishes may be very elegant as well as delicious. Such a dish may involve any number of special vegetables and become a party dish in itself. The famous dish called the Buddhists' Feast may have 15 to 20 (or more) different vegetables in it. We do not have to use quite that many items (and that much extra labor) to make a very festive meatless dish. As a matter of fact, if we leave out the meats in many of the recipes in this book, they can become vegetarian dishes for people who must follow certain diets for health or religious reasons. Conversely, all of the vegetable dishes given in this book may be changed to suit your mood and creative skill by the addition of meat or seafood. It is my hope that, after a while, you will take some liberties with my recipes, once you've mastered the basic concept of Chinese cooking.

The following recipe uses a few of the special Chinese canned and fresh vegetables, and should not be attempted unless you have most of the items on hand.

I   6   *dried Chinese mushrooms (about 1 inch in diameter, soaked in ⅓ cup water)*

     1   *medium-size onion, cut into 8 segments and separated into natural layers*

     ½   *cup thinly sliced canned bamboo shoots*

     ¼   *cup sliced water chestnuts*

     2   *cups snow peas†*

II   1   *clove garlic, minced*

     2   *slices fresh ginger, shredded*

III   1   *teaspoon sugar*

     1   *tablespoon cornstarch*

     1   *teaspoon monosodium glutamate*

     2   *tablespoons soy sauce*

     ½   *cup chicken stock*

       Liquid from soaked mushrooms

IV   ¼   *cup vegetable oil*

     ⅛   *teaspoon salt*

     2   *tablespoons sherry*

     2   *tablespoons chopped scallions or parsley, for garnish (optional)*

Soak mushrooms for 1 hour or longer, then squeeze dry. Save the liquid for the seasoning mixture. Remove and discard the hard stems from mushrooms, if any. Mix together ingredients in Group III and put aside.

Heat wok or pan hot and dry. Add the oil, then the salt. Turn heat to medium, put in the garlic and ginger, and stir-fry until golden brown. Add the onion and fry for ½ minute. Turn heat up high and add the mushrooms, bamboo shoots, and water chestnuts and stir-fry 1 minute. Pour in the sherry and quickly cover to cook 1 minute longer. Add the snow peas, then add immediately the mixture from Group III while stirring. As soon as the gravy has thickened, remove from cooking pan into serving dish. Sprinkle chopped scallions or parsley on top as garnish. Serve at once.

SUBSTITUTIONS AND VARIATIONS

Very few substitutions can be made in this recipe. Too many changes will alter its authentic Chinese character. The snow peas may be replaced by sliced baak choy or celery cabbage. The scallions or parsley is used as a garnish, and although either adds a fresh flavor, it is optional.

7

Pork

I WOULD like to introduce you to two Chinese characters. The first is written like this: 安 and is pronounced "on." The second one is written 家 and pronounced "ga." The two words combined, "on ga," mean "a tranquil and comfortable home." But what has that got to do with pork? Just this: the two Chinese characters have the top symbol 宀 ("min") in common. That top symbol represents a house roof. Under the roof of the first character is the symbol 女 ("nui"), which is Chinese for woman. Under the other roof is the symbol 豕 ("chi"), the symbol for swine. The meaning is quite clear: with the possession of a wife and a pig, a man's home is complete. The order in which these pieces of good fortune rank in a man's mind and heart must depend on the man, the wife, and the pig!

Pork is the most widely used meat in the Chinese cuisine. There are very good reasons for this. A pig grows very fast. It does not require a large pasture. It can eat almost anything and grow fat on it, and that fat can be used in many ways to supplement the diet of a poor country.

In China, the diet is so poor in animal fats that the craving for fat overwhelms a taste for anything more subtle. What would repel us as being too fat and greasy becomes a great delicacy in a fat-poor diet. In this connection I remember a story about the head of a proud and once-rich family, who were made destitute by the Chinese revolution against the Manchu dynasty. This former mandarin saved a piece of Chinese bacon, which could be kept for months, and rubbed his children's lips with it after each meal. Meatless though the family's meals were, to the outside world the greasy faces of the children reflected a rich diet. That was *some* face-saving!

Much more can be said about the importance of pork to the Chinese people, but I've left out the most important reason for pork's popularity in Chinese cooking, which is that it *tastes* good. It is also a very obedient and versatile meat as well. You can cook it almost any way you choose, and if you treat it with respect, it will produce wonderful eating. A glance at a Chinese menu is ample proof of pork's versatility. You will find pork boiled, braised, barbecued, breaded, fried, stewed, steamed, and cooked in every way man knows. Pork is also a most sociable food: it can mix and mingle with any other meats, seafood, or sauces, and through its pleasant personality everything it comes in contact with is transformed for the better.

What Cut of Pork to Buy

Any lean cut of pork will do nicely for Chinese cooking. In other meats, what part of the animal the meat comes from often makes a big difference in tenderness, taste, and texture. This is not true with pork, which is uniformly tender and good tasting. The main difference between the various cuts is the proportion of fat to lean meat; the higher the ratio of lean meat, the more expensive the cut. In buying pork, buy the leanest piece you possibly can—but not necessarily the most expensive cut. There will be enough fat in whatever cut you buy because pork is naturally fat. Trim off most (but not all) of the large pieces of solid fat before proceeding with a Chinese recipe.

The best cut of pork to use is the lean meat from fresh hams.

The drawback is that a fresh ham is a very large cut. An average-size ham weighs between 10 and 15 pounds. Pound for pound, it will yield more lean meat at a lower cost than other parts of a pig. It may not be a bad idea to buy this cut, large as it is, even if you have a small family, since it can be cut up and stored frozen. You may also inquire of your butcher or meat market if they would sell you only half of a fresh ham, since selling habits vary from city to city and store to store. If you can buy half a ham, the butt half yields slightly more lean meat proportionally.

The next best cut to use is known variously as "pork shoulder," "shoulder butt," or "Boston butt." This cut is very convenient, since the whole piece weighs 5 to 7 pounds, and you can buy only a portion of that (as little as ½ pound if you wish).

Pork loin or pork chops (which come from the loin) are wonderful for our purposes. Since the loin is available at all times, I would have recommended it first, except that it is the most expensive cut of pork to buy. If cost is not a consideration, by all means use this cut, especially if you need only a small amount of it in a recipe.

If a particular cut of pork is especially suitable for a given purpose, I shall mention it in the recipes.

Pork stores very well in the freezer. It does not keep well in the refrigerator. Two or three days should be its storage limit. I make it a habit to buy more pork than I need for one meal, then cut up the extra and freeze it for future use. The easiest and most practical way to do this is to buy a big piece of pork, then use a portion of the meat for each type of cut you are likely to use in cooking. I slice some, cube some, chop some, and cut some into strips for barbecuing. It is not only economical, but it is a great convenience and a timesaver. Separate the meat cut by each method into portions, then wrap in plastic or plastic bags. This way, you can thaw out a portion at a time for use. Pork when frozen will keep safely without loss of quality or flavor for up to 6 months.

Chopped Pork

Pork should be hand-chopped for certain purposes, as when making "lobster sauce" or fillings for won tons, and for steamed pork dishes. Pork may be coarsely ground for these purposes, but hand chopping is better if you have the time and inclination.

In chopping pork, first cut the meat into thin strips, then dice them into small cubes before chopping. The meat should be irregular and fairly coarse when the job is completed. The two medium-weight cleavers are excellent tools for this purpose.

Fried Pork Chops, Chinese Style   煎猪肉

DEEN CHI YUK

I hope I've made it apparent by now that learning to do Chinese cooking is not just a matter of following recipes, but rather is learning the concepts of *how* foods should be cooked—in other words, acquiring a *style* in cooking. It is style which distinguishes anything that has to do with man's creativity. We can tell without seeing the signatures who painted a certain masterpiece, wrote a particular book, or composed a piece of music—all by their style. Even the way in which an athlete moves shows his style.

This recipe is a good one to start with for any beginner learning to cook in the Chinese style. While in China the luxury of having *a* pork chop for each person was out of the question, let alone *two* as in this recipe, I suspect that it was only the circumstance of life in a poor country which prevented Chinese cooks from creating dishes made with steaks and chops. The new generation of Chinese boys and girls with whom I have come into contact prefer steaks and chops over anything else in American cooking. The pork chops in this recipe have plenty of Chinese style.

I   4   *pork chops ¾ inch thick (about 1½ pounds)*

II 1   *clove garlic, minced*

   3   *scallions, chopped*

III 1   *teaspoon sugar*

   ½ *teaspoon monosodium glutamate*

   ⅓ *cup soy sauce*

   2   *tablespoons sherry*

     Dash of Tabasco

IV 2   *tablespoons vegetable oil†*

Combine all the items in Groups II and III to make a marinade. Trim off some of the fat from the pork chops, but not all. Place pork chops in a shallow plate or platter. Pour marinade over, turning chops several times to coat all surfaces. Let stand for 2 hours or more.

When chops are ready to fry, remove from marinade. Dry with paper towel. Heat a heavy frying pan until hot and dry. Add the vegetable oil. Turn heat to medium and put in pork chops to brown on one side (about 7 minutes). Turn over and fry for 10 minutes more uncovered, lifting and moving each chop once or twice to keep it from scorching (reduce heat if necessary). Pour leftover marinade over chops, cover, turn heat low, and cook 1 minute more. Remove pork chops to serving plates, pour gravy over, and serve.

SUBSTITUTIONS AND VARIATIONS

The pork chops may also be broiled, in which case you need not dry them on paper towels and you will not need the oil. Brush some marinade on chops as they broil. The length of broiling time varies with the stove, distance of the meat from the heat source, and other factors. Generally, with chops placed at a normal broiling distance, 10 minutes on each side is about right. Overcooked pork chops become dry and tough. See page 96 on how to tell when pork is done.

Pork with Broccoli in Oyster Sauce   蠔油芥蘭

HO YAU GAI LAAN

I dwelt at some length on the virtues and preparation of broccoli in the vegetable section (page 70) but a little more should be said about it in relation to this recipe and the one which follows. These recipes were selected to illustrate the versatility of broccoli, and how easily it can be transformed by the use of a different sauce mixture and a slight change in the cooking time.

The first recipe, for broccoli using pork and oyster sauce, is more familiar since it is on most Chinese restaurant menus. The taste should be very delicate and slightly salty. The vegetable is cooked slightly longer, and is therefore softer and less green-looking than in the recipe which follows.

The second recipe is a sweet dish. When cooked properly, the broccoli should be deep bright green in color and very crunchy in texture. Just for your own edification and amusement, why not make both of these broccoli dishes for the same meal? Doing so can show you some of the concepts and subtleties of Chinese cooking better than all the words which I could muster. Your family and friends will be beneficiaries of your noble experiment.

I   2   *cups sliced lean pork (about 1 pound)*

     1   *bunch (about 2 pounds) fresh broccoli, sliced (see page 71)†*

II   2   *slices ginger, shredded*

     1   *clove garlic, minced*

III   1   *teaspoon sugar*

     1   *tablespoon cornstarch*

     1   *teaspoon monosodium glutamate*

     ¼   *cup oyster sauce*

     ½   *cup chicken stock*

IV   ¼   *cup vegetable oil*

     ⅛   *teaspoon salt*

     ¼   *cup water*

Mix together ingredients in Group III and put aside.

Heat wok or pan until hot and dry. Add the oil, then the salt. Turn heat to medium. Add the ginger and the garlic and fry until golden brown. Turn heat to high. Add the pork and fry until outside is lightly browned. Add the broccoli and stir-fry for 3 minutes. Add the water, cover, and cook for 4 minutes. Pour in sauce mixture from Group III; stir while cooking until gravy thickens. Turn heat down to low, cover, and cook for 2 minutes more. Place in covered serving dish until ready to serve.

SUBSTITUTIONS AND VARIATIONS

If this dish is to be tried with the other broccoli recipe as a test, no substitutions should be made, in the interest of science! But if science is of no interest to you, 2 packages of frozen broccoli spears, thawed and sliced, may be used in place of the fresh. Cut cooking time in half after adding broccoli if you're using the frozen kind.

You don't *have* to cook both of these dishes for one meal. Try them out for two separate meals if you like, but don't let too much time elapse in between.

Sweet Broccoli with Pork

炒甜芥蘭

CHOW T'IM GAI LAAN

Please read the preceding recipe and the discussion on how to buy and prepare broccoli on page 70 before tackling this recipe. Fresh broccoli must be used here, because the chief characteristics of this dish are its crunchiness and fresh-vegetable taste.

Some people shy away from the thought of a sweet dish for a meal, because they conjure up in their minds gooey candy or dessert. Chinese sweet dishes are not at all like that. This dish comes out light and pleasant, as good sweet and sour Chinese dishes should be, and, once tasted, it will become a favorite.

I   2   *cups lean sliced pork (about 1 pound)*
   1   *bunch fresh broccoli, sliced (about 2 pounds)†*

II   2   *slices ginger, shredded*
   1   *clove garlic, minced*

III   ½   *cup brown sugar*
   1   *teaspoon monosodium glutamate*
   ¼   *cup soy sauce*
   ½   *cup sherry*

IV   ½   *cup vegetable oil*
   Pinch of salt

Mix together ingredients in Group III and put aside.

Heat the wok or pan hot and dry. Add one half the oil, then the pinch of salt. Turn heat to medium and add the ginger and garlic; fry till golden brown. Add the pork, turn heat up high, and stir-fry until pork is lightly browned on outside. Put in the remainder of the oil. Add the broccoli and stir-fry only long enough for it to turn a bright, deep green (about 1 to 2 minutes).

Pour in sauce mixture while stirring rapidly, and cover at once. Turn heat off and let stand for 2 more minutes so the sauce and wine have a chance to penetrate the food before serving.

SUBSTITUTIONS AND VARIATIONS

This little item may be of only passing interest to you. There is also a Chinese broccoli that can be bought in Chinese grocery stores. There is a great difference in appearance, since the stalks are much smaller than American broccoli. In taste it is so similar that it would take an expert to tell them apart. In view of the great difference in price, and the fact that Chinese broccoli is not readily available, I suggest you stick to the American variety.

Pork with Pickled Greens or Sauerkraut 酸菜肉

SEUN CHOY YUK

In large cities where there are Chinese grocery stores, you can buy Chinese pickled mustard greens, called haam gai choy (page 59). In taste, they are sour and a bit salty. The texture is very crisp. Since this item is not available everywhere, I discovered there is something you can substitute for it which *is* widely available—sauerkraut. Fresh sauerkraut is better than the canned type, since the fresh sauerkraut is crisper, and crispness is one of the important qualities to seek in this dish.

If you are able to get the Chinese pickled greens, squeeze them dry and then slice the leaves and stems across to form thin slivers about ⅛ inch wide. Sauerkraut can be just squeezed dry and used without further cutting.

The pork should be quite fat for this dish, because the tartness of the vegetable requires a little extra oil, but at the same time this very tartness modifies the fat in the pork, so it will not be greasy. Any piece of pork that has fat lacing through it is suitable. Pork butt is an excellent cut for this dish.

I   2   *cups sliced pork (about 1 pound)*†
       3   *cups sliced pickled greens, or same amount of sauer-*
          kraut (both about 1½ pounds)

II   2   *slices ginger, shredded*
      1   *clove garlic, minced*

III ¼ *cup brown sugar*
      1   *teaspoon monosodium glutamate*
      1   *tablespoon cornstarch*
      2   *tablespoons soy sauce*
     ¼ *cup white vinegar*

IV ¼ *cup vegetable oil*
        Pinch of salt

If Chinese greens are used, be sure to separate the leaves and rinse the stems thoroughly to remove any sand which may be present. Drain and dry thoroughly.

Mix together ingredients in Group III and put aside.

Heat wok or pan hot and dry. Add the oil, then the salt. Turn heat to medium and add garlic and ginger; fry till golden brown. Add the pork, turn heat to high, and stir-fry for about 3 minutes until pork has browned on the outside. Quickly add the pickled greens or sauerkraut and fry uncovered for 1 more minute. Add the sauce mixture from Group III. Stir-fry only long enough to thicken the gravy. Turn heat off. Cover and let stand for a minute or two. Remove from pan and serve.

SUBSTITUTIONS AND VARIATIONS

It is important not to overcook the vegetables, since we want to maintain their crispness.

This basic recipe can be varied by changing the meat ingredient, using chicken, beef, fillet of fish, or shrimps. The procedure is almost the same. The substituted meat should be cooked in much less time (about 1 to 2 minutes), then removed from the wok or pan. The vegetables are then stir-fried, the sauce added and thickened. The meat or seafood can now be put back with the vegetables to complete the dish.

Chinese Roast (Barbecued) Pork

A purist will insist that roast pork must be barbecued on a special stove or over a charcoal grill, where some fat and juice will drip into the live coals and flare up momentarily to give the meat that slightly charred quality which is characteristic of good barbecue. I agree that is the best way. However, one of the delights of Chinese cooking is its adaptability, and good results can be obtained in your gas or electric oven or rotisserie.

One of the most colorful sights in a Chinese community is the display in restaurants and grocery stores of roast meats hung in show windows to attract customers. The reputation of the establishment often is based upon the quality and attractiveness of its barbecued meats. If you are a stranger in the community, and can speak Chinese, it is possible for you to inquire of old residents in the area which store is the most famous for its barbecued foods. If you live near a Chinese community, try asking anyway, and buy some roast pork or spareribs to try at home. The pork is cut into long strips and the spareribs are in banks, hung up by hooks. One can learn a lot about how barbecued meat should look and taste by looking and tasting some you purchase in a Chinese store. Roast meats are good eaten cold or warmed up again at home. It is quite a common practice for the Chinese themselves to buy rather than make their own barbecued meats.

Another hint here is that you may want to barbecue more roast pork than you plan to use at one time. Freeze the excess, and you can have roast pork at your disposal at a moment's notice. Frozen roast pork will keep for 2 to 3 months.

Any lean cut of pork may be used, since they will all be tender. The preferred cuts are fresh ham and shoulder (which is often called a pork butt). Both cuts have fat and bone which must be removed either by you or the butcher. Save the bones for making soup stock.

After the meat has been boned and the fat trimmed off, slice the meat into strips about ¾ inch thick by about 2 or 3 inches wide and up to 5 or 6 inches long. The thickness should not be any more than ¾ inch since pork has to be cooked thoroughly and it takes too long to cook thicker slices.

I   2-3   *pounds pork, cut into strips about 3 by 6 inches and no more than ¾ inch thick*

II   3   *cloves garlic, minced*

III 3   *tablespoons sugar*
     ½   *cup sweet bean sauce (hoi sin deung)*
     ½   *cup light soy sauce*
     1   *tablespoon red vegetable coloring†*
     ½   *cup sherry*

Mix all ingredients in II and III together in a bowl and pour over the pork. Make sure all the surfaces of each piece of pork are covered with the marinade. Let stand for 2 or 3 hours at room temperature before barbecuing.

(This recipe makes about a pint of marinade, which is enough for about 4 or 5 pounds of pork. If you are using less pork, store the extra marinade in a tightly covered jar and refrigerate. It will keep several weeks. Discard any marinade once it has been used as it would contain some juices from the raw pork.)

Method 1. To Barbecue in an Oven

Make "s" hooks of stiff wire or stainless-steel lacing pins, the kind used for lacing up roasts or fowl. They can be bought at a hardware or dime store. Bend wire or pins into "s" shape with pliers. Make one hook for each strip of meat (see illustration).

Place one oven rack close to the top of the oven and another rack at the position closest to the bottom (pan may be placed on bottom if your oven does not have sufficient height). Line oven roasting pan with foil. Add water to a depth of about ½ inch. Place pan with water on bottom rack. Preheat oven to 375° F.

Drain marinade from pork and push a hook into the top of each strip. (Do not double one strip on top of another.) Open oven and pull out top rack. Hang other end of hooks onto the rack, keeping the pork strips spaced so they do not touch each other. The strips of pork should hang over the water-filled pan, which will catch the drippings. The water in the pan keeps the meat from drying out and prevents spattering and smoking. Remember that the wire rack is hot when you are hanging the pork on it.

Push rack back, close oven, and cook at 375° for 45 minutes.

SUBSTITUTIONS AND VARIATIONS

The above method for barbecuing utilizes the kitchen oven, be it gas or electric. The methods below can be used if the equipment required is available to you.

The red vegetable coloring is optional. It doesn't affect the taste, but makes the meat look prettier and more appetizing.

Method 2. Using a Rotisserie

A whole family of "open hearth" appliances are now made by practically every major kitchen appliance manufacturer. They work on the principle of a charcoal grill, with an electric heating element either above or below the cooking surface. If you own one of these, barbecuing is easy. Just turn on the heat about 5 minutes before using. Then lay the pork strips across the wire rack. Turn the strips around every few minutes so that they will be seared evenly.

The time will depend on the make of your rotisserie. It may take longer than in an oven. Check for doneness by squeezing the meat with your fingers. If the meat feels firm all the way through when squeezed, then it is done. You may also pick out the thickest piece of meat and slice it in half with a knife to see if it is done.

Method 3. Using a Charcoal Grill or Hibachi Stove

A hibachi stove is nothing more than a portable charcoal grill used by the Japanese for centuries to cook indoors. It is now very popular in America. Most department stores have them in stock and they are quite inexpensive. The familiar back-yard barbecue grill needs no introduction. In both cases, make sure your charcoal briquettes are at optimum heat—which is after the charcoal has been burning for about 45 minutes and is now evenly lit and covered with a whitish ash.

The grill should be scraped free of previous cookout residue before the pork strips are put on it, and should be raised as high above the fire as possible.

Charcoal heat is intense. It is much hotter than the oven or rotisserie and more care must be given to watching and turning the meat, or it will burn. Test for doneness as in rotisserie cooking. This last method makes the most flavorful Chinese barbecued meats if you have the means to do it.

Roast Pork and Pea Fluff   叉燒鬆

CHA SHIU SOONG

There is a whole family of dishes called "yook soong," of which this one, made with barbecued pork, is representative. "Soong" in Cantonese can be translated as "loose" or "fluffy." When applied to cooking, it implies that the dish so named should be light and delicate.

I   1½   *cups diced barbecued pork†*
     1   *package frozen peas, thawed*
     4   *or 5 leaves of lettuce, to line serving dish*

II   ½   *cup diced canned bamboo shoots†*
     ½   *cup button mushrooms, drained*
     1   *clove garlic, minced*
     1   *small onion, diced*
     1   *sweet red pepper, diced*

III   1   *teaspoon sugar*
     1   *tablespoon cornstarch*
     1   *teaspoon monosodium glutamate*
     2   *tablespoons light soy sauce†*
        Dash of Tabasco
     ½   *cup chicken stock or water*

IV   3   *tablespoons vegetable oil*
        Pinch of salt
     2   *tablespoons sherry*
        Chopped scallions or parsley, for garnish (optional)

Mix together ingredients from Group III and put aside.
Heat wok or pan hot and dry. Add the oil, then the salt. Turn

heat to medium. Add the garlic, onion, and red pepper and stir-fry till onion is golden yellow (about 2 or 3 minutes).

Turn heat up high and add the meat, peas, bamboo shoots, and mushrooms. Stir-fry for 1 minute. Add the sherry. Cover quickly and cook for 1 minute more. Add the sauce mixture from Group III; stir well until gravy has thickened. Turn off heat; remove from pan into lettuce-lined serving dish. Top with parsley or chopped scallions and serve.

SUBSTITUTIONS AND VARIATIONS

You may make endless substitutions with this dish. Cooked ham, chicken, roast beef, in the same quantity and also diced, may be used in place of the pork.

The bamboo shoots are optional, but their inclusion upgrades the dish. Substitution of 3 tablespoons oyster sauce for the soy sauce also enhances the dish and gives it a more subtle flavor.

Foo Yung Eggs #1   芙蓉蛋

FOO YUNG DAAN

The Egg Foo Yung that is so popular in Chinese-American (as distinct from Chinese) restaurants deserves an honored place

in your repertoire. This type of omelet, together with Chop Suey
and Chow Mein, which were invented in America, serves to
bridge the gulf between Western and Chinese tastes.

In recent years, Egg Foo Yung has fallen in the esteem of
those who have become knowledgeable about Chinese food, perhaps because of its past associations. However, any dish is only
as good as the ingredients used and the skill of the cook. When
properly made, I think this dish is delectable.

Egg Foo Yung is not strictly a dish invented for the American
taste by Chinese cooks. There was a great tradition from which
it drew. An authentic version of it follows this recipe.

I	6	*eggs, beaten well*
	1	*cup shredded roast pork†*
	2	*cups fresh bean sprouts†*
II	2	*scallions, chopped, including the green ends*
	1	*medium-size onion, shredded*
III	1	*teaspoon sugar*
	⅛	*teaspoon ground pepper*
	1	*teaspoon monosodium glutamate*
	2	*tablespoons soy sauce*
	½	*cup chicken stock or water*
IV		*Vegetable oil*

Make gravy if desired (see end of recipe). Preheat oven to
200°. Line a platter with several thicknesses of paper towel.

Mix all the ingredients except the vegetable oil together in a
mixing bowl.

Heat a frying pan hot and dry. Put in vegetable oil to a depth
of about ½ inch. Keep oil at this level by adding more, as some
is absorbed in cooking. Bring oil temperature to medium. (If
a raw bean sprout or a sliver of onion is dropped into the oil,
it will sizzle and float.) Stir up the omelet mixture each time
before you take a scoopful of it out, in order to have the proper
ratio of liquid and solid ingredients in each omelet.

With a ladle or soup scoop, take a scoop of the egg mixture and gently put into the frying pan. When the first omelet has stiffened, gently move it over to make room for the next. The number of omelets you can make at once depends on the size of your frying pan. When one side of the omelet has turned golden brown, turn over gently with pancake turner to fry the other side. When done, transfer from frying pan onto paper-lined platter. Paper towels will absorb excess oil. Put platter into preheated oven to keep warm until all the omelets can be served together. Serve with or without gravy.

GRAVY

1½ *cups chicken stock*
1 *tablespoon cornstarch*
2 *tablespoons dark soy sauce*
1 *teaspoon monosodium glutamate*
⅛ *teaspoon ground pepper*
  Pinch of salt

Mix all the ingredients together in a saucepan. Bring to a boil slowly with frequent stirring. When gravy has thickened, turn heat to very low to keep it warm until ready to use.

SUBSTITUTIONS AND VARIATIONS

A cookbook could be written with just one basic Egg Foo Yung recipe, and a thousand ways to vary it. This recipe can be varied infinitely by substitution of everything except the eggs! Try substituting an equal amount of shrimps for the roast pork. A can of drained bean sprouts may be substituted for the fresh variety.

Foo Yung Eggs #2   芙蓉蛋

FOO YUNG DAAN

This is the Chinese version of Egg Foo Yung from which the modified version on page 98 was created. In serving this dish, no gravy is required.†

I   6   *eggs, very slightly beaten*
      ½   *cup chicken stock or water*
          Juice from canned mushrooms

II 1   *cup roast pork, shredded*
      1   *cup shrimps, cooked and shredded*
      ½   *package frozen French-style string beans, thawed*
      3   *scallions, cut in 2-inch lengths and shredded, including green ends*
      1   *small can sliced button mushrooms (save liquid for egg mixture)*
      ½   *cup shredded bamboo shoots†*

III 1   *teaspoon sugar*
      ⅛   *teaspoon ground white pepper*
      1   *teaspoon monosodium glutamate*
      2   *tablespoons soy sauce*
          Few drops of sesame oil

IV 1¼ *cups vegetable oil*

Break eggs into a large mixing bowl. Add chicken stock or water and the juice from the mushrooms. Add ingredients in Group III to the eggs and beat very slightly so the white and yolks are not completely mixed. Put aside.

Heat frying pan hot and dry. Add 2 or 3 tablespoons of the vegetable oil. Add all the solid ingredients in Group II and fry over high heat for just 1 minute. (The ingredients should be only partially cooked.) Empty this mixture immediately into the bowl containing the eggs. Stir gently together.

Clean frying pan and heat hot and dry again. Put in remainder of the oil. Heat oil to medium frying temperature. With soup ladle, scoop up a ladleful at a time of the mixture and gently pour into oil to make round thin omelets. Transfer omelets onto paper towels to drain and keep warm in oven (see p. 100). Serve as soon as all the omelets are done.

SUBSTITUTIONS AND VARIATIONS

Although no gravy is used with this dish, some Chinese enjoy it with a few drops of oyster sauce on top.

Barbecued Spareribs

In barbecuing spareribs almost all the processes for barbecued pork are followed. A few simple adjustments are made to give the spareribs a stronger, spicier flavor, because rib meat is not quite as delicate and tender as the other pork. Buy spareribs which come in one bank or slab. Supermarkets often package spareribs with the bones cracked and folded over, which is not suitable for this purpose. You can ask the butcher to give you spareribs which have not been cut in half, however.

The marinade below is enough for 2 banks of spareribs, of about 2 pounds each. I suggest you make the full recipe even if you intend to make only 1 bank of ribs. In that case, put half of the marinade away in a covered jar. Refrigerated, it will keep for several weeks.

I	2	*banks of spareribs, uncut, about 2 pounds each*
II	3	*cloves garlic, minced*
III	½	*cup sweet bean sauce (hoi sin deung)*
	½	*cup soy sauce*
	½	*cup ketchup*
	1	*tablespoon red vegetable coloring†*
	¼	*cup sherry*

Trim off excess fat from the thick edges of spareribs. Place ribs in a shallow pan or platter. Mix remaining ingredients for a marinade and spread over both sides of the spareribs. Let stand for at least 2 hours at room temperature.

Preheat oven to 375° F. Hook each bank of spareribs with 3 or 4 hooks across its width, on the thick edges, and suspend under oven rack. Use the same method to barbecue as for roast pork (see page 94). Cook for 45 minutes at 375° F.

SUBSTITUTIONS AND VARIATIONS

For rotisserie or charcoal grill, just lay the ribs on top of grill or rack. Turn over frequently. The timing is about the same. Test for doneness by cutting the thickest part of the largest rib. There should be no pinkness showing inside the meat.

You will need at least one bank of spareribs for each two persons. If the ribs are from baby porkers, allow ¾ bank for each guest.

The barbecued spareribs may be made the day before without loss of quality. To reheat, take out of refrigerator, bring to room temperature, and cut into separate ribs. Place on metal or oven-proof platter. Preheat broiler and slide the platter under broiler for 5 minutes. Serve with English mustard and plum sauce as a dip.

The vegetable coloring is optional.

Spareribs with Garlic Sauce 荳豉排骨

DAU SHE PAI GWAT

One of the most distinctive seasoning combinations in Chinese cooking is salted cured soybeans (dau she), garlic, ginger, and soy sauce. During a dinner hour in any Chinese community, the tantalizing smell of this sauce permeates the whole neighborhood. Every kind of meat, fish, or fowl will have many recipes using this combination of spices.

This sauce is highly spiced, and must be adjusted to the state of development of your own taste. The Chinese like it highly seasoned, and I know some of my non-Chinese friends have developed the same taste, so that when this sauce is modified for Americans in some restaurants, my friends now find it pallid and uninteresting.

Try out this sauce with spareribs in the recipe below. I've not tried to modify the sauce, but you can. I am giving it to you just as a Chinese family would make it. As I've stressed throughout the book, Chinese cooking is so flexible that it will bend over backward to suit your taste.

Have your butcher trim off the fat from the spareribs and crack or saw the bones crosswise at 1½- to 2-inch intervals. Then you can separate each bone into riblets with a knife at home.

I   1   *bank of spareribs (about 2 pounds) cut into individual riblets 1½ to 2 inches long*

II   2   *cloves garlic, minced*
      3   *slices ginger, shredded*

III   1   *teaspoon sugar*
      1   *tablespoon cornstarch*
      1   *tablespoon salted cured soybeans, rinsed well in a strainer*
      1   *teaspoon monosodium glutamate*
      2   *tablespoons dark soy sauce*
      ¼   *cup water*

IV   1   *quart water*
      1   *teaspoon salt*
      2   *tablespoons vegetable oil*
      1   *cup chicken stock*
        Chopped scallions or parsley, for garnish (optional)

Mix together ingredients in Group III and set aside.

In a saucepan large enough to accommodate the water and the spareribs, bring the water to a boil with the salt. Add the spareribs and bring water to a boil again. Turn heat to medium and cook 5 minutes longer. Drain off liquid and dry spareribs thoroughly.

Heat wok or frying pan hot and dry. Add the oil. Turn heat to medium and add the garlic and ginger. Fry till golden brown. Add the drained spareribs. Stir-fry until the outside is slightly browned. Turn heat to low.

Add the chicken stock and cover to simmer for 5 minutes. Add the sauce mixture from Group III; stir well. Cover and simmer for 5 minutes more. Top with chopped scallions or parsley and serve with white rice.

SUBSTITUTIONS AND VARIATIONS

The gravy over the rice is delicious. If you wish more gravy, add another ½ cup of water or chicken stock to the sauce mixture.

Diced Pork with Vegetables

猪肉鬆

CHI YUK SOONG

This dish belongs in the family of "soong" dishes as explained on page 97. By the addition of the sweet bean sauce (hoi sin deung) an entirely different flavor is achieved. This sauce is used a great deal in northern Chinese cooking.

Another characteristic of "soong" recipes is that all the solid ingredients used are either diced or minced to add to the lightness and delicacy of the dish. Since everything is cut so small, it gets done very quickly. Care should be used so that the food does not get overcooked. One pound of pork butt without bone, or 4 center-cut pork chops with most of the fat and bones removed will yield the correct amount of meat for this recipe.

I   1   *pound lean pork, diced*
      2   *cups diced Chinese cabbage (white stems only)†*
      1   *package frozen petite peas, thawed*
      1   *green pepper, seeded and diced*

II   ½ *cup Chinese mushrooms, soaked and diced†*
      ½ *cup canned bamboo shoots, diced*
      2   *scallions, diced, including green ends*
      1   *clove garlic, minced*
      2   *slices ginger, shredded*

III 1   *tablespoon cornstarch*
      1   *teaspoon monosodium glutamate*
      2   *tablespoons soy sauce*
      2   *tablespoons sweet bean sauce (hoi sin deung)*
      ½ *cup chicken stock or water*

IV 2   *tablespoons vegetable oil*
           Pinch of salt
      2   *tablespoons sherry*
           Several sprigs Chinese parsley, for garnish (optional)†

Mix together ingredients in Group III and put aside.

Heat wok or pan hot and dry. Add the oil. Turn heat to medium. Add the salt, then add the garlic and ginger. Stir-fry until golden brown. Turn heat to high and put in the pork, stirring rapidly and constantly until the pork is browned on the outside (about 1 to 2 minutes).

Put in all the diced vegetables and peas and stir-fry 1 minute more. Pour in the sherry and cover pan at once. Cook covered another minute. Pour the sauce mixture from Group III evenly on top of the food while stirring. When gravy thickens, turn off heat and serve at once. Top with Chinese parsley (optional).

SUBSTITUTIONS AND VARIATIONS

The Chinese cabbage (baak choy) must be bought from Chinese or Japanese stores. Substitute American celery cabbage if Chinese cabbage is not available. The white hearts of celery may also be used in its place.

See page 33 for information on Chinese mushrooms. The same amount of canned button mushrooms may be used instead. If the button mushrooms are small, use them whole. Larger ones should be quartered.

Chinese parsley has a wonderful fragrance. Use it not only for looks as a garnish, but eat it with the food. Cut or break the sprigs into short pieces and sprinkle over the food. The use of Chinese parsley is always optional, but do exercise the option if you can.

Steamed Eggs with Pork and Sausages 蒸臘腸蛋

CHING LAAP CHEUNG DON

This is a steamed dish which is easy to make and is a favorite of many people. We've covered this method of cooking rather thoroughly on page 9. Please refer to it before you use this recipe. The Chinese use preserved, salted duck eggs (available in Chinese stores), but I've used both the salted duck eggs and just fresh chicken eggs for American friends, and both dishes were equally enjoyed by the guests.

I   6   *eggs, slightly beaten*

    ½ *cup (about ½ pound) fresh pork, coarsely chopped, preferably by hand (see page 86)*

    1   *Chinese sausage, sliced thin†*

II   1   *small onion, minced*

    2   *scallions, chopped, including green ends*

III 1   *teaspoon sugar*

    1   *teaspoon monosodium glutamate*

    ⅛ *teaspoon salt*

    ½ *cup chicken stock or water*

    2   *tablespoons light soy sauce*

    1   *tablespoon vegetable oil*

Mix all the ingredients together in a mixing bowl. Transfer to a flat-bottomed, shallow dish which is large enough to accommodate the egg mixture with at least one inch of space above it for expansion of the food when cooked. Place the dish in a steamer, cover tightly, and bring the water to a vigorous boil to produce the steam. Turn heat down to medium low and allow to steam for 45 minutes. Serve at your leisure. This dish may be kept hot for hours until ready to serve, or can be made beforehand and resteamed without loss of flavor.

SUBSTITUTIONS AND VARIATIONS

Use ¼ cup minced ham or 2 slices minced bacon if Chinese sausage is not available. Five or 6 water chestnuts, chopped, will add a nice crunchy texture to the dish.

Sweet and Sour Pork

甜酸肉

TIM SEUN YUK

This dish is sometimes called "Sweet and Pungent Pork" and some Chinese restaurants call it "Old-fashioned Meat." But by any other name it'd taste just as sweet—and sour. It is a dish which pleases the occidental and the oriental palates alike, perhaps because it combines very subtly several flavors which our taste buds can detect.

While there are one or two more steps you have to take in the preparation of this dish than in some others, it really is not difficult to make. There may even be short cuts you can devise after one or two tries that will simplify its preparation. In any case, you will be delighted with the results, and the proof will be in the eating!

If you tackle this recipe in two stages, one for the sauce and one for the meat, and treat them as separate recipes, which will then be combined, the cooking and preparation will be easier. I've written the recipe with that thought in mind.

Pork butt, trimmed of excess fat, or pork loin with the bones and excess fat removed is suitable for this dish.

THE PORK

I	1½	pounds pork, cut into ¾-inch cubes
II	1	cup chicken stock or water
III	2	teaspoons monosodium glutamate
	¼	teaspoon ground white pepper
	⅛	teaspoon salt
	1	egg
	2	tablespoons cornstarch
IV		Oil for deep frying

Put the chicken stock or water, monosodium glutamate, pepper, and salt in a saucepan and bring to a boil. Put in the pork cubes and stir until the liquid mixture and pork boil again. Turn heat to medium, cover and cook for 3 minutes longer. Turn off heat, remove pork from liquid and let pork cool. (Save the liquid for the sauce.)

Put the pork cubes in a mixing bowl, add the egg and mix well. Sprinkle the cornstarch on the pork and stir to coat the meat with it. Preheat your oven to 200° F.

Heat the deep-frying oil to 350° F. Add the pork and fry until the outside turns golden brown. Remove from oil, place in paper-towel-lined oven pan and put in preheated oven until ready to mix with the sauce just before serving.

THE SWEET AND SOUR SAUCE

I   2   *cups marinated vegetables (see page 67)†,*
        or 2 medium-size carrots
    ½   *cup cauliflower*
    1   *green pepper*

II 1   *cup canned pineapple, drained, and cut into bite size*
    1   *cup sugar*

III 1   *tablespoon cornstarch, dissolved in 2 tablespoons water*
    1   *cup white vinegar*
    ¼   *cup ketchup*

IV   *Leftover liquid from pork*

To the saucepan with the leftover liquid from the pork add the sugar, cornstarch, vinegar, and ketchup. Bring to a boil while stirring. When the liquid has thickened, turn heat down to medium. (If you like a heavier gravy, add more dissolved cornstarch.)

If you use marinated vegetables, just add them and the pineapple and let the mixture come to a boil, then add the pork from the oven, mix together, and serve at once.

If the vegetables are fresh, cut all into bite size and cook them in the sauce for 5 to 7 minutes over medium heat. Add the pineapple and pork, mix well, and serve at once.

SUBSTITUTIONS AND VARIATIONS

As suggested on page 67, preparing and marinating vegetables for sweet and sour recipes and keeping them in your refrigerator is a great timesaver. If you have to use the fresh vegetables, any combination of the listed vegetables, in any proportion you desire, may be used for this dish.

The above recipe is for a light sweet and sour sauce. All sweet and sour sauces are basically made the same way. The variations are for individual whim or taste, or for color. Where the major ingredients are light in color, such as chicken or shrimp, a light sweet and sour sauce has more eye appeal. The darker meats, or those that do not have a particularly good-looking color in themselves, such as spareribs, may look less anemic if given a darker sauce. However, there is no set rule, and you are the master.

Dark sweet and sour sauce is made the same way as the light, except substitute 2 tablespoons dark molasses for the ¼ cup ketchup.

Pork with Bitter Melon

苦瓜猪

FOO KWA CHI

One of the five detectable tastes is bitterness. The Chinese consider all five tastes as essential to their cuisine. Since life is Yin and Yang, the contrast of the bitter and the sweet must be tasted and appreciated if one is to live a full life. One cannot exist without the other. Some people, like the Orthodox Jews, on certain religious occasions will eat something bitter as a reminder of a bitter event in their history. But not the Chinese. We think of a bitter taste as a treat. This taste is a shock much like the first plunge into a cold, crystal pool. This shock wakes up our taste buds much as the plunge into the pool wakens up our body and serves to make us fully appreciate being alive. The Chinese value bitter melon so highly that all authentic restaurants which have predominantly Chinese clientele will serve this vegetable in various ways.

Fresh bitter melon is a most unusual-looking vegetable, and its likeness is often portrayed in Chinese art motifs. It is dark green in color and glossy. It is about the size of a medium-sized cucumber. In fact, it is often called "bitter cucumber." The skin is rippled with smooth hills and valleys. Its shape is round and

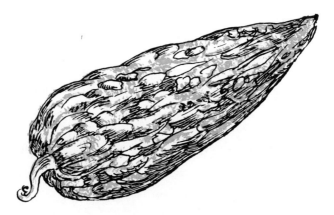

larger at one end, then gradually tapers to a point at the opposite end. The inside is hollow, with large hard seeds which must be discarded.

To cut fresh bitter melon, split it in half the long way. Remove seeds and cut across halves into about ¼-inch half circles. The skin is very thin and does not have to be peeled off. You may also buy bitter melon in cans, from stores listed in the back of this book. Just drain and cut up the canned variety, and it's ready for use.

The recipe below is my father's favorite.

I   2   *cups thin-sliced lean pork (about 1 pound)†*
    2   *fresh bitter melons, medium size, or 1 medium-size can of bitter melon (cut as instructed above)*

II 1   *clove garlic, minced*
    2   *slices ginger, shredded*
    1   *medium-size onion, shredded*

III 1   *teaspoon sugar*
    1   *tablespoon cornstarch*
    1   *tablespoon salted cured soybeans, rinsed and crushed†*
    2   *tablespoons soy sauce*
    1   *teaspoon monosodium glutamate*
    ½   *cup chicken stock or water*

IV 2   *tablespoons vegetable oil*
    2   *tablespoons sherry*
        Chopped scallions or Chinese parsley, for garnish (optional)

Mix together ingredients in Group III and put aside.

Heat wok or pan until hot and dry. Add the oil. Turn heat to medium and add the garlic, ginger, and onions. Fry till golden brown. Turn heat to high and add the pork. Stir-fry until pork is browned on outside. Add the bitter melon and stir-fry for 1 minute. Add the sherry and cover pan at once. Cook for 2 minutes covered. Add the sauce mixture from Group III. Stir-fry until gravy thickens. Garnish with Chinese parsley or chopped scallions (optional). Serve with boiled rice.

SUBSTITUTIONS AND VARIATIONS

Bitter melon is often cooked with chicken, beef, or seafood. Vary the recipe by changing the meat to suit your own preference.

The salted cured soybeans may be left out. In that case, you need not add to or alter the recipe otherwise. The dish will just be more bland. Add salt to taste.

Triple Dragon   三及第

SAAM GUP DAI

Some Chinese dishes are very hard to classify, since they are neither fish nor fowl. To add to this confusion, in many cases the same thing may be called by different names, depending on the poetic ability of the chef. I understand that the name "Triple Dragon" was invented by a certain chef working in a

restaurant on Long Island. Another chef called it "Triple Crown." The waiters still call the dish into the kitchen by the more popular Chinese name "Saam Gup Dai." The closest literal translation I can make of it is "The unity of the big three." But by any name it is still delightful and elegant.

Originally, this dish, as made in China, used the three major ingredients from the pig: pork, pork liver, and a certain portion of the pig's small intestine. That last item is no longer used in this country because it is not easy to obtain. In some restaurants, fresh pork liver is still used, but now the most popular combination is, as given below, chicken meat, lobster meat, and roast pork.

I 1 *cup sliced lobster meat, fresh, frozen (thawed), or canned, sliced†*

1 *cup sliced roast pork†*

1½ *cups sliced cooked chicken breasts (about 2 small breasts)*

2 *cups sliced Chinese cabbage†*

1 *cup snow peas†*

II ½ *cup sliced bamboo shoots†*

⅓ *cup sliced water chestnuts†*

1 *small can button mushrooms, sliced or whole*

2 *slices ginger, shredded*

1 *clove garlic, minced*

III 1 *teaspoon sugar*

1 *tablespoon cornstarch*

1 *teaspoon monosodium glutamate*

¼ *cup oyster sauce†*

IV 3 *tablespoons vegetable oil*

⅛ *teaspoon salt*

2 *tablespoons sherry*

Chopped scallions, Chinese parsley, or nut meats, for garnish (optional)

Mix together ingredients in Group III and put aside.

Heat wok or pan until hot and dry. Add the oil, then the salt. Turn heat to medium and add the ginger and garlic; stir-fry until golden brown. Turn heat up and add the Chinese cabbage, bamboo shoots, water chestnuts, and mushrooms. Stir-fry for 2 minutes. Add the sherry; cover and cook 1 minute more. Put in all the remaining solid ingredients except garnish and stir well (about ½ minute; don't overcook). Pour in the sauce mixture from Group III while stirring. Turn heat off as soon as gravy has thickened. Remove from pan into serving dish at once. Top with the scallions, Chinese parsley, or nut meats and serve immediately.

SUBSTITUTIONS AND VARIATIONS

Crabmeat or shrimp may be used in place of lobster meat. The roast pork should be Chinese roast pork (page 93), but regular roast pork is all right too. In place of oyster sauce, you can use 2 tablespoons light soy sauce.

Some of the items marked with the symbol † may be eliminated. But don't eliminate too much, or else your dish may turn out like the story about the farmer who gradually lessened the amount of oats he fed his horse until one day he didn't have to give it any oats at all! Guess what had happened.

8

Beef

BEEF (ngau yuk) is highly prized in Chinese cooking. Pork is more extensively used but this fact has more to do with economics than with taste or choice. Cattle in China were—and are—too valuable to be employed primarily as food. Only countries endowed with a relatively small population and rich grazing land can support herds of cattle for milk and meat.

When I was a boy in China—and for generations before my time—our beef came from tough old water buffaloes. A water buffalo was usually the only other source of labor that the farmer and his family had. At that not every farmer could afford to own one to harness to his plow. Water buffaloes were so necessary and valuable that they were not permitted to graze alone but were usually accompanied by a little boy cowherd who perched on the back of one of the animals and played his flute.

A water buffalo was only slaughtered for food after it was too old to work. In order to make its meat tender enough to eat, our ancestors devised the method of cutting which is used today on all meats. It is the long stringy fibers in a piece of meat that make it tough. If the meat is cut very thin and across the fibers it will break down easily when chewed, and therefore be far more tender. This method of cutting also made a small amount of meat stretch so that everyone could have at least a tiny bit. It also cooked faster, thereby conserving fuel.

Any cut of beef which can be broiled or roasted may be used for Chinese stir-fry cooking. These cuts naturally include the choice, expensive cuts, such as sirloin and porterhouse steaks, but it is not always necessary to use them. (It is not only the price per pound but the *yield* per pound of usable lean meat that makes these cuts expensive. In a good prime sirloin or porterhouse steak the fat and bones may weigh as much as the edible meat, so the cost is really twice as much as for a flank steak, which has almost no waste, if both cost exactly the same price a pound originally.) In general, when the recipe calls for "lean beef," try buying boneless cuts such as flank steak, skirt steak, London broil, and any cut which is meant to be roasted in the oven. Do not use pot roasts or other cuts that are meant for braising or stewing. Generally they are tough and do not have as good a flavor.

Do not trim off all the fat from a piece of beef unless your health or diet requires it. I am not competent to discuss all the pros and cons of animal fat and its effect on health, and on such questions I am a fence sitter and put my faith in the old Chinese concept of 中 ("chung" or "middle course"). Aside from the health issue, there is no question but that a small amount of fat enhances the meat's flavor.

How to Stir-Fry Beef

The chief point to bear in mind in cooking beef by the stir-fry method is not to allow the meat to overcook. Since it is sliced very thin in many Chinese recipes, little cooking time is required.

Usually, when beef is a main ingredient, it is put into the frying pan or wok first, then removed as soon as the outside has browned, and put aside until the other ingredients are cooked, whereupon the beef is put back in to complete the recipe.

Beef is never left to cook with the other ingredients. When other meats are used, which do not overcook as easily, it is usually not necessary to remove the meat from the pan before completing the recipe.

Chinese-Style Sirloin Steak

HONG JONG SE DIK

A good way to start learning to cook Chinese food (or any other cuisine, for that matter) is to take a familiar dish and cook it the Chinese way. I've suggested before that cooking ingredients do not have a single citizenship; they can change uniforms to become allies of a number of nationalities.

There are people who are aghast at the thought of "ruining" a perfectly good steak by the addition of any condiment except salt. While I respect their feelings I do suggest that it is perfectly permissible to marinate meats to give them a special flavor. There really is no argument between the two views if we think about it in a broader sense: cannot a woman be a wonderful wife and also a good mother?

The Hawaiians of Chinese descent are particularly fond of the following recipe.

I 1 *sirloin steak, about 2 pounds*

II 2 *slices ginger, shredded*
1 *clove garlic, minced*
2 *scallions, chopped*

III 1 *teaspoon monosodium glutamate*
2 *tablespoons soy sauce*
2 *tablespoons sherry*

IV 2 *tablespoons vegetable oil*

Trim steak of most excess fat, leaving some on, since it will improve the taste and prevent the steak from being too dry. Mix all the ingredients in II and III together to be used as a marinade.

Place steak on a platter, pour marinade over it, and let stand for 15 minutes (minimum). Turn steak over and marinate for 15 minutes more. Drain off marinade and save. Brush steak with the oil. It may now be broiled, barbecued, or fried as you choose. While cooking, brush on more of the marinade from time to time for stronger flavor.

If the steak is fried, a gravy can be made from the marinade by the addition of 1 tablespoon cornstarch mixed with ½ cup chicken broth. After the steak has been removed, add the mixture to the frying pan, and cook over medium heat until gravy has thickened. The gravy is excellent over boiled rice.

Steak with Oyster Sauce   蠔油牛

HO YAU NGAU

Most Chinese dishes are meat extenders, but this dish is one of the closest to the "all meat and no potatoes" category. Even the scallions are used more for decoration and flavor than to extend the meat.

Porterhouse steak or filet mignon can be used instead of sirloin. In slicing the steak, make the slices at least twice as thick as is usual in other Chinese dishes: at least ¼ inch and up to ½ inch. This makes it easier to control the degree of rareness.

I   2   *cups trimmed and sliced sirloin steak (about 1½ pounds before trimmed of fat and bone)*

II   3   *scallions, split into quarters lengthwise, then cut into 1-inch lengths, including green ends*

     2   *slices ginger, shredded*

     1   *clove garlic, minced*

III   1   *teaspoon sugar*
       1   *teaspoon monosodium glutamate*
       ¼   *teaspoon ground white pepper*
       2   *tablespoons light soy sauce*
       2   *tablespoons sherry*
       1   *tablespoon vegetable oil*

IV   2   *tablespoons vegetable oil*
       ⅛   *teaspoon salt*
       ¼   *cup oyster sauce*
       ½   *cup chicken broth or water*
       1   *tablespoon cornstarch*
         Chinese parsley sprigs, for garnish (optional)

Mix together ingredients in Group III and marinate the steak in the mixture for about ½ hour before cooking. Drain, mix marinade with oyster sauce, chicken broth, and cornstarch, and put aside.

Heat wok or frying pan hot and dry. Add the oil. Add the salt, ginger, and garlic. Fry till golden brown. Put in the steak and fry for 1 minute (more or less according to doneness preferred), or until meat has browned on outside. Remove beef from pan and set aside. Add scallions and fry ½ minute. Add the mixture of Group IV items and marinade while stirring. When gravy has thickened return beef to pan, turn off heat, then remove food to serving dish. Top with Chinese parsley (if desired) and serve.

Beef with Fresh Bean Sprouts   芽菜牛

NGA CHOY NGAU

This is a very simple dish to make, since so little preparation is needed. The bean sprouts need no cutting. Only fresh bean sprouts should be used for this dish (see how-to-grow information on page 60), since one of the desired characteristics of this dish is a crisp texture, which canned sprouts do not have.

Please don't overcook. When the bean sprouts become almost translucent (their original color is white) they are done. All the ingredients used here are edible raw.

I	1-1½	*cups sliced lean beef (about ¾ pound)*
	2	*pounds fresh bean sprouts, washed and drained*
	4	*scallions, cut into 1½-inch lengths, including green ends*
II	2	*cha kwa (see page 35),† shredded (about ⅛ cup)*
	1	*slice ginger, shredded*
	1	*clove garlic, minced*
III	1	*teaspoon sugar*
	1	*tablespoon cornstarch*
	1	*teaspoon monosodium glutamate*
	2	*tablespoons soy sauce*
	½	*cup chicken broth or water*
IV	¼	*cup vegetable oil*
	⅛	*teaspoon salt*
	2	*tablespoons sherry*
	½	*teaspoon ground white pepper*

Mix together ingredients in Group III and put aside.

Heat wok or pan hot and dry. Add about ½ the oil to pan. Add salt, then garlic and ginger, and fry till brown. Put in beef and stir-fry over high heat till just browned on outside (about 1 minute). Remove beef at once and put aside.

Heat wok or pan hot and dry again. Add remainder of oil. Put in bean sprouts, scallions, and cha kwa. Stir-fry for 1 minute. Add sherry. Cover and cook for 1 minute more. Put back beef and stir in Group III sauce mixture. Cook until thickened. Add pepper and mix well. Serve with boiled rice.

SUBSTITUTIONS AND VARIATIONS

If you do not have cha kwa, use 2 shredded sweet gherkins. Gherkins and cha kwa are similar in size, weight, and taste.

Beef with Tomatoes and Green Peppers   茄椒牛

K'E DEUL NGAU

Tomatoes are not native to China. The first encounter I had with them was when my father brought some home for the first time, about forty years ago. I was nine and my father had returned from the United States to take us to America. He spotted some tomatoes in a Chinese market. None of the rest of my family had ever seen or eaten them before. Since that time, of course, tomatoes and their by-products, such as ketchup, have become prized items in a Chinese kitchen.

Did you know that the word "ketchup" or "catchup" was invented by Chinese cooks in America? (I am getting as nationalistically possessive as the Russians. Pretty soon I may even claim that the Chinese invented gunpowder!) It was originally two Chinese words: 茄汁 ("k'e chup"), meaning "tomato juice, sap, or gravy."

We are familiar with the uneven quality of tomatoes, varying according to season and species and where they are grown. Tomatoes at their best are an incomparable vegetable, but some hothouse varieties are not worth eating. Fortunately, when tomatoes are at their best they are also the cheapest. So take advantage of good tomatoes in season. They should be red but firm for this recipe.

Be sure to dry the tomatoes, peppers, and scallions before cooking. The tomatoes give off a lot of liquid, especially if your stove is not hot enough, or when they have been cooked too long. In case your vegetables do get too watery, discard some of the liquid before you add the sauce mixture.

I   1½-2   *cups sliced lean beef (about 1 pound)*
    2   *pounds tomatoes, stem tops cut off, cut into 4 or*
            more pieces each, depending on size
    2   *medium-size green peppers, seeded and cut into*
            irregular pieces, smaller than the tomatoes

II   4   *scallions, cut into 1½-inch lengths, including*
            green ends
    1   *clove garlic, minced*
    2   *slices ginger, shredded*

III 1   *teaspoon sugar*
    1   *tablespoon salted cured soybeans, rinsed and*
            crushed
    1   *tablespoon cornstarch*
    1   *teaspoon monosodium glutamate*
    1   *tablespoon light soy sauce*
    ½   *cup chicken broth or water*

IV   2   *tablespoons vegetable oil*
    2   *tablespoons sherry*

Mix together ingredients in Group III and put aside.

Heat wok or pan hot and dry over high heat. Add oil. Add garlic and ginger and fry till brown. Add beef; stir-fry quickly till brown on the outside. Turn down heat and remove beef and put aside. Reheat wok or pan over high heat. Add the tomatoes, green peppers, and scallions. Stir-fry over high heat for 1 minute. Add the sherry. Cover and cook for 2 minutes more. Add the sauce mixture and stir till it thickens. Put back beef. Mix gently. Turn off heat and serve with plain cooked white rice.

Beef with String Beans   荳仔牛

DAU TSAI NGAU

This is a classic example of a Chinese stir-fry (chow) dish. You can make a wide range of Chinese dishes using the meat and vegetables of this recipe. If you should want to experiment on your own, to test out how flexible Chinese cooking really is, use this dish as the core of your research. You'll discover that no matter what ingredients you add to upgrade it, or what you subtract for simplicity and economy, as long as the beef, string beans and seasoning are there, it will still be basically the dish you started out to make.

In buying the string beans, be sure they are slender, tender, and fresh. The big broad beans are old and tough and shouldn't be used. If a bean snaps easily, and is full of moisture, the beans are young and fresh. Remove ends and strings, break in half, then wash and dry thoroughly before cooking.

I 1½-2 *cups sliced lean beef (about 1 pound boneless beef to 1½ pounds with fat and bone as in a sirloin steak)*

  1 *pound string beans, prepared as above*

II 6 *dried Chinese mushrooms, presoaked in 1 cup water and shredded†*

  1 *cup bamboo shoots, shredded†*

  4 *scallions, cut into 1½-inch lengths, including green ends*

  2 *slices ginger, shredded*

  1 *clove garlic, minced*

III 1 *teaspoon sugar*

  1 *tablespoon cornstarch*

  1 *teaspoon monosodium glutamate*

  2 *tablespoons soy sauce*

  ½ *cup chicken stock or water*

IV ¼ *cup vegetable oil*

  ⅛ *teaspoon salt*

  2 *tablespoons sherry*

   Sprigs of Chinese parsley (optional)

Mix together ingredients in Group III and put aside.

Heat wok or pan hot and dry. Add half of the vegetable oil.

Add the salt. Turn heat to medium and add the ginger and garlic to fry until golden brown. Turn up heat to high and add the sliced beef, stirring constantly until the outside has browned. Shut off the heat, remove beef from pan, and put aside.

Heat wok or pan again and add remainder of the oil. Add the string beans, mushrooms, bamboo shoots, and scallions and fry for 2 minutes while stirring. Check for doneness by observing color of the string beans. When they've turned a deep bright green, they're done. Add the sherry and cover quickly to cook 1 minute longer. Put back the beef. Stir well and add the sauce mixture from Group III. Cook until gravy thickens. Turn off heat. Put in serving dish, top with Chinese parsley (optional) and serve.

SUBSTITUTIONS AND VARIATIONS

If Chinese mushrooms are not available, use a small can (4 ounces) of button mushrooms instead.

Bamboo shoots are optional.

Beef with Chinese Cabbage

BAAK CHOY NGAU

A fine example of how a lovely vegetable becomes more beautiful when it gets "all dressed up to go to town" is given below. Baak choy, cooked with a minimum of adornment as in the recipe on page 77, is already a wonderful dish. Add a few choice items like good beef and Chinese mushrooms, and perfume it with a little ginger and garlic, and it becomes irresistible. We can add more items to it, such as bamboo shoots and the like, but after a certain point this kind of addition becomes subtraction. (I call it Lee's new math!) We want this to be a baak choy dish, escorted by hearty slices of beef. They make a handsome couple.

I   2   *cups lean beef, sliced (about 1 pound)*
     2   *small heads Chinese baak choy or celery cabbage,*
          sliced (about 1 pound)†

II   6   *medium-size dried mushrooms, soaked in ⅓ cup*
          water and sliced
     2   *scallions, cut into 1-1½-inch lengths*
     1   *clove garlic, crushed and minced*
     2   *slices fresh ginger, shredded*

III 1   *teaspoon sugar*
     1   *tablespoon cornstarch*
     1   *teaspoon monosodium glutamate*
     1   *tablespoon dark soy sauce*
     2   *tablespoons oyster sauce (optional)*
     ½   *cup chicken broth and ¼ cup water from mushrooms*

IV   ¼   *cup vegetable oil*
     ⅛   *teaspoon salt*
     2   *tablespoons sherry*
          Chinese parsley sprigs (optional)

Mix together ingredients in Group III and put aside.

Heat wok or frying pan hot and dry over high heat. Add ½ the oil. Add salt, then garlic and ginger; stir and brown quickly. Add beef and brown on outside (about 1 minute). Turn off heat and remove meat and juices into a bowl or dish. Put aside.

Reheat wok or pan hot and dry again. Add remainder of oil. Add the baak choy, scallions, and mushrooms. Fry over high heat for 2 minutes while stirring. Toss in the sherry and cover to cook 1 minute longer. Remove cover, put back the beef slices and juice. Pour in the sauce mixture from Group III, and stir while frying until gravy thickens. Turn off heat and serve at once.

If you have Chinese parsley, a few sprigs on top of most dishes enhance their looks and flavor.

SUBSTITUTIONS AND VARIATIONS

Chinese baak choy (see page 58), commonly called "Chinese cabbage" by Westerners, is misnamed. Its cousin, the celery cabbage, is closer in looks to a cabbage, but tastes more like the Chinese baak choy. Since baak choy can be bought only in Chinese or Japanese stores, use celery cabbage, which you should not have any trouble finding in American markets.

When you do have a chance to get the real baak choy, by all means use that, because there is a difference.

Beefsteak in Curry Sauce   咖喱士的

GA LEI SE DIK

Curry powder is strictly an Indian flavoring, but the Chinese ability to assimilate the best in foreign cultures is vividly illustrated in the curry dishes concocted by Chinese chefs. These dishes are unmistakably Chinese, even though we don't even have an exact written Chinese character for curry. The above "ga lei" is only a phonetic transcription of the word, just as we have no written characters for the word "steak." The best we can do here is the two words "se" and "dik"!

Use sirloin or flank steak for this recipe, and cut the slices thicker than generally done in stir-fry Chinese dishes (about ¼ inch).

More or less curry powder may be used for individual taste.

I   2   *cups sliced steak (about 1 pound trimmed meat)*
     1   *cup onions (sliced and separated into rings)*

II   1   *clove garlic, minced*
     2   *slices ginger, shredded*

III   1   *teaspoon sugar*
     1   *teaspoon monosodium glutamate*
     2   *tablespoons light soy sauce*

1 *tablespoon vegetable oil*
1 *tablespoon cornstarch*
1 *tablespoon curry powder*
½ *cup chicken stock or water*

IV 3 *tablespoons vegetable oil*
⅛ *teaspoon salt*
Chopped scallions or Chinese parsley, for garnish

Mix the first 4 ingredients in Group III as a marinade.

Marinate the sliced beef for about 30 minutes before cooking. Mix together remaining ingredients in Group III and put aside. Drain beef and combine marinade with the curry mixture.

Heat wok or frying pan hot and dry. Add ½ of the oil from IV. Put in salt, garlic, and ginger and stir-fry till golden brown. Put in beef to brown quickly on outside (about 1 minute). Remove at once into a bowl and put aside.

Clean wok or pan. Heat hot and dry again. Add the remainder of oil and fry onion rings till golden brown. Stir in curry mixture and heat until it has thickened. Put beef back in pan and mix thoroughly. Serve with chopped scallions or parsley as garnish.

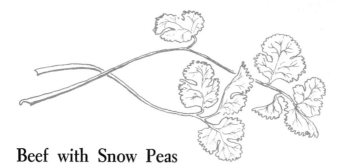

Beef with Snow Peas

雪荳牛

SUET DAU NGAU

Snow peas are one of the most delicate and fragile of vegetables. When cooked just till the color changes, they are sweet and crisp. Overcooked, they are soggy and uninteresting. Snow peas are also known as sugar peas, and very recently they became a frozen-food item in many supermarkets and fancy-food stores. The frozen are not as good as the fresh, but if you live in an area where only the frozen kind are available, by all means try them in this recipe. If frozen snow peas are used, thaw them and drain well before use. Add to the other ingredients only long enough to get them just warmed through. Any further cooking will make them limp.

I   2   *cups sliced beef (about 1 pound)*
    2   *cups snow peas (about ⅓ pound), washed*

II   1   *clove garlic, minced*
     2   *slices fresh ginger, shredded*

III   1   *teaspoon sugar*
      1   *tablespoon cornstarch*
      1   *teaspoon monosodium glutamate*
      2   *tablespoons light soy sauce*
      3   *tablespoons water*

IV   3   *tablespoons vegetable oil*
     ⅛   *teaspoon salt*
     2   *tablespoons sherry*
     ½   *cup chicken broth*

Mix together ingredients in Group III and put aside.

Heat wok or frying pan hot and dry. Add 1 tablespoon of the oil, then the salt, garlic, and ginger. Stir quickly till golden brown (don't let garlic burn). Add beef quickly. Stir constantly till beef is brown on the outside. Shut off heat at once and remove from wok or pan into bowl or dish. Put aside.

Heat wok or pan again. Add remainder of the oil. Add snow peas and stir-fry a minute or less. Watch color of fresh snow peas carefully. As soon as the color begins to turn a darker green, put back the beef and add the sherry and chicken broth. Stir and add the sauce mixture from Group III. When gravy thickens shut off heat and remove food from wok or pan. Serve at once.

Beef with White Radish

LOH BAAK NGAU

In the past, Chinese vegetable farmers in the United States had to continually replenish their vegetable seeds from China to maintain pure strains. Now the farmers have become expert seed producers themselves. Through careful, selective breeding, the vegetables grown from their seeds now rival the best the farmers in China can produce.

Sometimes two strains of the same vegetable may vary greatly in size, yet taste alike. White radishes provide a case in point. One white radish bought at a Chinese grocery store can equal in weight several bunches of the American variety. Either variety may be used in this recipe.

If Chinese white radishes are available, 1 medium-size radish will yield about 4 cups. Small American white radishes are widely available. They come in bunches like their red cousins. You may need 2 or 3 bunches of these to make 4 cups sliced.

This dish has a very tempting appearance, and its flavor is a delightful contrast to the blander vegetables ordinarily used. The translucent slices of radishes almost reveal the opaque slices of beef under them. And the bright green of the chopped scallions used as a garnish crowns the dish with a jadelike tiara!

Radishes should be scrubbed clean but need not be peeled before slicing.

I   2   *cups sliced lean beef (about 1 pound)*
      4   *cups sliced white radishes (sliced into ⅛-inch-thick dominoes)†*
      4   *cups water*
      ½   *teaspoon salt*

II   2   *slices fresh ginger, shredded*
      1   *clove garlic, minced*

III   1   *tablespoon sugar†*
      1   *teaspoon monosodium glutamate*
      3   *tablespoons light soy sauce*
      1   *tablespoon vegetable oil*
      1   *tablespoon cornstarch*
      1   *cup chicken broth or water*

IV   2   *tablespoons vegetable oil*
      ⅛   *teaspoon salt*

Mix together the first 4 ingredients in Group III. Marinate the beef in mixture for 10 minutes or longer before cooking. Drain off marinade and save. Boil the 4 cups water in a saucepan; add the ½ teaspoon salt to water. Put in sliced white radishes, and when water boils again cook 1 minute more. Drain radishes. Refresh radishes in cold water. Drain and put aside.

Heat wok or frying pan hot and dry. Add oil and the ⅛ teaspoon salt. Put in ginger and garlic to fry till brown. Add the beef, and stir constantly until brown on outside. Turn off heat and remove beef from wok or pan at once and put aside.

Mix the marinade liquid with the cornstarch and chicken broth. Put the mixture into wok or pan with the drained, half-cooked radishes. Turn heat to medium and bring to boil while stirring constantly (the gravy will thicken in the process). Put back beef and mix well for ½ minute. Turn off heat, place in serving dish and top with the chopped scallions before serving.

SUBSTITUTIONS AND VARIATIONS
Turnips may also be used, but the flavor is not quite as deli-

cate. Turnips, if used, should be boiled twice as long as the white radishes.

More sugar is used here than in most other recipes to heighten the natural sweetness of the radishes. Reduce the sugar to 1 teaspoon if you wish.

Ginger Steak with Peas 生薑牛

SAANG GEUNG NGAU

The Chinese palate can tolerate food that is very hot—if by "hot" we mean "a burning sensation on the tongue." The Mexicans and Indonesians eat food that is even hotter. Fortunately, the degree of hotness can be easily controlled without drastically altering the character of a dish.

It is wise to make hot dishes as mild as possible for the first try. Then as your tolerance increases, the hot ingredients can be increased correspondingly. I suggest that when you use this recipe for the first time you use only about half the ginger called for, and increase the amount in subsequent tries. Young ginger, which is usually available at the end of August, or canned ginger is preferable to the older ginger roots, but the dish may be made with the older variety, in which case only about ¼ as much of the ginger is needed. The potency of ginger roots increases with the age at which it is harvested. All the candied and pickled (canned) ginger is of the young variety, and has a "peaches and cream" complexion, as compared to the light brown and thicker skin of older ginger.

The beef used should be sirloin, flank steak, or other choice tender cuts, since the meat is most important. Very few Chinese dishes call for so much meat in proportion to the vegetables used. The beef slices should be twice as thick (about ¼ inch) as usual in Chinese stir-fry recipes for two reasons: the beef used is tender by itself, and it is easier to control the degree of doneness when the slices are thicker.

I 3 *cups sliced beef (about 1½ pounds)*

   ¾ *cup (about ⅓ pound) very thinly sliced young ginger, fresh or canned; or ¼ cup older ginger (see above)*

   1 *package frozen peas, thawed†*

II 2 *cloves garlic, minced*

   2 *scallions, cut into 1½-inch lengths, including green ends*

   3 *sprigs parsley, chopped†*

III 1 *teaspoon sugar*

   1 *tablespoon cornstarch*

   1 *teaspoon monosodium glutamate*

   ⅓ *cup oyster sauce*

   ½ *cup chicken stock or water*

IV ¼ *cup vegetable oil*

   ¼ *teaspoon salt*

   3 *tablespoons sherry*

Mix together ingredients in Group III and put aside.

Heat wok or pan over high heat until hot and dry and add ½ the vegetable oil. Add the salt. Add the garlic and stir quickly until golden brown. Add the sliced beef at once and stir-fry until the outside is browned (about 1 minute; don't overcook). Turn heat to low, scoop out the beef and juice into a bowl and put aside.

Heat wok or pan dry and hot again. (It ought to be washed after the beef has been taken out, but this is not absolutely essential.) Add the remainder of the oil. Put in the ginger and fry for 1 minute. Add peas, scallions, and parsley. Stir-fry 1 minute more. Add sherry, stir, and cover. Let cook 1 minute longer.

Put back the beef and juice. While stirring, add the sauce mixture from Group III, and cook until gravy thickens. Turn off heat and serve.

SUBSTITUTIONS AND VARIATIONS

One cup of fresh snow peas or a package of frozen snow peas may be used in place of the regular frozen peas. Less time is required to cook snow peas. See Beef with Snow Peas recipe, p. 129.

Chinese parsley is preferable, but American parsley may be used.

Since this is a hot dish, and highly spiced, it is a good idea to serve another dish with it which is very bland, such as a sautéed vegetable or dau foo (bean curd). Serve it with lots of boiled rice.

Sirloin Steak Cubes

SE DIK KAU

This is a most elegant dish. It is one of the most expensive dishes in a restaurant's menu, if it is listed at all. It is a happy marriage of East and West, because the Chinese do enjoy a steak, yet they do not want to abandon completely the Chinese system of cooking. Conversely, a Westerner can identify the chunks of steak as something familiar and enjoyable. If I were a diplomat, I would serve such a dish during a Sino-American conference!

If you like your steak rare, after you've cut the steak cubes put them in the freezer or ice-cube compartment for about ½ hour before cooking. The meat, being cold, will get brown on the outside but stay rare on the inside.

To make 2 cups of pure steak, a sirloin will have to weigh about 1½ to 2 pounds including bone and fat.

I   2   *cups sirloin steak, trimmed and cut into 1-inch cubes*†
      1   *cup snow peas*
      1   *cup diced baak choy hearts or celery cabbage*

II   1   *small can button mushrooms, drained, liquid saved*
      ½   *cup diced bamboo shoots*
      ¼   *cup diced water chestnuts (fresh or canned)*

III   1   *teaspoon sugar*
      2   *teaspoons cornstarch*
      1   *teaspoon monosodium glutamate*
      2   *tablespoons oyster sauce*
      ¼   *cup chicken broth or water*
           Liquid from mushrooms

IV   3   *tablespoons vegetable oil*
      3   *tablespoons light soy sauce*
      2   *tablespoons gin or vodka*
      ¼   *cup parsley or chopped nut meats (optional)*

Mix together ingredients in Group III and put aside.

Heat wok or frying pan hot and dry. Add 1 tablespoon of the oil and heat till very hot. Add steak cubes; let sear on one side, then turn to another side until cubes are brown on all sides. Mix together soy sauce and gin or vodka and pour over the steak; turn off heat immediately. Remove steak and juice from wok or pan into bowl and put aside.

Wash wok or pan and reheat till hot and dry. Add remainder of oil. Put in all the canned and fresh vegetables except the snow peas. Fry for 2 minutes. Cover and cook 1 minute more.

Remove cover and stir in Group III sauce mixture until sauce thickens. Add snow peas and stir thoroughly. Put back steak and juice and mix thoroughly. Remove from pan to serving dish. Top with parsley or chopped nut meats (optional).

SUBSTITUTIONS AND VARIATIONS

There should be very little substitution in making this recipe. Only the very best of ingredients should go into the making of it. Sirloin steak is generally used, but porterhouse or filet mignon may be used to upgrade it, if you are feeling flush.

While the ingredients should not be changed, the ratio of meat to vegetable may be altered as you wish. But remember, this is a *steak* kau and not a *vegetable* kau!

Stewed Shin Beef, Peking Style   北京牛肉

PAK KING NGAU YUK

A common challenge to cooks of every nationality is to take a less desirable cut of meat and make it not merely edible but delicious. Shin beef presents such a challenge, and Chinese cooks have met it superbly. This dish is easy to make and can be done in advance; therefore, more time is saved for you to do the other more complicated dishes in your dinner plan. The only way to cook shin beef tender is by long, low-heat simmering with liquid which covers the meat. What you would normally cut away and discard in American cooking, such as tendons and the fibers which encase the meat, is prized in this dish. It is the difference in the textures of the various components of the shin beef which gives this dish its character.

Buy the boneless shin beef. Leave the beef (which may come in 1 or 2 pieces) uncut.

This is one of the Chinese dishes that can be made in advance and reheated without any loss of quality. In fact, reheating actually improves the dish. There are other advantages to making it beforehand, too. If the meat is taken out of the liquid and refrigerated, it is easier to slice. Also, the liquid can be cooled after straining (in this case it should not be thickened until later), and the fat in the liquid will harden into a layer on top, which can be easily lifted off.

To serve, bring the liquid to a boil. Thicken it with cornstarch. Slice the beef and reheat in the gravy.

I   2   *pounds shin beef, rinsed†*

II   3   *slices ginger*
     1   *medium-size onion, chopped*
     2   *cloves garlic, skinned and crushed*
     3   *scallions, cut in halves, including green ends*
     3   *sprigs parsley (Chinese parsley preferable)*

III ½   *teaspoon cracked black pepper*
     2   *star anise seeds*
     1   *teaspoon monosodium glutamate*
     2   *tablespoons brown sugar*
     ¼   *cup dark soy sauce*
     ¼   *cup sherry or 2 tablespoons whiskey*
     ½   *teaspoon sesame oil*
     2   *tablespoons wine vinegar*

IV   2   *tablespoons vegetable oil*
     ¼   *teaspoon salt*
     2   *tablespoons cornstarch, mixed with ¼ cup water*
          Chopped scallions, for garnish (optional)

Heat wok or frying pan till dry and hot. Add oil, then salt. Turn heat down to medium and add the ginger, onion, and garlic. Fry till golden brown. Remove from pan and set aside.

Turn up heat again. Put in shin beef and brown the outside. After the beef has browned, put in all the ingredients in Group III and cook covered for 2 or 3 minutes. Put back the garlic, ginger, and onion, and add scallions and parsley. Stir thoroughly and shut off heat.

Transfer everything into a deep pot with cover. Add enough water to cover the meat. Bring to a boil, then reduce heat to a slow simmer. Cook for 2 to 3 hours, covered, until beef is tender. When ready to serve, remove meat onto a platter. Strain the liquid and discard the solids. Put liquid back in the pot and reheat to boiling; skim off excess fat. Stir up the cornstarch mixture and add to liquid to thicken. Slice meat with sharp knife. Serve with rice and plain boiled spinach, peas, string beans, or other green vegetable. Ladle gravy over meat, rice, and vegetables and sprinkle chopped scallions (optional) over it.

SUBSTITUTIONS AND VARIATIONS

This is a good example of "red cooking" (see p. 10). Fresh picnic ham, fowl, or tough cuts of meat may be cooked using this basic recipe.

Steamed Chopped Beef with Pickled Bamboo

SUN YEE NGAU YUK

While you may not use this recipe much, just as you may not use the recipe for Pork with Bitter Melon on page 111 frequently, trying this recipe out a few times may give you more insight into the Chinese appreciation for the five fragrances that our taste buds can detect. Most Chinese people are very fond of this dish because of its slightly sour-salty flavor, and you may find it to be a wonderful change of pace in your menu.

Sun yee, the ingredient that determines the flavor in this dish, is literally translated as "the garment of the bamboo shoot," which is the thin layer of skin on each bamboo shoot. It looks like fine broad egg noodles in color and shape. Its texture is velvety and slightly *al dente*. You can buy it in Chinese stores in cans, under the name pickled bamboo and the first two characters listed above. Leftover pickled bamboo should be transferred to a jar with cover. It will keep very well for months with or without refrigeration.

Do not use regular hamburger meat for Chinese cooking, since there is too much fat in it. Chopped stew beef, well-trimmed chuck, or round steak is an ideal cut for this dish. The meat may be ground by machine, but it should be ground as coarsely as possible.

No added liquid is needed for steamed dishes, as in the steaming process the steam will condense, and the natural juices are retained within the food to give enough gravy.

I   1½   *pounds lean chopped beef†*

II   ¼   *cup pickled bamboo shoot (use as it comes
          from the can)*

III   1   *teaspoon sugar*
      1   *teaspoon monosodium glutamate*
      1   *teaspoon cornstarch*
      ⅛   *teaspoon salt*

IV   2   *teaspoons vegetable oil*

In a mixing bowl, place chopped beef. Pour oil on top of the beef. Mix together all the ingredients in Group III and sprinkle evenly over the beef. Use a fork and fold the meat and seasoning together several times. Transfer meat to a shallow uncovered dish. Sprinkle the pickled bamboo on top and steam for 30 minutes. See page 9 for instructions for steaming.

SUBSTITUTIONS AND VARIATIONS
Chicken cut into pieces may be used in place of the beef.

Five Fragrances Beef

MM HEUNG NGAU YUK

This is a dish with multiple virtues. It may be eaten hot or cold, as a main dish or as an appetizer. The principal difference between it and American pot roast is in the five fragrances seasoning used, which gives it a unique fragrant taste. Use a boneless chuck roast for economy. Any other cuts of lean beef roast, such as top round, may be used. Trim off most, but not all, of the fat before cooking. Some fat on a piece of meat when eaten hot is pleasant to taste, but cold fat has the opposite effect. Discard the liquid, unless you wish to cook more of this dish within a week. Keep refrigerated until reused. The stock is too insistent for use with other dishes.

I   3   *pounds boneless chuck roast (or other beef cut, above)*

II   3   *slices fresh ginger*
     2   *cloves garlic, crushed*
     3   *whole scallions*
     3   *sprigs of Chinese parsley (optional)*

III 3   *tablespoons sugar*
     1   *teaspoon monosodium glutamate*
     ½   *teaspoon cracked pepper*
     1   *tablespoon five fragrances spices, tied in cheesecloth (saam lei, but kok, page 33)*
     3   *tablespoons vinegar*
     ¼   *cup soy sauce*

IV   2   *tablespoons vegetable oil*
     ½   *teaspoon sesame oil*
     1   *teaspoon salt*
          Water to cover meat in saucepan
     ½   *cup sherry (optional)*

Use a heavy saucepan large enough to contain meat and water to cover. Heat pan hot and dry. Add the vegetable oil and sesame oil, then add the salt. Turn heat to medium and add the ginger and garlic. Stir-fry until golden brown. Remove pan from stove to cool. Place the beef and all remaining ingredients except parsley garnish and sherry (if used) in the pan and cover with cold water. Bring liquid to a boil. Reduce heat to a simmer and cook for 2-3 hours until beef is tender. Drain off liquid, slice beef, add sherry (if used), and serve.

If you wish to serve it cold, when meat has cooled place in refrigerator for 3-4 hours. Slice as you would cold roast beef. Arrange slices on platter and pour on the sherry. Garnish with parsley and serve.

9

Chicken

I
N the villages of old China (and in all parts of the rural world,
I guess) chicken and other fowl were greatly in evidence. The
cocks proudly stalked the village compounds, and ducks placidly
swam the communal ponds. Each Chinese farmer, no matter
how poor, would keep two or three chickens in his house for
special occasions like birthdays and the New Year. Chickens
required no upkeep in a Chinese village; they could literally
"scratch for themselves." Besides the earthworms and insects,
there were always those few grains that even the most frugal
farmer spilled when he laid rice or beans out to dry in baskets
in the sun.

One of the jobs little boys had to assume in a village was to
chase chickens, ducks, geese, and birds away from the drying
grain. At night, the chickens would come home—be it to a hovel
or a middle-class house. The houses always had little open ter-
races. Beneath a hole in the roof like an open skylight was a
stone-paved area where the chickens roosted. This was a common design in Chinese architecture.

To come back to the present, chicken is one of the best bar-
gains and best-tasting meats available for any type of cooking.

In recent years in the U.S.A., chicken has been downgraded because of its abundance and availability, but not so many years ago the golden dream was "a chicken in every pot," symbolizing all the good things of an ideal and affluent society.

I am reminded of a line by Shakespeare. ". . . If all the year were playing holidays, to sport would be as tedious as to work." Perhaps this is another way of saying familiarity breeds contempt, and chicken is too available. But chicken cooked well and in a variety of ways can give your menu wings!

How to Buy Chicken

There is some justification for people who are complaining that chicken doesn't taste as good as it used to. Chicken raising is a large-scale business today, efficiently and scientifically controlled from the time an egg is laid to the point where neatly packaged chicken parts are displayed for sale at your supermarket. Fed on vitamins, hormones, and chicken-feed mixtures, a chicken can be brought to market size in three or four months, whereas it would take twice as long if it were grown on a farm and fed only on grain. The economic advantage of such high-speed production is simple to understand, but in this fast growth some of the flavor is lost. There may be further loss of flavor in the mass cleaning, packaging, refrigerating, and distribution processes.

The above is a reality of modern life, but there are ways out of this dilemma if we use a little extra care and effort in selecting our chickens. Here in New York, right in my neighborhood, there are many live poultry markets for the Chinese, Jewish, and Italian peoples. One may select a chicken, duck, or squab and have it freshly killed and cleaned for just a little more than a chicken would cost in a regular supermarket. There may be markets like these in your area too, or fresh-killed chicken may be ordered through your regular butcher.

Some of the reasons why fresh-killed chicken is superior to the frozen and packaged ones have been loosely covered above.

A little more light should be shed on the subject. The flavor of chicken is very fragile and delicate. In this respect, it's like fresh fish vs. frozen fish, although the qualities of fish can be lost much more easily. Unlike beef, which is not really at its best until it has been aged, chicken and fish are at the peak of their flavor when fresh-killed. When a duck or chicken is roasted, even the golden brownness of the skin is handsomer when fresh-killed fowls are used.

Since a good cook must be resourceful, she has to take her real world as it comes—but she'll try to improve it! Cooking and eating can be only one part of a person's life (albeit a large part); we should not spend all our time and energy in the pursuit of gastronomy. If fresh-killed chickens are not easily available, by all means use the best-quality chicken that is available.

There are certain hints on buying chicken. The Chinese divide chickens into two categories, "high chicken" and others. The high chickens are the fully matured ones, such as those used for roasting. Females are the best, but they must not have laid eggs yet. The ideal weight, cleaned, should be from 4½ to 6½ pounds. In appearance, the skin should be a rich yellow, and the feet should be yellow, too. If the chicken has feathers you can see, they should be dark or colored. Originally these chickens came from Peking, China, I understand. If this is the case, what more appropriate chicken can you buy for Chinese cooking?

The original name for this breed of chicken has been lost. I doubt that even poultry farmers know that the chickens they raise had a Chinese ancestry. But they will know them by their English names. The favorite breeds the Chinese people use for their cooking are Wyandotte, Jersey Plymouth, and New Hampshire Hen, in that order.

Besides the high chicken described above, the others include young fryers under 4½ pounds each used for frying in halves, as in the recipe called "Jah Tz Gai" on page 160. Old, tough chickens are also usable, but only to make soup stock; after the flavor has been extracted, the meat is discarded or can be fed to your cat (I keep a cat just for that purpose!).

What about the very small chickens weighing only 1-1½ pounds that you may find in your supermarket? The Chinese cook would not ordinarily use such a small chicken because it is not "chickeny" enough.

The Chinese people have loved capons from time immemorial. A detailed discussion on capons is given with the recipe on page 169.

When a recipe in this book calls for a whole chicken, please use a roasting chicken. Get one as large as you can, because the larger-sized ones yield more meat per pound than the smaller ones. If you buy a chicken larger than you need for one meal, the leftovers make for good snacking or can be used in another recipe.

If only the meat of chicken is called for in a recipe, use chicken breasts. It was not always so, but now chicken in parts may be bought almost anywhere. This makes for great convenience, since you can buy several chicken breasts, instead of having to buy several chickens in order to get enough white meat for a recipe. The chicken breasts have another advantage; they are very easy to bone and cut. They do not have the complicated bone structure and sinews of the other parts of the chicken. When buying, pick the largest breasts you can find among the packages. They yield more meat, plus better flavor, because the larger chickens from which they come were more mature and had a longer time to develop the "chickeny" taste.

Refrigerating and Freezing

In a remote village compound in China the ideal of a fresh-killed chicken can be attained without any problems. It would be impossible there to get a *frozen* chicken even if a cook *should* desire one. There are very few items whose flavor and texture are actually improved by being frozen. There are many items that will lose only a tiny bit of their quality by being subjected to freezing. Fortunately fowls fall into this category. Poultry may be kept frozen for 6 to 8 months. If the fowl has been cut up, then the storage time is shortened by 2 months. Boned, cubed, or sliced meat should not be kept frozen for more than 2 months.

When storing packaged poultry in the refrigerator, always remove the plastic wrappers or else the skin will become slimy, and an unpleasant odor will develop. Poultry should not be kept in the refrigerator for longer than 2 days.

Frozen poultry may be defrosted in the refrigerator or at room temperature. An average-size roaster (4-6 pounds) will defrost in the refrigerator within 24 hours. Placed outside at room temperature it will defrost in 6 to 8 hours.

To compensate for the slight loss of flavor in a chicken which has been stored, sprinkle a teaspoon or so of monosodium glutamate on the chicken after it has been cut into pieces and let it soak into the meat for about half an hour before use to bring out its best flavor.

Boning a Chicken

Anyone can bone a chicken. But to do it fast, with the utmost efficiency, takes great skill. I feel that I am fairly competent in boning a chicken, but when I go and visit my chef friends in restaurants and see them do it, I feel like an amateur with ten thumbs. I timed Mr. Lee Lum once, without his knowledge, and he boned a chicken in less than a minute and a half. I am not going to tell you what my speed record is.

While you may never get to be very deft at it, you should know how to go about boning a chicken. By that I mean removing the bones from the chicken so that the meat can be cut into the various shapes for Chinese cookery. In some Chinese recipes, the bones are deliberately left in, and that kind of cut is called "luk" (see page 42).

Boning a chicken can mean something else. All chefs engage in tours-de-force, and Chinese chefs are no exception. Some highly skilled chefs have perfected the art of removing all the bones of a chicken from the *inside* so that when they are presented at the table a line from a folk ballad, "I gave my love a chicken without any bones," becomes literally true. However, I think the time needed to perfect this skill can be better used toward mastery of some other phases of cooking.

I know a race of people who claim that "a picture is worth a thousand words." I may add that a demonstration by a skilled teacher is worth many pictures.

NOTES AND COMMENTS

Not only skill is necessary to perform a good job; the proper tools in the best of condition are also essential. In this case, the knife must be razor sharp; the cutting surface on which the chicken rests must be secure and nonslippery. Wipe off excess moisture from time to time. Remember to cut only where and what you can see plainly.

A good trick to learn when slicing raw fowl or other meats is to semi-freeze them first. Meat tends to be wet and slippery when fresh. Freezing partially firms the meat, and will make the slicing or cutting easier.

Pure-Cut Chicken 白切鷄

BAAK CHIT GAI

There are certain foods that are so good in themselves that everything possible should be used to preserve their individual character and flavor. A good prime steak just broiled over charcoal or a fresh Maine lobster boiled in ocean water cannot be surpassed. This is not to say that you should never do anything else with lobster or steak, because good foods have many talents and can play many roles. We've often said to ourselves, "What can I do to dress up this (or that) food so it'll be different?" We

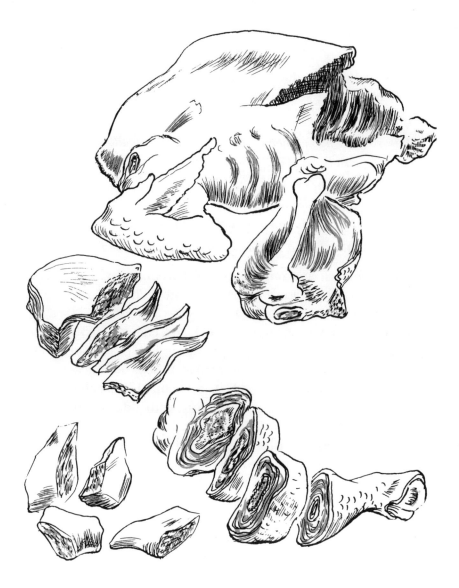

usually answer that query by *adding,* be it spices, other meats, vegetables or sauces. Sometimes it is equally important to know when to *subtract* in order to add to your culinary luster. This recipe is plainly a case of subtraction. It's almost like putting chicken on stage center, with a spotlight on it, without props or costumes, to let it captivate your audience with only its own goodness. You, as the director, must select the best chicken possible for the role. See the advice on how to select chickens, page 144.

I   1 *roasting chicken (fresh-killed, if available), 4 to 5 pounds, cleaned and drawn*

II   2 *tablespoons salt*
     1 *teaspoon ground pepper*
     2 *tablespoons monosodium glutamate*

III   *Water, about 4 quarts (amount determined by pot used)*

Clean chicken and remove loose fat from cavity. Let chicken reach room temperature before cooking. (Chicken fat can be saved for other use or discarded.)

Place chicken in a large pot and add enough cold water to cover by at least 1 inch. (This process is just to measure quantity of water needed for your utensil.) Remove chicken from pot and bring water to a boil. Add Group II seasoning.

Put chicken into pot, cover tightly with lid, and turn heat down to low at once. Cook for 1 hour. Remove from pot. Carve at table Western style or cut into pieces Chinese style (see page 43) and serve plain, with a salt dip made as below:

Do not open the lid to peek while the chicken is cooking. Remember Pandora's box! Let Hope and Faith remain.

The liquid in which the chicken is cooked should be discarded. It should contain no chicken flavor. We were making *chicken*— not chicken *soup.*

SALT DIP

2   *tablespoons table salt*
½   *teaspoon ground white pepper*
¼   *cup vegetable oil*

Mix salt and pepper together, then add the oil and stir well. Spoon out into individual small dishes so that each diner can dip the chicken into it according to personal preference.

Chicken Slices with Vegetables

炒鷄片

CHOW GAI PEEN

Most Chinese dishes start out with raw meats as ingredients, but in this recipe the chicken meat is precooked before being combined with the fresh vegetables. It is an excellent recipe for using up leftover chicken, or you can start out with uncooked chicken breasts.

The unused portion of the chicken broth used to boil the chicken breasts should be saved for soups or gravies. The flavor of the broth has been enriched in the cooking process.

After the chicken breasts have been cooked and cooled, it will be very easy to separate the meat from the bones by peeling with your fingers.

I 3 *chicken breasts, whole (about 2-2½ pounds)†*
   1 *can chicken broth*
   ¼ *teaspoon salt*
   ⅛ *teaspoon ground white pepper*
     Liquid from canned mushrooms

II 2 *cups sliced baak choy hearts (see page 58)*
   ½ *cup snow peas*
   1 *can button mushrooms, drained, liquid saved*
   1 *clove garlic, minced*
   2 *slices ginger, shredded*
   ½ *cup sliced canned bamboo shoots†*
   ¼ *cup sliced fresh or canned water chestnuts†*

III 1 *teaspoon sugar*
   2 *teaspoons cornstarch*
   1 *teaspoon monosodium glutamate*
   ¼ *cup light soy sauce*
   1 *cup stock from Group I*

IV 3 *tablespoons vegetable oil*
   2 *tablespoons sherry*

In a saucepan, bring Group I ingredients (except the chicken breasts) to a boil. Add chicken breasts. Turn heat down very low and cook covered for 20 minutes. Remove chicken, reserving broth. Let cool and remove bones. Cut meat into slices. Put aside. Mix together ingredients from Group III and put aside.

Heat wok, add oil. Fry together all ingredients in Group II (except the snow peas) for 3 minutes while stirring. Add chicken. Add sherry and cover at once. Cook for 2 minutes longer. Lift cover and put in snow peas. Add the sauce mixture in Group III, stirring constantly until gravy thickens. Turn off heat and serve at once.

SUBSTITUTIONS AND VARIATIONS

Chicken may be fried instead of poached before being cooked with the other ingredients. In that case, see Chow Gai Kau recipe on page 176 for instructions on frying the meat.

The bamboo shoots and water chestnuts are optional.

If leftover cooked chicken is used, the dark meat and the white may be used together.

Deep-Fried Fluff Chicken   炸浮鷄

JAH FAU GAI

The breading of deep-fried foods should stay light and crisp, even after the food has cooled. Nothing detracts from one's pleasure in good food as much as a limp, soggy crust. The secret in making a fluffy crust which will stay crisp for hours lies in the mixing of the batter, which must be followed exactly as outlined here. The oil must be mixed with the flour first, before the water is put in. Do not reverse this process.

If you are serving only chicken without other dishes, allow half a chicken to each diner.

I   1   *frying chicken, about 3 pounds, disjointed, breast split in half†*

II   3-4 *quarts water, or enough to cover chicken in saucepan*
     2   *tablespoons salt*
     1   *teaspoon monosodium glutamate*

III 2   *tablespoons light soy sauce*
     1½   *cups flour*
     ¼   *teaspoon salt*
     1   *tablespoon baking powder*
     ½   *cup vegetable oil*
     1   *cup cold water*

IV   *Oil for deep frying, about 2 quarts*

Bring water, salt, and monosodium glutamate (Group II) to a vigorous boil in a heavy saucepan with cover. Add the disjointed chicken and turn heat down to low at once (don't let water boil again). Cover and allow chicken to poach for 35 minutes. Remove chicken from water and allow to cool. Discard water. After chicken has cooled, pat dry with paper towels. Pour the 2 tablespoons soy sauce (from Group III) over the chicken, and rub with fingers to cover all parts of the chicken evenly with it.

Mix remaining Group III ingredients as follows: In mixing bowl put everything except the oil and water. Mix thoroughly. Add the oil a little at a time while stirring with a wooden spoon, until all the oil is used, and flour has turned into dough. Add all the cold water a little at a time while stirring. The dough will turn into the consistency of pancake batter.

Heat oil from Group IV to medium frying temperature (350°-360° F.) in deep fryer. Dip chicken into the batter; let excess batter drip off each piece just before putting into oil. Fry till breading becomes golden brown. Remove from oil onto absorbent paper towels. Season with plain or spiced salt at table (see page 162 for Spiced Salt recipe).

Chicken in parts may be used instead of 1 chicken. You may prefer chicken breasts or legs. Buy the equivalent of a 3-pound chicken and the recipe will not have to be altered.

Chicken Slices with Mushrooms

冬菰鷄片

TUNG KOO GAI P'IN

On page 33 we discussed the different types of mushrooms used in Chinese cooking. This recipe can be made into several different dishes just by choosing different mushrooms and different kinds of meat. While it is legitimate to write a separate recipe for each of the possible combinations, it is not my purpose to see how thick a book I can make. Rather, it is hoped that after being provided with a solid grounding in cooking techniques and basic recipes, the reader may eventually use his or her own skills and imagination to create variations to basic recipes.

There are certain basic concepts (rather than rules—I don't think you can make rules for cooking) that should be followed. If the dish is to be a "p'in" dish, then the mushrooms, whether canned or dried, should be thin sliced, as the word "p'in" designates. If it's a "k'au" dish, meaning balls or chunks, whole button mushrooms or small whole dried mushrooms should be used. This is known as "harmony of cut" (see page 38).

I	3	*chicken breasts†*
	1	*can chicken broth*
	⅛	*teaspoon salt*
	1	*teaspoon monosodium glutamate*
	⅛	*teaspoon pepper*
II	1	*pound fresh bean sprouts†*
	2	*packages frozen French-style beans, thawed*

1 *clove garlic, minced*

2 *slices ginger, shredded*

1 *small can sliced button mushrooms (save liquid) or 6-8 dried mushrooms, soaked in ⅓ cup water ½ hour or longer (save water)*

III 1 *teaspoon sugar*

1 *tablespoon cornstarch*

1 *teaspoon monosodium glutamate*

½ *cup broth from chicken (save remainder for other gravies and soups)*

Liquid or water from mushrooms

3 *tablespoons light soy sauce*

IV 3 *tablespoons vegetable oil*

2 *tablespoons sherry*

3-4 *sprigs parsley, ¼ cup crushed nuts, or 2 chopped scallions, for garnish (optional)*

Mix together ingredients in Group III and set aside. Combine in a saucepan all ingredients in Group I except chicken breasts. Bring to a boil. Add chicken breasts. Turn down heat to low. Cook covered for 15 minutes. Remove chicken breasts and put aside to cool. Save liquid. When chicken has cooled, remove bones and slice meat into thin strips. Put aside.

Heat wok or pan hot and dry. Add oil. Add garlic and ginger and stir until brown. Add remainder of items in Group II. Fry while stirring for 3 minutes. Add sherry and cover to cook for 2 minutes more. Add chicken; mix thoroughly. Add mixture from Group III. Stir until gravy thickens. Serve topped with chopped scallions, crushed nuts, or parsley (optional).

Serves 3-4 people.

SUBSTITUTIONS AND VARIATIONS

If fresh bean sprouts are not available, canned bean sprouts may be used. A 1-pound can is equivalent to 1 pound of fresh bean sprouts. Drain well before using.

Tender celery hearts are a good substitute for Chinese vegetables such as Chinese cabbage and bean sprouts. Shred the celery hearts very fine, and cook only briefly (1-2 minutes) with the other ingredients so that they will still be crisp and slightly crunchy for best texture, contrast, and flavor.

Please notice that most vegetables and fresh and dry seasonings are the same in stir-fried dishes. You can just as well use 2 cups beef, pork, or seafood as substitutes for the chicken.

Barbecued Chicken   燒雞

SIU GAI

Chickens lend themselves to the barbecue method of cooking particularly well. The Chinese are very fond of barbecued food, but some of us feel maligned whenever foreigners repeat to us the old story about how Chinese learned the art of barbecuing by accident, when a farmer's house burned down and the family pig was trapped and roasted in the holocaust. The story goes that the meat salvaged from this disaster was so delicious that all the neighboring farmers set their houses afire and had a community barbecue! I believe that actually barbecuing was accidentally discovered by our common primitive ancestors as a result of forest fires, when animals were trapped and roasted. Barbecuing is still one of the best methods of cooking today.

The marinade below is a modification of the one used for barbecued pork on page 93.

I   1   *frying chicken, about 3 pounds, split in half*
II 1   *tablespoon sweet bean sauce (hoi sin deung)*
    ½   *cup ketchup or chili sauce*
    2   *tablespoons soy sauce*
    2   *tablespoons sherry or 1 tablespoon whiskey*
    ½   *teaspoon salt*
    2   *cloves garlic, minced*
    ¼   *teaspoon Tabasco (optional)*

Mix the marinade, using all ingredients in II. Rinse and dry chicken halves with paper towels. Coat a large, shallow dish or platter with 2 tablespoons of the marinade. Place chicken halves on it split side up. Pour remainder of marinade evenly on chicken. Let stand at least 1 hour at room temperature before cooking.

Preheat oven to 400°. Turn on broiler. (Some ovens have broiling and roasting units together in the oven; others have separate spaces for broiling and roasting. This recipe assumes that the oven and broiler are separate. Adjust cooking instructions to best utilize your equipment.)

Place chicken halves on wire rack of broiler pan, split side up. Put chicken into broiler compartment as close as possible to heat source. Sear for 5 minutes, then turn chicken halves over to sear the skin side for 5 minutes. Remove broiler pan and chicken. Place in preheated oven. Turn heat down to 325°. Leave in oven for 35 minutes. Test for doneness by sticking fork into chicken thigh. If fork goes in easily, and the juice running out is not red, the chicken is done. Don't overcook, or else the chicken will be stringy and dry.

It is not necessary to baste the chicken while it is being cooked, because the seared skin would prevent penetration of the marinade anyway.

Barbecued chicken is best when cooked slowly. But it should be seared on both sides to seal in the juice. If a rotisserie is used, preheat and place chicken as close to the fire as possible for about 5 minutes on each side. Then lower or raise the spit (as the case may be) so the chicken will not scorch or cook too quickly. Allow about 45-50 minutes for cooking.

If the chicken is to be barbecued over charcoal outdoors, lower the grill to sear the chicken on both sides, then raise the grill a few notches to permit longer cooking. The amount of time varies according to the heat of your charcoal fire. Test for doneness after 30 minutes as outlined above in oven cooking.

Celestial Chicken 鳳凰鷄

FUNG WONG GAI

Continuing the Chinese tradition of inventing new dishes, or revising old ones, a chef created this dish in recent years right here in the United States. It caught the fancy of gourmets, and most high-class Chinese restaurants now have a version of this dish. Since recipes cannot be copyrighted or patented, we can only send our compliments to the chef—whoever he was.

The name "Fung Wong Gai" is also a fanciful invention. "Phoenix Emperor Chicken" is the literal translation, implying a celestial chicken dish for the emperor.

Buy the chicken breasts in parts, and choose them to be all about the same size. Chicken breasts usually come from broilers or fryers about 2 to 3 pounds in size, whole. When the bone has been removed (see page 147 on boning), the meat on either side of the breastbone will be about ¾ inch thick. When the ¼-inch-thick ham slices are inserted in the chicken meat, the total thickness of the "sandwich" will be about an inch. Use raw chicken. The ham is already cooked, and the chicken will be nicely done once the breading becomes golden brown in the frying oil.

I	4	*whole chicken breasts, raw, skin and bone removed*
	8	*slices cooked ham, 2 inches by 3 inches and about ¼ inch thick*
	1	*cup fresh snow peas†*
	1	*package frozen leaf spinach, thawed*
II	1½	*cups flour*
	¼	*teaspoon salt*
	2	*teaspoons baking powder*
	1	*egg*
		Water, enough to mix a batter of pancake consistency (about 1 cup)
III	3	*cups water*
	1	*teaspoon vegetable oil*
	1	*teaspoon salt*
IV		*Oil for deep frying, about 2 quarts*

Make a lengthwise slit in each piece of raw, boned chicken to form a pocket for the ham. Insert the ham slices into the pockets.

Mix all ingredients in Group II to form a batter about the consistency of pancake batter.

Place water, oil, and salt from Group III in saucepan and bring to a boil. Put in snow peas for about ½ minute, or until they turn a nice green color. Remove at once from pot and rinse with cold water.

Bring water to boil again, and put in the spinach. Bring to boil again and turn off heat. Drain spinach, but leave in pot to keep hot until ready to serve.

Heat oil in IV to medium temperature (350°-365° F.). Dip chicken-ham sandwiches into batter. Let excess batter drip off for a few seconds before putting sandwiches into oil. Fry till golden brown. Remove from oil and onto absorbent paper towels. Cut each chicken-ham sandwich crosswise twice to form 3 short, smaller sandwiches.

Place spinach on bottom of serving platter. Place chicken-ham sandwiches on top with slight space between each sandwich. Insert snow peas between and serve.

SUBSTITUTIONS AND VARIATIONS

If fresh snow peas are not available, packages of frozen snow peas may be found in your supermarket. If they are not available either, a good substitute would be frozen French-cut string beans. Blanch the same way as the snow peas.

The dish may be sprinkled with 2 or 3 teaspoons oyster sauce, and garnished with scallions or crushed roasted nuts. This is optional.

Chinese-Style Fried Chicken 炸子鷄

JAH TZ GAI

It is the subtle variations of a cuisine that make it different from all others, and give it its national character. The process of deep frying is universal, so how can Chinese-style fried chicken be so different? The answer lies in the spices used to prepare it *before* it is fried. By being immersed in hot liquid below the boiling point, the chicken is partially cooked, and all the spice flavors have a chance to penetrate deep into the flesh of the chicken, without toughening the flesh and extracting the flavor.

I find it convenient to make 2 or more chickens at one time, even if we have no company. Since the marinating liquid will serve for 1 or 10 chickens, without any addition or changes, it is a time and money saver to make an extra chicken or two, and wrap and freeze them for future use. Don't make too many extra, because that would use up too much freezer space, even though the chicken will keep frozen without loss of quality for 2 or 3 months. Thaw thoroughly before deep frying. Spring or frying chicken is used instead of the larger ones used in other recipes. Allow ½ chicken to each person.

I   1 *chicken (about 3-3½ pounds), split into halves†*

II   4 *quarts water*
        2 *tablespoons five fragrances spices (page 33)*
        4 *slices fresh ginger*
        3 *cloves garlic, crushed*
        1 *teaspoon salt*
        1 *tablespoon monosodium glutamate*
        1 *cup dark soy sauce*
        3 *scallions, cut in half*

III   2 *tablespoons light soy sauce*

IV   *Oil for deep frying (about 2 quarts)*
          Spiced salt (see recipe page 162)†

Put all ingredients in Group II in large pot with cover. Pot should be large enough to hold the liquid mixture with enough space left over to accommodate the chicken halves without spilling over. (Cook only 2 halves of chicken at one time—if you are making more than one.) Bring mixture to a boil. Turn heat down to a simmer for 10 minutes. Turn up heat until liquid boils vigorously again. Immerse chicken halves in it. Turn heat down very low at once. Cover and let chicken stay in liquid for 30-40 minutes, depending on size of chicken.

Remove chicken from liquid. Discard liquid. Pat dry with absorbent paper. Rub the 2 tablespoons of light soy sauce all over the chicken halves.

Heat oil in wok or deep fryer to medium heat (about 350°-360° F.). Use long tongs to pick up chicken halves and lower into oil. CAREFUL! Stand back as far as possible because the oil may spatter when the chicken is placed in it. Turn chicken over to cook evenly.

Cook chicken until golden brown all over. Turn off heat. Remove chicken onto paper towels to drain off excess oil. Serve whole halves or cut up into pieces, Chinese style. Season individually with spiced salt, which was made beforehand.

SUBSTITUTIONS AND VARIATIONS

Any small fowl, such as Rock Cornish hens or game birds, may be used instead of chicken. The special tastes of the birds and fowl will still be maintained.

The spiced salt is not an absolute necessity. Regular table salt will do.

Spiced Salt

HEUNG YIM

This is known also as "fragrant salt." It is used as a table spice whenever fried chicken or squabs are eaten, and is a welcome change from plain salt or soy sauce. Once made, it will keep indefinitely, like plain salt. Make a jar of it and have it on hand in your cupboard.

2 *cups uniodized plain table salt*
1 *tablespoon five fragrances powder (Mm heung foon) (page 32)*

Heat wok or pan till hot and dry. Place in salt and stir. Heat for 5 minutes until salt is very hot. Shut off heat. Sprinkle in the five fragrances powder while stirring rapidly. The yellowish powder will turn into black specks like pepper. Let cool and store in a jar. When serving, place in small dishes or salt cellars, to be dipped into or sprinkled onto the food just like salt.

Chicken with Almonds 杏仁鷄

HAANG YAN GAI

This is a classic recipe in which most of the concepts of Chinese cooking are called into play. Here you will find the textural contrasts, especially the crunchy, roasted almonds arrayed against the other softer, yet varied textures of the chicken meat and vegetables. Please also note the harmony of cut of the various ingredients. Since it is not possible to make the almonds, the button mushrooms, or the peas larger, the meat is cut smaller.

Fresh chicken breasts are used. In boning and dicing the meat, refer to instructions on page 147 and drawing on page 149.

I	3	chicken breasts, boned and diced
	1	egg white
	⅛	teaspoon salt
	1	teaspoon monosodium glutamate
		Pinch of ground pepper
	2	tablespoons cornstarch

II	1	can button mushrooms, drained, liquid saved
	½	cup diced bamboo shoots
	½	cup diced water chestnuts
	1	package frozen petite peas, thawed
	1	clove garlic, minced
	1	slice ginger, shredded

III	1	teaspoon sugar
	1	teaspoon monosodium glutamate
	1	tablespoon cornstarch
	¼	cup oyster sauce
		Liquid from mushrooms plus ¼ cup water

IV	1½	cups vegetable oil
	2	tablespoons sherry
	⅓	cup roasted almonds†
		Chinese parsley or chopped scallions, for garnish (optional)

Mix together ingredients in Group III and put aside.

Place in mixing bowl all items in Group I. Mix well. Heat wok or pan and add all the oil. Turn heat to low and add chicken mixture to fry slowly. When chicken has turned slightly white on outside surfaces, remove from pan at once and set aside. Remove all the oil except about 2 tablespoonfuls. Save extra oil for another use. If particles are in oil, strain off when oil has cooled.

Turn up heat to high. Add garlic and ginger first, then all the vegetables in Group II. Stir while frying for 2 minutes. Add the sherry, cover and cook for 3 more minutes.

Put back chicken. Pour in slowly, while stirring, the mixture in Group III. When gravy has thickened, add the nuts. Top with Chinese parsley or chopped scallions just before serving.

SUBSTITUTIONS AND VARIATIONS

You may find three different listings in a Chinese menu for this one dish. It is listed as Chicken with Almonds; Chicken with Walnuts and Chicken with Cashew Nuts. There would be a difference in price between them also. Actually, the only justification for listing them separately is the cost factor of the different nuts used. The walnut meats are the most expensive. Everything else used in these three dishes is exactly the same, and the cooking procedure is the same. You may use whichever kind of nuts suits your fancy.

Some chefs like to mix the nuts throughout the dish. Others prefer to sprinkle them on top. It is a matter of personal whim.

Soy-Sauce Chicken 豉油鷄

SHE YAU GAI

The ability to adapt and modify a recipe, to make it practical and economically feasible, is the hallmark of a good cook. Many Chinese recipes are thus converted for home use from restaurant recipes. This chicken recipe as made in restaurants requires 10 to 15 pounds of soy sauce. But a restaurant prepares many chickens from this one pot of sauce, so the cost is negligible per chicken. Although we cannot always capture 100 percent of the qualities of a recipe by substitutions and adaptations, we can come close enough to justify the saving and the slight change in taste. We only need 2½ cups of soy sauce here.

Rock sugar comes in crystals of irregular size. Some are clear as glass and others are shades of light amber. In fact, rock sugar resembles uncut semiprecious stones. There's a subtle taste difference between it and granulated sugar. The other reason for using rock sugar in cooking is that it melts slowly, and gradually releases its sweetness, so that food cooked with it will not become overly sweet. Seldom do Chinese use sugar in their tea, but when it is used in such teas as jasmine or chrysanthemum, a lump of rock sugar is placed in the teacup, and cup after cup of tea can be consumed before the sugar is used up. Try it yourself, and taste the difference between it and granulated sugar. Rock sugar can be bought in fancy-food stores or from your local confectioner.

I	1	*whole roasting chicken, 4 to 5 pounds, cleaned and drawn*
II	2	*slices fresh ginger*
	1	*clove garlic, crushed*
	3	*scallions, cut into 2-inch lengths*
	1	*leek, quartered lengthwise, cut in half†*
III	2	*lumps of rock sugar, about ¾ inch in diameter†*
	1	*tablespoon monosodium glutamate*
	½	*teaspoon ground pepper*
	3	*star anise seeds*
	1	*cup light soy sauce*
	1½	*cups dark soy sauce*
	1	*can condensed chicken broth (about 10½ ounces)*
	1	*can water*

Place all Group II and III ingredients in a 4-quart or larger saucepan or Dutch oven. Bring mixture to a boil. Turn down heat and carefully put chicken on its side into pot of liquid (the liquid will not cover all of the chicken). Bring liquid to a boil again. Cover and turn heat down to very low at once. Liquid must not boil any more. Cook for 45 minutes. Turn chicken over on other side and cook covered 30 minutes longer. If chicken is more than 4 pounds, allow about 5-10 minutes more on each side. Remove chicken from pot. Drain dry. It may be served hot or cold, and may be carved at the table, Western style, or chopped into strips and pieces with the bone, Chinese style (see "Boning a Chicken," page 147).

SUBSTITUTIONS AND VARIATIONS

If rock sugar is not obtainable, use 2 tablespoons granulated sugar.

If leeks are not available, double the amount of scallions and garlic. Leeks are closely related to both, perhaps with a slightly closer kinship to the scallion.

The liquid in which the chicken is cooked is saved for dipping the chicken into while eating, or used as a gravy over the chicken. It also makes an excellent gravy over plain rice.

Velvet Chicken or Smooth Chicken   滑鷄

VOT GAI

This is a method of cooking pieces of boned raw chicken into a velvety-smooth finished product. The meat also retains all its marvelous juiciness.

The chicken thus cooked is not used exclusively for one recipe. It becomes the central item in a whole series of dishes which call for "vot gai" or smooth chicken. The dishes made from it range from soups, vegetable dishes and noodle dishes to appetizers. You will find recipes calling for Velvet Chicken under those different classifications. The basic method of cooking is the same, but the method of cut of the chicken can be varied for specific recipes.

Remove bones from chicken and cut the meat into chunks, slices, or shreds as the recipe may specify. It takes about 1½-2 pounds of raw chicken with bones to yield 2 cups of meat.

I   2   *cups raw chicken (see above)*
     ⅛   *teaspoon salt*
     1   *teaspoon monosodium glutamate*
     1   *teaspoon light soy sauce*
     1   *egg white*
     2   *tablespoons cornstarch*

II   2   *quarts water in saucepan*

III   *Sinkful of cold water ready*

Mix all the ingredients in Group I in mixing bowl. Bring water in saucepan to a vigorous boil. Put in chicken. (The chicken will have stuck together, but once in the boiling water it will separate with gentle stirring.) As soon as water starts to boil again, turn off heat immediately. Let stand in water for 1 minute.

Drain meat in a strainer. Put chicken into the sinkful of cold water at once to cool. Remove and drain dry. The chicken is now ready for any recipe you may choose to use; you will have 2 cups of Velvet Chicken. It needs no further cooking, so all you do is add it to the other ingredients *after* they are cooked. Stir to mix together. The heat from the rest of the cooked items will warm up the chicken pieces.

Try out these pieces of Velvet Chicken in conjunction with the recipe for Chicken with Almonds (page 163). Now the recipe can be called Velvet Chicken with Almonds. This is not a substitution, unless you believe that replacing a painting by Rembrandt with one by Da Vinci is a substitution. For Velvet Chicken with Almonds, follow the recipe on page 163 exactly except for the instructions on cooking the chicken, which have now been replaced by the instructions for Velvet Chicken.

Two more recipes using Velvet Chicken can be found in this book: Velvet Chicken Stir Fried Noodles on page 302 and Velvet Chicken Cucumber Soup on page 263.

Roast Capon with Vegetable Stuffing 焗餡鷄

GUK YIM GAI

A capon is a eunuch, brought up with great care and allowed to grow to full maturity before being marketed. Capons have been raised in China since before the time of emperor Shih Huang Ti (259-210 B.C.), of the Ch'in Dynasty. He was the ruthless emperor who built the Great Wall and burned all the books in China, so everything and every date in Chinese history would begin with his reign. According to legend a scholar, at the risk of death, managed to hide one book and save it from being burned, and that book contained instructions on how to castrate chickens.

A man who caponized chickens in China was a wonderful craftsman. He learned his special craft from his father, who in turn learned it from his father. The caponizer traveled from village to village on a regular schedule. I recall with what fascination we children followed him about when he came to our village. He would catch a rooster with speed and deftness from an owner's flock, put it on the ground and gently but firmly step on the chicken with his bare foot. He would then lift its wing and pluck a few feathers away, make a tiny incision at the exact spot, and, with the aid of a nooselike thread at the end of a pencil-sized bamboo stick, extract the male gland. All this was done in seconds, and the rooster would then be released to run away squawking, but apparently none the worse for his experience! There wasn't even a drop of blood spilled. I had a chance to talk to a young man who had come from a village in China recently, and he told me that the same age-old system was still used to create capons.

The Chinese highly prize capons as a food. The flesh is rich, flavorful, and velvety smooth. In cooking, capons are treated with great respect and almost always cooked whole. Use the plain boiled chicken recipe on page 148, or else just roast a capon Western style. There is not much difference between the way a Chinese chef cooks a capon and the way his Western counterpart does it. The following recipe is a compromise between the two styles.

Capons are very fat. Remove all the fat you can from the cavity and around the base of the neck. Save a piece of the fat (about 2 ounces) to render and use to fry the vegetables for the stuffing.

I	1	*whole capon, about 6 pounds, cleaned and drawn*
	1½	*cups shredded celery hearts*
	½	*cup shredded green pepper*
	½	*cup diced onions*
	3	*scallions, cut into 1½-inch lengths, including green ends*
	1½	*cups cooked rice*
II	1	*small can sliced button mushrooms, drained†*
	1	*clove garlic, minced*
III	1	*teaspoon monosodium glutamate*
	1	*teaspoon sugar*
	⅛	*teaspoon ground pepper (white or black)*
	2	*tablespoons soy sauce*
	2	*tablespoons water*
IV	1	*piece of fat from capon (about 2 ounces)*
	⅛	*teaspoon salt*
	2	*tablespoons sherry*

Mix together ingredients from Group III and put aside.

After the capon has been drawn and cleaned, pat skin dry with paper towels. Let skin air-dry thoroughly for 1 to 2 hours at room temperature (an electric fan or hair dryer trained on the capon will dry it in 30 minutes).

In the meanwhile make the stuffing. Cut and combine all the vegetables from I and II, including the rice and mushrooms but not the garlic. Heat wok or pan hot and dry over high heat. Turn heat to medium and add the raw chicken fat. Stir with spatula all around the wok or pan until the cooking surface is coated with chicken fat. Turn heat down to low and let the chicken fat render its oil. Remove residue of chicken fat. Add the salt and turn heat up to high. Add garlic to brown, then quickly add all the vegetables. Stir-fry for 2 minutes; add Group III mixture while stirring. Add the sherry and cover at once. Allow to cook 1 minute more. Turn off heat. The stuffing is ready to be used.

When skin of capon has dried, fill the neck cavity with part of the cooked stuffing. Sew or skewer opening. Fill the stomach cavity with remainder of stuffing and sew or skewer that opening. Place capon on wire rack of roasting or broiling pan. (This assures that heat can circulate under the capon, and the fat can drip away from it.)

Preheat oven to 425° F. Place capon in oven and roast for 30 minutes at this temperature to seal in the juice. Turn heat down to 350° F. and roast for 2 hours.

Serve either by carving Western style, or by cutting into pieces Chinese style. If Chinese style is preferred, remove all the stuffing into a bowl and keep warm in the still hot oven. Let capon cool slightly (about 5 to 10 minutes) before chopping into strips.

SUBSTITUTIONS AND VARIATIONS

Fresh mushrooms may be used, sliced, in place of the canned ones. The gizzard and liver may be simmered for 30 minutes, then minced, to be combined in the stuffing. The gizzard and liver may also be frozen and used on another occasion.

Chicken Livers and Scallops

鷄肝海鮮

We use the phrase "neither fish nor fowl . . ." always in a derogatory sense, implying indecision and lack of character. The Chinese combine seafood, meats, and fowls with great frequency, so the quote definitely could not have been of Chinese origin. The following recipe weds chicken livers with scallops to form a light and delicate dish.

Be sure to use only fresh chicken livers. Chicken livers which have been frozen become crumbly when fried. Livers of any kind must not be overcooked, else the result will be dry and leathery.

I   ½ *pound chicken livers*
      1 *pound sea scallops, whole (if small) or cut in half (if large)*
      ½ *pound string beans, ends removed, broken in halves†*

II   3 *scallions, cut into 2-inch lengths, including green ends*
      ½ *cup shredded bamboo shoots (optional)†*
      1 *small can button mushrooms, drained, juice saved*
      1 *clove garlic, minced*
      1 *slice ginger, shredded*

III 1 *teaspoon sugar*
      1 *tablespoon cornstarch*
      1 *teaspoon monosodium glutamate*
      ½ *cup oyster sauce, or 2 tablespoons light soy sauce*
      ¼ *teaspoon sesame oil*
         Liquid from mushrooms
      ¼ *cup stock, chicken broth, or water*

IV 1 *cup vegetable oil*
      ⅛ *teaspoon salt*
      2 *tablespoons sherry*

V   *Blanching stock:*
      1 *teaspoon salt*

½ teaspoon monosodium glutamate

1 slice fresh ginger (optional)

1 pint water

½ cup crushed roasted nuts or few sprigs Chinese parsley, for garnish (optional)

Mix ingredients from Group III and put aside.

Cut chicken livers roughly into 1-1½-inch pieces, regardless of thickness. In a saucepan, bring the pint of blanching stock (Group V) to a boil. Add chicken livers, turn heat to low, stir and cook for 1½ minutes. Drain, discarding liquid, and put aside.

Heat wok or pan hot and dry. Add oil from Group IV. Turn heat to medium and add scallops. Fry until the outside of scallops turns creamy white (about 2 minutes). Don't overcook. Remove from oil at once and put aside. Put in chicken livers and fry for 2 minutes. Turn off heat. Remove chicken livers and put with scallops.

Scoop out all the oil except for about 3 tablespoonfuls. Turn on heat again. Add salt. Add the garlic and ginger and fry till golden brown. Add the string beans and all remaining items in Group II. Stir-fry for 2 minutes over high heat. Add sherry. Cover and cook for 2 minutes longer. Put in the precooked liver and scallops and mix well.

Add Group III mixture, stir and cook till gravy thickens. Serve topped with crushed roasted nuts or Chinese parsley (optional).

SUBSTITUTIONS AND VARIATIONS

If bamboo shoots are not available, try shredded carrots. They have a crunchy texture and also will add a nice color to the dish.

Use snow peas in place of string beans if available. In that case, the snow peas should be put in last, just before the gravy mixture thickens.

Chicken Three Ways

一鶏三味

YAT GAI SAAM MEI

"One chicken, three flavors" is the literal translation of the name for this group of three dishes, all made from one large chicken of good quality. The idea of making several different dishes from one large thing is not limited to a chicken; frequently a duck or large fish may also be so treated. One can easily entertain four people adequately and elegantly with the three dishes from this one chicken.

This method of making several dishes from one thing has another advantage. It gives the cook an opportunity to select the proper cut of meat for each dish. The chicken's liver, gizzard, and heart are used in a soup; the soft, tender, meaty parts are used for stir-frying; and the bony parts, from which the meat is hard to extract, are chopped into fairly large pieces, bones and all, for a sweet and sour dish.

Following are the instructions and recipes for making the three separate dishes in Chicken Three Ways. It should be emphasized that you do not *have* to follow this sequence. You can make any *one* of the dishes singly if that is your wish, using chicken parts, and not make the other two.

CUTTING UP THE CHICKEN

The illustration on page 149 should give you a clear idea of how to cut up the chicken for Chicken Three Ways. A few hints and comments are in order here.

The chicken should be a roasting chicken about 5 to 6 pounds.

Knives must be sharp, and cutting surface dry and nonslippery. You will need your sharp cleaver to cut through the bones in one of the operations, and a boning knife to separate meat from the bones in another.

Do not try for speed at first. This will come with experience.

Meat from the breast, drumsticks, and thighs is used for the stir-fried dish. All bones and skin are removed from those parts. Boil the bones for the soup stock, then discard. The skin which clings to the bony parts of the chicken (the neck, wings, and back) is left on. These parts are chopped into pieces with the bones, then are deep fried before being made into the sweet and sour dish. The skin will be crisp and tasty.

Way # 1: Bean Curd Chicken Soup (*Dau Foo Gai Tong*)

荳腐鷄湯

Chicken livers, gizzards, hearts, and other variety meats should always be blanched in boiling water before being used, to remove gamy or fishy tastes from them. Cut the liver and gizzard into slices. Cut the chicken heart in quarters. For blanching boil 1 pint water in a saucepan with 2 slices ginger and ½ teaspoon salt. Add the liver, heart, and gizzard while water is boiling. Shut off heat and allow meats to stay in the hot water for 2 minutes. Drain and rinse in cold water. Discard ginger. Put aside until ready to add to the soup.

The baak choy and snow peas are put in last. Keep them separated since the cooking time for each is different. Snow peas cook very quickly. They should be the last item to be put in any recipe.

I   *Liver, gizzard, and heart from large chicken, blanched*
     ½   *cup sliced lean pork (about ¼ pound)*
     3   *cakes fresh bean curd (dau foo), cut into smaller cubes (about 1-inch square)†*

II   4   *or 5 dried mushrooms, presoaked in 1 cup water*

III   1   *teaspoon light soy sauce*
     1   *teaspoon monosodium glutamate*
     ⅛   *teaspoon salt*
     1   *can clear chicken broth*
     2   *cups stock (from the chicken bones) or water*

IV   1   *cup sliced choy hearts†*
     ½   *cup snow peas†*

Place all the items in Group III in a saucepan. Add the mushrooms and their liquid. Bring to a boil. Add the pork and dau foo. Bring to a boil again, turn off heat, and let stand until the other two dishes are almost done. Then turn heat back on, bring the stock to a boil again, add the baak choy hearts, and the chicken heart, liver, and gizzard, and simmer for 3 minutes. Turn off heat and add the snow peas. Stir and allow to stand for 1 minute longer. Serve at once, alone or with the other two dishes.

SUBSTITUTIONS AND VARIATIONS

If no baak choy or snow peas are available, a package of frozen French-cut string beans may be used. Be sure the string beans are thawed beforehand. Put into the soup at the time baak choy hearts would have been put in.

If you cannot get bean curd, substitute 2 medium-sized cucumbers, peeled and cut into domino shape (see recipe for Velvet Chicken Cucumber Soup, page 263), or you may use 2 cups sliced celery cabbage.

Way # 2: Stir-Fried Chicken and Vegetables (*Chow Gai Kau*) 炒鷄球

This dish is the main one of Chicken Three Ways. As suggested, it may be made by itself with white meat of chicken breasts if you wish. However, the meat, white and dark, from a large chicken, rather than the breasts from smaller chickens (as the case with chicken in parts), makes the dish decidedly better.

Although many of the ingredients used here are the same as those used in the soup dish, the taste, texture, and flavor will be quite different, because of the different methods used to cook the two dishes.

Baak choy grows in a bunch, like celery. Each bunch may vary greatly in size and weight. Baak choy hearts have the coarser, larger outside leaves and stalks removed, so only the tender center stalks remain. Tear off enough stalks to make 2 cups for this recipe and keep the remainder for other dishes.

I   1½   *cups raw chicken meat, cut into chunks†*
     1   *tablespoon cornstarch*
     1   *egg white*
     ⅛   *teaspoon salt*

II   1   *clove garlic, minced*
     2   *slices ginger, shredded*
     2   *cups sliced baak choy hearts*
     1   *can button mushrooms, drained (save liquid)*
     ½   *cup sliced bamboo shoots*
     ¼   *cup sliced water chestnuts*
     ½   *cup snow peas*

III   *Liquid from mushrooms*
     ½   *cup chicken broth*
     1   *teaspoon sugar*
     1   *teaspoon monosodium glutamate*
     ¼   *cup oyster sauce*
     1   *tablespoon cornstarch*

IV   1½   *cups vegetable oil*
     2   *tablespoons sherry*

In mixing bowl, place all ingredients from Group I. Mix thoroughly. Mix together ingredients from Group III and put aside.

Heat wok or pan hot and dry. Add all the oil. Heat only to moderate temperature (see pages 8 and 16 on sautéing). Turn heat down to low, and add the chicken mixture. Fry slowly until chicken turns slightly white. Remove at once from wok or pan. (Do not overcook the chicken. It should be only about half done at this point.)

Remove all the oil except for about 2 tablespoonfuls (save excess oil for future use). Add garlic and ginger to brown slightly. Turn up heat high and add remainder of ingredients, except snow peas, from Group II. Stir-fry for 2 minutes.

Sprinkle in the sherry. Cover pan and cook for 2 minutes more. Put back chicken, add snow peas, and mix thoroughly.

Slowly pour in Group III mixture while stirring. When gravy has thickened, turn off heat at once and serve.

SUBSTITUTIONS AND VARIATIONS

Some substitutions can be made or some ingredients can be eliminated, but in that case the dish will be down-graded. This is one of the most expensive dishes in a Chinese restaurant's menu. You should try to use all the ingredients listed if at all possible.

Chances are you will have more raw chicken meat than this recipe calls for from the large roaster you have cut up. The extra meat may be wrapped up and frozen for another time, or the meat may be added to the sweet and sour dish which follows.

Way # 3: Sweet and Sour Chicken—Bones In (*Tim Seun Gai Kwat*) 甜酸鷄骨

The Chinese fully utilize every bit of food that is available. To make use of even the least desirable parts and make them yield delightful eating is a challenge and the pride of a good cook. This dish does not have to be made from the bony parts of a chicken, because it will taste equally well if it is made with prime chicken meat. But in that case what would you do with the perfectly good chicken carcass after you'd made the other two dishes in Chicken Three Ways?

To chop up the chicken, refer to cutting instructions on page 38 and special instructions and illustrations on page 149.

Most Westerners expect Chinese food not to have any bones in it. The Chinese, however, believe that some food is preferable *with* the bones attached. So warn your guests that these chicken pieces have bones, and to be careful.

I   *Wings, neck, and back from 1 chicken, cut into chunks with bone*

   1   *egg (use white and yolk)*
   2   *tablespoons cornstarch*
  ¼   *teaspoon salt*
     Pinch of white pepper

II 1   *cup pickled vegetables, drained (see page 67)†*
   1   *small can pineapple chunks (save liquid)*
   2   *scallions, cut into 1½-inch lengths*

III ½ *cup sugar*
   ½ *cup vinegar*
   ½ *cup chicken broth*
     Liquid from pineapple
     Dash of Tabasco
   ¼ *cup ketchup†*
   ⅛ *teaspoon salt*
   1   *tablespoon cornstarch*

IV 2 *cups vegetable oil*

In making sweet and sour dishes, after all the ingredients are prepared and ready for use, always make the sweet and sour sauce first. To make the sauce, mix all the ingredients in Group III (be sure cornstarch lumps are not present or else the sauce will not be smooth) in a saucepan. Heat over medium flame. When almost boiling, stir continuously until sauce has thickened. Turn heat very low, cover, and keep hot till ready for use.

Put chicken and all other Group I ingredients in mixing bowl and mix thoroughly together.

Heat wok or pan hot and dry. Add oil. Heat till quite hot. Add chicken and stir to separate pieces. Brown one side, then turn over to brown the other. When chicken pieces are golden brown all over, remove from pan onto absorbent paper to drain. Save oil for future use.

Turn up heat on sweet and sour sauce. Add all ingredients

from Group II and heat until sauce reboils. Turn off heat and put in the chicken. Mix and serve.

SUBSTITUTIONS AND VARIATIONS

If you do not have the pickled vegetables on hand, use fresh carrots, white radishes, and cauliflower, sliced. Place in prepared sauce and cook a little longer than with the pickled vegetables.

The ketchup is optional. It adds a nice color to the sauce. If you prefer a clear sauce, eliminate the ketchup. Another way to make the sauce is to mix 1 tablespoon cornstarch with ¼ cup of water. Bring the sauce to a boil, and slowly stir in the cornstarch mixture a little at a time until the desired consistency is reached. This method of thickening sauces and gravies may be used in any other recipe in this book.

10

Duck

ONE of the world's great delicacies is a dish called "Peking Duck." It is, however, more shadow than substance: the diner never sees the duck itself. This dish, eaten by wealthy Chinese, consists of just the crisp skin, roasted to a beautiful glossy brown in a long process which takes a whole day's labor. The meat of the duck is of such secondary importance that it used to be given to the servants for their meal in the kitchen. This intriguing phenomenon of waste of food and effort took place in a country ruled by the very rich, with a population that was very poor. Such excess is not limited to China; pursue the histories of all such cultures and similar examples can be found. While it is impractical to make Peking Duck at home, a recipe which produces a good homemade equivalent is given on page 185, in which the delicious meat is eaten, too.

Actually, if you've ever eaten duck, it's likely to have been a Peking duck, though not the cooked kind described above. Almost all the ducks raised in this country are of the Peking variety; very few other breeds of ducks are raised for food in the United States. These ducks were originally imported from China, and they adapted to the American climate and way of life so easily that the other varieties were relegated to being novelties or pets. In China, the children made pets of ducks and geese, too, especially the children of the "Boat People." Large populations used to live on boats in the rivers and harbors of China, and one of the "crops" the Boat People could harvest was ducks. The flock (usually no more than ten to a boat family) were let out to pasture in the water, where they subsisted on the minnows or shrimps which swam by, and the children were their shepherds. I've watched the boys gather their ducks and drive them back to their cages, which were strapped to the sides of the boat. Each boy knew his ducks so well that there was never any risk of mistaken identity. Those boy "duckherds" also acquired a certain caution: they swam absolutely naked, and the near-sighted ducks did not make distinctions between minnows and other things.

How to Buy Duck

Ducks will vary greatly in size, weighing anywhere from 3 to 7 pounds each, if you buy them live at a poultry market. But most of the ducks sold throughout the country are frozen, and the sizes available are very limited. The growers and processors will market the ducks when they are between 4½ and 5½ pounds, which is an ideal size for most recipes. If you can get a fresh-killed duck, all the better. If only frozen ducks are available to you, they are perfectly acceptable. Thaw a frozen duck by leaving it out at room temperature for 6 to 8 hours for a 4½- to 5½-pound duck, or allow a day for it to thaw in the refrigerator. Be sure to remove the plastic covering as soon as possible after the duck begins to thaw.

Roast Duck, Chinese Style

唐裝焗鴨

T'ONG CHONG KUK APP

Of all the domestic fowls, duck lends itself to roasting the best. By nature ducks are fatty, and in the roasting process the fat is extracted, leaving the flesh sweet and moist. The ideal way to roast a duck is to hang it up by the neck and let it sear and cook by open heat, while the fat drips off from the tail, as is done in Chinese restaurants. Since houses (Chinese as well as American) do not have this kind of stove, necessity has forced cooks to devise means of roasting ducks with the kinds of stoves that are available. While you will not be able to reproduce the duck at home exactly as you can buy it in a Chinese restaurant or Chinese grocery store, the recipes below will make your duck come out very close to it in taste and crispness.

I strongly recommend that the hoi sin deung and yuen shaai she deung be used. Although the duck will still be good without these two flavorings, it will not really be Chinese roast duck.

I 1 *duckling, whole, 4½-5½ pounds, cleaned and drawn*

II 2 *cloves garlic, minced*
¼ *peel of an orange, shredded*
2 *scallions, cut into 1½-inch lengths, then shredded*
½ *leek, cut into 1½-inch lengths, then shredded*

III 1 *teaspoon sugar*
1 *teaspoon monosodium glutamate*
½ *teaspoon salt*
½ *cup sweet bean sauce (hoi sin deung)*
2 *tablespoons yellow bean sauce (yuen shaai she deung)*

IV 4 *quarts water*
3 *tablespoons honey*
1 *tablespoon vegetable oil*

Preheat oven to 425° F. Remove liver, gizzard, and neck, which have usually been packed in cavity of frozen duck. (The liver and gizzard may be placed inside the duck and roasted. The neck I usually discard.) Remove any fat from cavity. Bring water and honey to a boil in a saucepan large enough to hold the duck. Lower duck, back first, into the water. When the water returns to a boil, if the duck is not completely covered by the water use a soup ladle to scoop up some water and pour over the exposed part. Do this for 5 minutes. Discard water and dry duck with paper towels. Blanching the duck in this manner removes some of the fat from the skin, and the honey penetrates into the pores to give the skin crispness and a beautiful golden color.

Heat a small saucepan and add the 1 tablespoon oil. Add all the seasonings in Group II. Fry over medium heat for 3 minutes, while stirring. Turn heat to low. Add all the ingredients from Group III, mix well into a thick paste, and cook 1 minute longer. Turn off heat and let cool.

Spoon the sauce mixture into the duck cavity, and coat the inside thoroughly, using your hand.

Place duck on a wire rack or similar device to elevate it so air can circulate around it to thoroughly dry the skin for 1 to 2 hours. (An electric fan or hair dryer trained on the duck will reduce the time required by half.)

Line roasting pan with aluminum foil for better heat reflection and ease in cleaning. Place duck on wire rack of roasting pan. Roast at 425° F. for 30 minutes. Turn heat to 350° and roast 1 hour longer.

Remove duck from oven and let cool slightly (about 5 minutes). Drain any liquid from duck and save. Cut duck up into strips with the bones, Chinese style (see page 43), or cut into quarters, Western style. Serve while hot. The duck liquid makes a tasty gravy over rice or boiled vegetables.

SUBSTITUTIONS AND VARIATIONS

Duck may be roasted also in a rotisserie or cooked on an outdoor grill. Here are the procedures.

In a rotisserie: If your rotisserie has a motor-driven spit, do as follows:

1. After the mixture in Group III has been placed in its cavity, allow duck to marinate for at least 2 hours at room temperature. Then drain the marinade from duck cavity and discard.

2. Turn on your rotisserie 5 minutes before you are ready to begin roasting.

3. Stick spit through duck, balance and anchor securely with end prongs of spit. Arrange spit rests so that the duck is as close as possible to heating element, but so it can turn unobstructed. A 4½-pound duck may take 1½ to 2 hours cooked this way. It will be drier and less fatty, as well as having a crisper skin.

On outdoor grill: Build a charcoal fire about ½ hour before it is to be used. When the charcoal briquettes have been evenly ignited, and a white ash appears on them, the fire is ready for the duck.

The duck should be marinated for at least 2 hours at room temperature before cooking. Drain excess marinade from duck cavity and then split duck in half. Put the halves skin side up and barbecue for 30 minutes, with the grill about 4 inches above the charcoal, then raise grill to 6 inches. Turn duck halves over and cook till skin is brown and crisp (about 15-20 minutes). Allow ½ duck to each diner.

Fire Duck (Chinese Barbecued Duck)   火鴨

FOH APP

I often wonder if "Fire Duck" was just a very poetic invention of an imaginative Chinese chef, who drew upon the legend of the phoenix, the "fire bird" which never died but burned itself up periodically, then rose from the ashes to be more alive and beautiful than ever. Only with this method of cooking ducks and chickens do the Chinese refer to "fire." Usually, the more common words "roast" or "bake" are used to describe dry-cooked food. In truth, "fire duck" rises from the ashes (charcoal ashes in the old Chinese stoves) more beautiful than ever, but thankfully not alive!

It is a prerequisite that the duck used in "fire duck" be fresh-killed and intact with the neck and the head. Have your poultry man or butcher make as small a hole as possible in the stomach cavity, and only a small slit in the neck, when drawing the duck. The smaller the openings, the easier it is to skewer or sew the duck up water-tight, so the marinade sauce will not run out. The butcher should also remove the oil sacs from the duck's tail. They have an unpleasant taste.

The secret of getting the duck skin crisp and delicious is to pump a layer of air between the skin and flesh. This serves to isolate the skin from the fat and juices of the meat, which can make the skin less crisp. However, it is not an absolute necessity to go through this pumping process. If you do want to go through with it, first put the marinade sauce in the cavity, and skewer or sew the opening. Use a bicycle or tire pump; stick the air hose into the slit in the duck's neck, hold the loose skin tight around the hose, then pump. (Get your children to help you. It's better than LSD!) Once the duck has been pumped full of air, tie a cord very tightly around its neck just below the slit and then remove the pump hose.

I   1   *duckling, 5-6 pounds, cleaned and drawn*

II   ½ *orange peel, finely shredded*
      2 *scallions, cut in 2-inch lengths, then shredded,*
          including green ends
      ½ *leek, cut in 2-inch lengths, then shredded*
      1 *clove garlic, minced*
      1 *tablespoon vegetable oil*

III ½ *teaspoon salt*
      2 *teaspoons sugar*
      2 *tablespoons yellow bean sauce (yuen shaai she deung)*
      ¼ *cup sweet bean sauce (hoi sin deung)*
      2 *tablespoons soy sauce*
      ¼ *cup water or stock*

IV   *Water, about 2 quarts*
    3   *tablespoons honey*

Heat the tablespoon of vegetable oil in a small saucepan. Add the remaining ingredients from Group II and stir-fry 3 minutes. Add all the ingredients from Group III except the water or stock and fry 1 minute more. Turn off heat and add the water or stock a little at a time and mix well. Let cool to touch. Fill the cavity with this mixture and skewer or sew tight. Then pump air into duck as described above (optional).

In a pot large enough to hold the duck, add enough water to cover it halfway. Remove duck and add the honey to the water. Bring water to a boil. Using large tongs or a sling made of cheesecloth, dip the duck in first on one side, then the other. (Keep the water over high heat.) Repeat several times, making certain the duck's back is particularly well scalded. Be careful not to puncture the skin. This process should take 5 to 7 minutes.

Remove duck from water. Drain on wire rack. Pat dry with paper towels and allow the duck to air-dry at least 2 hours. (Electric fan or hair dryer will speed this process.)

While duck is drying, arrange the racks in your oven so that the top rack is about 7 inches from the top. Put bottom rack as far down as possible. Fill broiler pan with about ½ inch of water (the water helps prevent smoke and spatter) and place on lower rack. Preheat oven to 425° F.

When duck has been air-dried (touch with your finger; if no moisture can be felt, it's dry enough), place, breast side up, on top rack, directly over the broiler pan in the oven. Roast for 30 minutes at 425° F. Turn oven temperature down to 350° and roast 1½ hours more for a 5-pound duck. Add 15 minutes for a 6-pounder.

Take duck out of oven and let cool for 5 minutes. Cut cord lacing at cavity or remove skewers and drain off liquid. Save. Cut duck strips with bones, Chinese style (see page 43), and arrange on platter. Strain the duck liquid and ladle over duck before serving hot. Duck may also be served Western style by disjointing and carving at the table. The duck liquid makes a delicious gravy over cooked rice or mashed potatoes.

Diced Fluff Duck or Squab 鴨，鴒丁

APP, KOP TING

There is a subtle difference between duck and squab, but the difference is so small in a dish like this that I normally only use duck, because it is more available and much cheaper than squab. (However, the difference becomes much greater in a deep-fried recipe, and you cannot substitute duck meat for squab.) If possible, use uncooked duck or squab for the meat needed here, but cooked meat may be used in a pinch. The raw meat lends its juice to the other ingredients during cooking to give the whole dish more flavor.

This dish is classified with "soong," or light, fluffy dishes. If you have a food grinder and can set it to "coarse," the meat and vegetables listed as "diced fine" may be ground in it for this recipe, as well as others in "fluff method" cooking.

Since ducks are not sold in parts as chickens are, you will have to buy 1 duck for this recipe. However, the extra raw duck meat may be frozen for future use. You will need 2 squabs to get enough meat for this recipe.

See page 147 for instructions on removing bones from fowl.

I   2   *cups finely diced duck or squab meat*
    1   *package frozen peas (thawed)*
    ½   *head of lettuce, shredded, placed in serving dish*

II   1   *small can button mushrooms, drained, liquid saved*
    ½   *cup finely diced bamboo shoots*
    ½   *cup finely diced water chestnuts*
    1   *clove garlic, minced*
    1   *slice ginger, shredded*

III 1 *teaspoon sugar*

    2 *teaspoons cornstarch*

    1 *teaspoon monosodium glutamate*

    3 *tablespoons oyster sauce, or 2 tablespoons light soy sauce*

    Mushroom juice plus stock or water to make ¾ cup of liquid

IV ¼ *cup vegetable oil*

    ⅛ *teaspoon salt*

    2 *tablespoons sherry*

    ¼ *cup crushed nuts (walnuts, almonds, cashews) (optional)*

Mix together in a bowl ingredients in Group III and put aside.

Heat wok or pan hot and dry. Add the oil. Add salt. Add garlic and ginger and fry till brown. Add duck or squab meat. Fry till meat has browned (about 2 minutes). Put in peas and all remaining items in Group II. Stir well, add the sherry, cover and cook for 2 minutes more. Lift cover and stir in Group III mixture. Cook until gravy has thickened. Scoop from wok or pan into lettuce-lined serving dish. Top with crushed nuts (optional).

Boneless Pressed Duck 窩燒鴨

WOH SHIU APP

This seems like a troublesome dish to make, but it is worth it. Duck is a wonderful meat, but usually so fatty that people, especially Americans, shun it. When it is cooked this way, all the fat is removed, the skin becomes very crisp, and the flavor of the meat is fragrant and subtle.

There are 3 methods used in restaurants for this party dish. It depends entirely on the chef, because the end results are quite similar. The methods differ only in getting the duck ready for the final process. One recipe is sufficient here, but the 2 other methods will be briefly mentioned at the end of the recipe.

To make this dish, there are 2 separate steps. If desired, the duck can be done the night before, or cooked and frozen in advance.

DUCK PREPARATION

I   1 *young duckling, 4½ to 5½ pounds, split in half*

II 4 *quarts water*
    2 *tablespoons five fragrance spices (saam lei, but kok)*
    4 *slices fresh ginger*
    3 *cloves garlic, crushed*
    1 *tablespoon salt*
    1 *tablespoon monosodium glutamate*
    1 *cup dark soy sauce*
    3 *scallions, cut in half, including green ends*

In a large pot, put all ingredients in Group II. Bring to a vigorous boil and put in duck halves. Bring liquid and duck to a boil again, and immediately turn heat to low. The liquid should not boil any more. Cover and let cook 1½ to 2 hours. Remove from liquid and let cool. Remove bones. The duck should be thoroughly done at this point, so that the bones may be removed with the fingers.

COOKING DIRECTIONS

I   ⅔ *cup water-chestnut flour†*
    ⅓ *cup cornstarch*
    2 *egg whites, beaten till frothy*

II ¼ *cup oyster sauce*
    1 *cup soup stock or chicken broth*
    2 *teaspoons cornstarch*

III ½ *cup roasted nuts (almonds, cashews, or walnuts), crushed*

IV *Oil for deep frying, about 2 quarts*

Mix flour and cornstarch together. Put through a flour sifter if necessary to remove all lumps.

Brush the boned duck halves with the beaten egg white. Sprinkle the flour-cornstarch mixture onto both sides of duck halves to cover evenly.

Place duck on a platter and steam covered for 20 minutes. (See "Steaming," page 9.) This steaming cooks the coating on the duck and makes for crispness. Let cool. Dry off any moisture with paper towels.

Make gravy in saucepan with Group II ingredients. Have ready and hot.

Heat oil for deep frying to 350° to 375° F. Carefully slip the duck halves into the oil with long tongs. Be careful and stand back. Oil may spatter. Fry until golden brown and crisp. Remove from oil and drain on absorbent paper. Cut across duck into manageable strips (about ¾ inch wide) and arrange on serving platter. Pour gravy over duck. Top with crushed nuts and serve.

SUBSTITUTIONS AND VARIATIONS

The other two methods used in duck preparation are either to roast the duck in an oven until done or to deep-fry the raw duck halves till done. Then when cool remove the bones with boning knife and complete process by following deep-frying directions for pressed duck.

There is no substitute for water-chestnut flour, but it is available in all Chinese food stores or by mail. See back of book for addresses.

11

Seafood

OF the three elements, Earth, Sky, and Sea, from which man harvests his food, I think the sea yields the most exciting treasures for his table. The Chinese have been aware of the sea's bountifulness from time immemorial, and we have always included seafood in our meals. When I speak of "harvest," I mean it literally. Almost every Chinese village had a pond to raise fish in, and periodically these ponds were "harvested" by being drained so that the fish could be gathered. Other food items were included in the harvest, such as shrimps, snails, and eels.

Freshness of fish and seafood cannot be overemphasized. These foods lose quality very rapidly, and, once it is lost, no amount of skill can regain it or mask the inferiority of the food. This does not apply to frozen foods like shrimps or king crabs, because if properly processed and kept they will retain their quality over a long span of time (up to 6 months).

There are a few simple observations to make on selecting fresh seafood. You will find them under "Buying Fish" (page 195), "Buying Lobster" (p. 213), and 'Buying Shrimp" (p. 224).

National tastes and food habits change, and this change is usually reflected in the price of a given food. I recall that shrimp used to cost less than 50 cents a pound ten years or so ago, and the price is now up to three times that much or more. Similarly, African rock lobster tails used to cost about 75 cents a pound a decade ago, and now the cost has skyrocketed to almost $3 a pound. Even taking into consideration that the cost of everything has gone up a lot, the cost of these two items is so disproportionate that it can only reflect much greater demand. A casual check among my acquaintances shows that this rather unscientific survey is valid.

Using the same yardstick as a measurement of change, the relative cost of most fish has not gone up at all. This tells the sad story that the American public has not yet learned how wonderful fish can be! Now that the traditional meatless Fridays are being eliminated, many fish dealers are afraid that there will be a decline in the consumption of fish. What a shame! A fish cooked properly and with imagination cannot be surpassed. But most people have never eaten properly prepared fish, so how are they to know? When cooked badly, fish could hardly be worse.

I hope that you will try to use more and more fish and seafood in your menu planning, once you discover how delicious and easy they are to prepare. Take the time to master the cooking of seafood, if your aim is to be a superior cook.

Removing Fishy Taste and Smell

Fishy smell and taste are unpleasant to almost everybody. The Chinese have worked out several methods of cooking and seasoning that minimize this unpleasantness. The use of ginger, garlic, and hot oil is considered a necessity whenever seafood is cooked in the Chinese way. The addition of a few drops of sesame oil further removed any fishy smell. And of course, a very fresh fish is seldom "fishy."

Some fishy smells are so insistent that the odor lingers in the pot or pan where the seafood was cooked, and if that smell is not exorcised from it any food cooked in it next may have a fishy flavor. It is quite simple to purify your pan or pot again as follows:

Heat pot or pan till hot and dry. Add 3 tablespoons oil. Spread the oil over the entire cooking surface of the pan or pot. Add 3 slices of fresh ginger and fry for 2 minutes. Stir to keep ginger from burning. Turn off heat and let cool. Drain oil, discard ginger, and wipe clean with paper towels.

FISH

Buying Fish

Since there is an infinite variety of fish, of necessity we can only touch lightly on the subject in this book. Many fishes are localized, and even seasonal, so where you live and when you cook can have a bearing on the matter. You may recall that in recent years there were several fishes caught off the African coast that scientists thought had been extinct for seventy million years. That type of fish we may ignore, because I don't have a recipe for it anyway.

There are two major categories of fresh fish used in Chinese cooking. The first group is used in the form of a boned fillet, sliced or cut into chunks, to be fried with vegetables or used in soups. In this group the fish must be fairly large and firm-fleshed so that it will not fall apart in cooking. The most commonly used fish for this type of cooking is yellow pike. However, other fishes, whether fresh or salt-water varieties, which have the two desired characteristics of size and firmness can be used. Ask your fish dealer to see if he can recommend other varieties if he does not have pike at the moment. He may have, for example, pickerel, which is related to the pike, or striped bass (which is much larger than the sea bass, therefore too big for cooking whole). Bluefish, cod, and halibut are also good for filleting and may be used for this category of Chinese cooking. Fillet of sole or flounder cannot be used here. The fillet is thick enough for slicing and cubing, but the meat falls apart as soon as fried. However, sole and flounder are good for other types of Chinese cooking, which we shall discuss later.

How can you tell if a fish is fresh? When fresh, the eyes are clear and bright. Lift the gills to make sure that they are red and clean. The scales should be tight and flat against the body. There are fish stores and fancy restaurants where fishes such as trout and carp are kept alive in tanks. If the fish swims, forget the other tests!

The larger fishes such as cod, bluefish, and halibut are sold by the slice, and you may order as much as you need. Since you cannot inspect the eyes and gills of large fishes (they're usually displayed without heads) you can tell freshness by look, smell, and feel. The flesh of the fish looks moist and close textured; it should not have a strong odor, and when pushed with a finger the flesh will feel firm and resilient. A little experience will teach you to judge freshness of fish quite easily.

Fishes of the other group are cooked and eaten whole. They are delicate, soft, smooth-fleshed fish. They may be steamed, poached, or fried and served with all kinds of sauces, from the pungent soybean-garlic sauce to the delicate sweet and sour sauce that so many people enjoy.

Within this group of fishes are the sea bass, carp, porgy, red snapper, butterfish, pompano, and flounder. These are the most commonly used fish in Chinese cooking. There may be fishes available in your locality, either from fish stores or caught by you and/or friends on fishing trips, that may lend themselves admirably to Chinese cooking. I can only suggest that you try out a few Chinese recipes with the types of fishes listed above, then other fishes will suggest themselves for some of the recipes.

The fishes in this second category are all relatively small, and therefore can be used whole rather than cut up. Most of these are readily available in a good fish market, except pompano,

whose habitat is restricted to tropical waters off the coast of
Florida and which is not easy to buy in other areas of the
country.

When buying whole fish, have the fish man clean it for you.
The fish should have its scales removed, the fins snipped off and
the entrails and gills discarded. Leave the head on, unless you
or your guests are so squeamish that the fish head interferes
with your eating pleasure. The eyes of the fish serve as an in-
dicator of doneness. The head left on helps to retain the natural
juices of the fish.

If you must clean the fish yourself, it is an easy job, if somewhat messy. The first thing to do is put several layers of news-
paper on top of your counter, near the sink. Use poultry shears
and cut off the fins close to the fish's body. Grab the fish by the
tail. Use a fish scaler (most sporting-goods and department stores
sell them) and rub the teeth of the scaler against the scales of
the fish from tail to head. This action lifts and removes the
scales. Rinse off the scales. Make a slit in the fish's stomach from
near the tail all the way up to the head where the gills begin.
Cut off the gills and remove the entrails. Rinse and pat dry.
The fish is now ready for cooking.

The cleaned fish may be refrigerated and kept overnight—but
no longer! Put the fish on a platter, wet several layers of paper
towels with cold water, and cover it to keep it from drying out
while being stored.

Frozen fish may be used, but it will not be as good as the
fresh fish. Since we all must work within limitations, by all
means use frozen products when you cannot get fresh ones.

The larger fishes, such as swordfish and tuna, are not popular with the Chinese.

Fish should never be overcooked. Here are some indicators
which will help you to tell when fish is done.

Fish, if cooked whole, is done when the eyes become hard,
turn white, and can be easily removed from their sockets. If
you stick a fork into the thickest part of the fish, it should go

in easily and not meet any resistance. If the fish is sliced for Chinese cooking, it is done as soon as the translucent gray turns whitish and opaque. This of course does not apply to fresh salmon, which loses some of its bright orange pink on cooking. The same advice about not overcooking applies.

Sea Bass with Garlic and Soybean Sauce　　豆豉魚

DAU SHE YEE

The Chinese are so intimate with sea bass that they sometimes call it by its initials! Many Chinese menus list this fish as "C.B. with garlic sauce," etc. (The letter "C" is phonetically close to the word "sea.") If that is a status symbol, it is well deserved. There are certain foods that have the ability to bend with the whim of the chef, be smothered by strong seasonings, yet still retain their own wonderful character. Sea bass is one of them. Compare this recipe, which is highly seasoned, with the poached fish recipe on page 204, which is hardly seasoned at all. You will find them both wonderful—and unmistakably sea bass!

Be sure to use a large enough frying pan or wok so that the fish does not get mangled in the process of being fried. A good fish deserves elbow (or fin) room!

I	1	*whole sea bass, about 2 pounds*
II	4	*slices ginger, shredded*
	3	*cloves garlic, minced*
	4	*scallions, cut into 1½-inch lengths, including green ends*
III	1	*teaspoon sugar*
	1	*tablespoon salted cured soybeans, washed and crushed*
	¼	*cup soy sauce*
		Pinch of salt

IV   *Oil for deep frying (about 1 quart)*
⅓   *cup sherry*
Chinese parsley or chopped scallions for garnish
(optional)

Have sea bass split open and cleaned, with head left on. Dry fish thoroughly with paper towels. Rub the inside with the pinch of salt.

Heat deep-frying oil to medium hot (350°-365° F.). Gently slide fish into the oil. Turn down heat so fish will only gently sizzle, not sputter. Fry until brown on one side, then turn over gently to brown other side. This will take about 7 minutes on each side.

Heat another wok or large frying pan hot and dry. Scoop about ⅓ cup of oil from the deep-frying oil (while the fish is still frying). Put in the ginger and garlic and turn heat to medium. Fry until brown. Add the scallions in II and the soybeans. Stir-fry for 1 minute longer. Add the sugar and soy sauce. Cover and turn heat down very low until fish is ready. Transfer fish from deep-frying pan into the other with the sauce. Turn up heat to medium and fry fish 1 minute on one side, then turn over and fry for another minute so the fish will soak up the sauce. Quickly pour in the sherry and cover pan. Turn off heat and let fish stand for 2 minutes more before serving.

Remove fish gently and place on serving platter. Scoop all the sauce from pan and pour over the fish. Top with Chinese parsley or chopped scallions (optional) and serve.

When transferring or removing fish from pan, use two pancake turners or Chinese "wok chons" (see page 15). Have the other pan or platter ready nearby to receive the fish. Hold one utensil in each hand; slip the utensils under the fish gently and lift fish to transfer or remove.

Steamed Fish   蒸魚

CHING YEE

Smaller, flaky fish lend themselves beautifully to steaming. In steaming, the fish is not touched while cooking, so that the problem of turning it over or handling, when it might fall apart, is eliminated. This method of cooking also makes the fish moist and smooth in texture, which are very desirable characteristics. Porgies, flounder, pompano, trout, sunfish, and butterfish are some of the many fishes which can be used for steaming. The 2 pounds of fish needed for this recipe may be just one fish or several, depending on the type selected. In any case, the fish should be split and cleaned, and the head or heads left on. Choose any of the above-mentioned fish. Let freshness, price, and availability be your guide.

I   2   *pounds fish, left whole, split, and cleaned (any fish
          mentioned above)*

II   3   *slices ginger, shredded*
     2   *scallions, chopped*

III ½   *teaspoon monosodium glutamate*
     1   *tablespoon salted cured soybeans, washed and crushed*
     2   *tablespoons soy sauce*
     2   *tablespoons hoi sin sauce (sweet bean sauce)*

IV   2   *tablespoons vegetable oil*
     ¼   *teaspoon sesame oil*

Mix together all ingredients from Group III.
Slash each fish across the body several times on each side

about 1½ inches apart to allow for the sauce to penetrate and for faster cooking. Rub the insides of the fish with some of the Group III mixture. Place fish in heat-proof bowl or pan which has high enough rim to accommodate fish and the resulting juices. Pour remainder of sauce from Group III on top of the fish, and scatter the ginger and chopped scallions on top.

Place prepared fish in a steamer (see page 9). Cover and bring water in steamer to a boil. Lower heat to medium and let steam covered for about 25 minutes.

Heat the vegetable oil and sesame oil (hot but not smoking) in a separate pan, and pour over the fish just before serving.

NOTES AND COMMENTS

In serving fish this style, the Chinese just pick off the meat communally with their chopsticks, and when the first side of a fish has been picked clean someone will deftly turn the fish over with his chopsticks for all to get at the other side. Serving Western style, use a fork and a large spoon. Carefully lift off the skin with the fork and discard. Then gently push the side of the fork down near the spine of the fish until it touches the bones. Use the spoon as a scoop. Use the fork to sweep the fish flesh from the bones and catch the meat with the spoon held in the other hand. Turn fish over by slipping the spoon under the fish, holding the fork on top to form a pair of tongs. Practice with chopsticks, using a wet kitchen sponge as a stand-in for the fish, when you have time. You'll be surprised at how skillful you can become in a short while. You may never need to polish silver again!

Sweet and Sour Fish   甜酸魚

TIM SEUN YEE

Sweet and sour fish is a favorite with many people. While the fish used may be boneless chunks cut from a fillet, if you can, use a whole sea bass for this sweet and sour recipe. Sea bass is one of the favorite fish of the Chinese people. It has all the virtues that a good Chinese cook admires in a fish. These virtues include sweet, firm flesh and not too many bones, and the fish comes in different sizes for every cooking purpose. As with all fish, sea bass must not be overcooked or else its wonderful qualities will be lost beyond recall.

Use a sea bass about 1½ to 2 pounds in size. Bigger sea bass can be used, but most home kitchens are not equipped to deep fry such big items. It is better to make two smaller fish in such cases, when you have company. When using a whole fish, make two or three fairly deep slashes diagonally across the fish's body on both sides before breading and deep-frying, to speed the cooking.

You must adjust the frying time according to the size of the fish. Generally, the fish is done, regardless of size, when the skin with the breading becomes golden brown.

I　1　*fresh sea bass, about 1½ to 2 pounds, cleaned and slashed†*

II　2　*carrots, sliced*
　　1　*green pepper, sliced*
　　3　*scallions, cut into 1½-inch lengths, including the green ends*
　　2　*slices canned pineapple, cut into wedges*

III　½　*cup vinegar*
　　½　*cup sugar*
　　½　*cup chicken stock*
　　⅛　*teaspoon salt*
　　1　*tablespoon cornstarch*

IV　　　*Vegetable oil for deep-frying (2-3 quarts)*
　　½　*cup flour*
　　　Pinch of salt and pepper

Prepare the sweet and sour sauce with the vegetables first. In a saucepan place all the items in Groups II and III, except the cornstarch and the green pepper (the pepper will lose its beautiful green color if cooked too long). Bring to a boil. Turn heat to low and simmer for 15 minutes. Add the cornstarch, stirring thoroughly until the sauce has thickened. Turn heat to very low, just high enough to keep the sauce hot until ready for use.

Dry the fish with paper towels. Sprinkle a pinch of salt and pepper inside and outside the fish. Spread ½ cup flour on a piece of wax paper or aluminum foil. Roll the fish on the flour to cover the skin thinly.

In a large deep-frying pan heat the oil to about 375° F. With a pair of tongs or long-handled kitchen utensil, gently lower the fish into the oil. Cook until skin turns golden brown (about 5 minutes). Remove fish onto absorbent paper to drain off excess oil.

Turn heat to high under the sweet and sour sauce. Add the green pepper slices. Stir and cook for 1 minute. Turn off heat. Place fish on a serving platter, ladle the sweet and sour sauce over it, and serve at once.

SUBSTITUTIONS AND VARIATIONS

If you prefer boneless pieces of fish, the best type to use is pike fillets. The flesh of this fish is firm and sweet, and will not crumble as easily as the flakier fillets from sole, for example. But it is possible to make a good sweet and sour fish dish from the fillets of other fish that one normally encounters in a fish market. The larger fish, such as swordfish, tuna, or cod, are not suitable for this purpose. Use 1 pound of fillets for this recipe.

For either the boneless or whole sweet and sour fish, you must have the sweet and sour sauce ready before you fry the fish. The prepared sauce will wait patiently for the fish, but the fish cannot wait for the sauce.

Poached Sea Bass

白水魚

BAAK SUI YEE

Fish should never be overcooked, if you are to get the best out of it. Poaching comes closest to the ideal method for cooking a fish. In poaching, the temperature never reaches the boiling point, so the flavor and velvety smoothness of the fish are retained. The addition of the oil and seasoning removes any fishy taste, without destroying the fish's original goodness. Once you've learned to make this dish properly, you will find that it is hard to surpass.

If sea bass is not available, or if what is available is not of the best quality, use a porgy, which is also a very good fish for this recipe.

The fish should be left whole with the head on. Fish-cleaning instructions can be found on page 197.

I   1   *fresh sea bass, whole, about 1½ pounds†*

II   2   *cloves garlic, crushed and peeled*
    4   *slices ginger, shredded*
    4   *scallions, cut into 1½-inch lengths, including green ends*
    2   *whole preserved cucumbers (cha kwa), shredded†*

III   2   *tablespoons dark soy sauce*
    2   *tablespoons light soy sauce*
    1   *teaspoon monosodium glutamate*
    1   *teaspoon sugar*

IV   ½   *cup vegetable oil*
    ½   *teaspoon sesame oil (optional)*
        Water enough to cover fish entirely when placed in a large pot or wok (about 3 to 4 quarts)

Have all your vegetables cut and ready before you start to cook the fish. Put the water in a large pot, which should accommodate the length of the fish without too much bending, and bring to a vigorous boil. (A fish cooker is wonderful if you have one, or use a Chinese wok if you have that.)

Make a sling out of cheesecloth. Place fish in the sling and tie two corners of the cloth together (for lowering and lifting the fish). Gently lower the fish into the boiling water. Turn heat to lowest possible *immediately!* The water should not boil again. Cover the pot and let fish remain in the water for 15-20 minutes. Test for doneness after 15 minutes by inspecting the fish eyes. If the eyes have turned white and protrude from their sockets and can easily be removed with a fork, the fish is done. Another way to test for doneness is to stick a fork into the thickest part of the fish. If the fork goes in easily to the bone without meeting resistance, the fish is done.

In a mixing bowl, combine the light and dark soy sauces, monosodium glutamate, and sugar. Have ready while fish is cooking.

Heat the oil in a small frying pan to medium-low temperature, about 325° F. Add the 2 cloves of garlic and let them get brown. Remove garlic from oil and discard. Keep oil hot.

Remove fish from water when done, and let drain for a few minutes. Place on serving platter and remove cheesecloth sling. Ladle the soy-sauce mixture over the fish.

Turn up heat under oil in frying pan to high temperature. Quickly add the shredded ginger. When the ginger is light brown, remove pan from fire, and immediately pour oil and ginger over fish. *Be careful!* The oil may spatter, so hold pan at arm's length.

Scatter the scallions and preserved cucumbers over fish, and serve.

SUBSTITUTIONS AND VARIATIONS

Fish fillets can also be used for this dish. They will not be quite as succulent or as handsome to look at as a whole fish. Use a pound of fillets and poach in water for only 7 to 10 minutes. When the fillets flake easily and the color has turned opaque, the fish is done. (If I've made too much of the point that fish should never be overcooked, it's because that point *cannot* be overemphasized.)

The Chinese preserved cucumbers (cha kwa, page 35) can be replaced by 2 sweet gherkins, shredded.

Fish Balls with White Radishes 蘿蔔魚餅

LOH BAAK YEE B'ENG

Fish balls and fish cakes are frequently used in Chinese cooking. All methods are used for cooking them, since they can be fried, boiled, or steamed, depending on the recipe. Whenever a recipe calls for a mixture of seafood, meats, and vegetables, it is safe to assume that fish balls or fish cakes can be added to improve the dish.

Fish balls are often used in soups like the Young Jewel noodle soup (page 295). Chopped fish is also used for stuffing bean curds and mushrooms for appetizers. After being stuffed, they're then steamed.

Fish cakes are usually fried in deep oil until golden brown on the outside, then sliced and cooked with meats and vegetables. One particularly happy combination is to cook them with sliced white radishes, scallions, and oyster sauce.

This recipe will be broken into two parts. The first part will give instructions for making the fish cakes or fish balls. The second part will deal with combining the cooked fish balls with the other ingredients into a delightful dish.

FISH BALLS OR FISH CAKES

The best type of fish to use for chopping is yellow pike. Have the fish dealer fillet the fish and you can either chop it or put it through a grinder. The addition of 3 or 4 medium-size shrimp to the fish as it is being chopped or ground serves two very nice purposes. First, they add a wonderful flavor to the fish. Second, shrimp have more natural adhesiveness than fish, so that they help to bind the other meat or seafood together and make the balls or cakes less crumbly. Chinese chefs very frequently add shrimp to chopped pork or beef for the same reason. In order of natural adhesiveness, shrimp comes first, followed by fish, pork, then beef. The chopped fish should resemble cooked oatmeal in texture.

1   *pound pike fillets*
3   *or 4 shelled shrimp*
3   *scallions, chopped*
½   *teaspoon salt*
1   *tablespoon cornstarch*
¼   *teaspoon sesame oil*
½   *teaspoon monosodium glutamate*
    Vegetable oil for deep frying (about 1 quart)

Cut fish fillets and shrimp into small cubes. Sprinkle on all the other ingredients, except vegetable oil, and mix together. Either chop together or put through grinder. Shape the chopped-fish mixture into ¾-inch balls. Heat oil to medium low (about 325°-350° F.). Add the fish balls a few at a time. Separate with Chinese chon or pancake turner so each fish ball can brown on all surfaces. When fish balls are golden brown, remove with slotted spoon or strainer onto absorbent paper to drain. Put aside until ready to add to recipe.

To make fish cakes, shape the chopped fish into strips about 2 inches wide by 4 inches long and ¾ inch thick. Fry the same way as fish balls. When fish cakes have cooled, slice across width into ¼-inch slices and add to recipe. If the chopped fish is to be used for stuffing, just scoop up as much as needed and fill whatever cavity you desire. Other foods which can be stuffed with chopped fish are won tons and whole fish, whose cavities are sometimes filled before frying.

FISH BALLS WITH WHITE RADISHES

White radishes are much used by the Chinese people. The variety you will find in Chinese stores can weigh as much as 2 or 3 pounds each. The ones you can buy in vegetable stores or supermarkets are usually much smaller, and come in bunches like their red cousins. They are bigger and long (instead of round). Generally they are about 4 or 5 inches long with a tapered tail. However the sizes may vary, the taste is exactly the same. Radishes do not have to be peeled. Just scrub well or scrape blemishes and dirt off with a stainless-steel sponge. If the radishes are quite large, split in halves before slicing. Cut the slices crosswise about ⅛-inch thick.

I   *Fish balls from above recipe*
   1½ *pounds white radishes, sliced (about 3 bunches of the American variety)*

II 2   *slices ginger, shredded*
    1   *clove garlic, minced*

III 1   *teaspoon sugar*
    1   *tablespoon cornstarch*
    1   *teaspoon monosodium glutamate*
    ⅛   *teaspoon ground white pepper*
    ¾   *cup chicken broth or stock*
    ¼   *cup oyster sauce (or 2 tablespoons soy sauce)*

IV ¼   *cup vegetable oil*
    ⅛   *teaspoon salt*
    2   *tablespoons sherry*
    3   *scallions, chopped, including green ends*

Mix together ingredients in Group III and put aside.

Heat wok or pan hot and dry. Add the oil, then the salt. Put in the ginger and garlic to brown. Add the sliced white radishes and stir-fry for 4 minutes. Add the sherry and cover quickly to cook 2 minutes more. Put in the cooked fish balls. Add the sauce mixture from Group III; cook, stirring, until gravy thickens. Sprinkle on the chopped scallions and mix well. Remove from pan and serve.

Sea Bass with Bean Curd   荳腐魚

DAU FOO YEE

I've stressed the importance of contrasts in Chinese cooking. Just to prove the exception, there are certain recipes in which *similarities* of tastes and textures are deliberately combined, to create the subtleties that make a cuisine great. The velvety smoothness of a sea bass done to perfection is heightened by the addition of bean curd, which is also smooth and bland. In combination the two enhance each other.

I   4   *cakes fresh bean curd (dau foo), each cake cut into 9 cubes*
    1   *whole sea bass, about 1½-2 pounds, cleaned and slashed*

II 1   *clove of garlic, minced*
    2   *slices fresh ginger, shredded*
    2   *scallions, cut into 1-inch lengths, including green ends*

III 1   *tablespoon salted cured soybeans, washed and crushed*
    1   *teaspoon monosodium glutamate*
    2   *tablespoons dark soy sauce*

IV ½   *cup vegetable oil*
    ¼   *cup sherry*
        Chinese parsley or chopped scallions, for garnish (optional)

Heat wok or frying pan hot and dry. Add oil and turn down heat to medium. Add bean curd cubes gently to pan. Turn over gently to brown all surfaces. Remove from pan and put aside.

Fry the garlic, ginger, and scallions in the same pan until golden brown. Turn heat up and lower sea bass gently into hot oil. Brown on each side for 5 minutes. Mix the ingredients in Group III and pour over the fish. Cook until the liquid bubbles. Put back the bean curd. Add sherry and quickly cover pan. Turn down heat to low and cook another 5 minutes.

To serve, place fish on platter. Surround fish with bean curd and pour gravy over fish and bean curd. Garnish with parsley or chopped scallions.

Live Carp with Chicken Fat   鷄油鯉魚

GAI YAU LEI YEE

All fish is better fresh. With carp, it is imperative that it be fresh, because the quality of its delicate flesh deteriorates

quickly. Fortunately, nature has made compensations by endowing this fish with an ability to live outside its native home. Therefore, in some fish stores, carp is kept alive in tanks until the customer picks one out and has it killed and cleaned. In New York City, on the Lower East Side, where I live, there are many ethnic groups who love carp, and it is very easy to get live carp, or very fresh carp on ice. Try this recipe only if the above conditions can be met.

Chicken fat should be rendered beforehand to save time. Next time you use a fat chicken, remove the fat from the chicken cavity and save for this purpose. To render the fat, heat a pan until hot and dry. Add the raw chicken fat and turn heat to medium. Let it fry until the fat has turned liquid. When the residue has turned dry and brown, remove and discard. When the rendered chicken fat has cooled enough, pour into jar with cover and store in refrigerator until needed. It will keep a long time.

I	1	fresh carp, scaled, split, cleaned, and dried
II	4	slices ginger
	3	cloves garlic, crushed
	4	scallions, cut into 1½-inch lengths, including green ends
III	1	tablespoon sugar
	1	teaspoon monosodium glutamate
	1	teaspoon cornstarch
	1	tablespoon salted cured soybeans, washed and crushed
	2	tablespoons dark soy sauce
	2	tablespoons oyster sauce (optional)
	½	cup chicken broth
	¼	teaspoon sesame oil (optional)
	¼	cup sherry
IV	½	cup chicken fat
	¼	teaspoon salt
		Sprigs of Chinese parsley or chopped scallions, for garnish

Mix together all ingredients in Group III and put aside.

Heat wok or large frying pan hot and dry. Add the chicken fat, then the salt. Add the items in Group II and cook till just browned. Remove from pan and save. Gently lower the carp into the chicken fat. Turn heat to high so the fish will brown quickly on one side, then turn over and brown the other side (about 5 minutes on each side).

When fish has browned on both sides, pour the Group III sauce mixture onto the fish. Put back the ginger, garlic, and scallions. Lift fish slightly to let the sauce spread under it. Cover and turn heat down to low. Let cook covered for another 10 minutes. Check occasionally to see if liquid has exaporated. If so, add a little water so that the bottom of the pan is never dry. Test for doneness after 10 minutes by sticking a fork into thickest part of fish. If fork goes in easily without meeting resistance, fish is done.

Remove fish to serving platter. Scoop up sauce from pan and ladle over fish. Top with Chinese parsley or chopped scallions. Serve while very hot.

The sauce for this dish should be very thin. Add more liquid if it is too thick. Sesame oil is optional, but its nutty flavor and ability to mask fishy taste make it a good addition for all fish.

Carp come big! An average carp weighs about 3-5 pounds and will serve 4-6 people.

Carp thrive in almost every country in the world. They are frequently caught by fishermen in all parts of the United States, and then a magical thing often happens: the carp turns into a white elephant! Most cooks do not know what to do with it. This recipe will help you be a sorceress in the kitchen, undo the black magic, and turn the carp back into a prince of fish.

LOBSTER

Buying Lobster (*Lung Ha*)   龍蝦

Lobsters have so sky-rocketed in price in the last few years that many restaurants are not making any money serving them. Some Chinese restaurant owners tell me that the margin of profit on lobsters is so low that they wish customers would not order them. Sometimes restaurants have to serve them at a loss.

But the demand goes up all the time, as more and more people discover what delicious eating lobsters are.

Most of the lobsters generally available are what are known as "chicken lobsters." This designates the size of the lobsters, which are amazingly uniform in weight at about 1 pound. Lobsters grow very slowly. A lobster takes about seven years to reach this 1-pound weight, and has shed its old shell for a new one about 10 times. There are soft-shell lobsters, just as there are soft-shell crabs, which are caught during the shell-changing process. The soft-shell variety is not as full and succulent, because it takes a lot of effort on the lobster's part to change shells, and a lot of weight is lost because of this exertion. Lobsters mate when the females have just changed shells, and the young are hatched only every other year, which accounts for lobster's scarcity and high price.

Although various species of lobsters are found all over the world, the best, often called "Maine lobsters," come from the New England coast and Canadian waters. Lobsters are not wanderers, and stay all their lives within a few miles of their birthplace.

The dark greenish matter inside the head of the lobster is called "tomalley" or liver. It has a rich, wonderful flavor and smooth texture. Don't discard it, as it is one of the nicest things to eat in a lobster. In some female lobsters you will find a set of "corals." These are the eggs of the female, and are equally prized by gourmets. The set of corals are oblong, caviarlike, greenish roe, found in both sides of the head when the lobster is split open. The green color turns into a beautiful coral when cooked.

How to Remove Lobster Meat from Shell

Some recipes call for the use of lobster meat without the shell. (See recipe for Lobster in Jade and Pearls, p. 222). In such cases, buy live lobsters. Bring pot of water to a boil. Immerse live lobsters in boiling water and cook until shell becomes red. Remove from water and let cool. Snap off the claws. Use nutcracker to break shell and remove meat from claws. Snap off the head of the lobster with a twist. Do the same thing to the fan of the tail (the last section of the lobster). Use finger to push meat out from tail through other end. Now the meat can be cut in any style for a particular recipe.

The meat of the head section and the legs is not in large enough pieces to use for this type of cooking, but these make for wonderful snacking when cold, when you have the time to pick on them. Save for that purpose.

Frozen Lobster Tails and Lobster Meat

Lobster tails come from rock lobsters, which thrive in tropical waters, such as off the coast of Africa or the Caribbean islands. Since it is not feasible to keep them alive and ship them as is done with Maine lobsters, the tails are quick-frozen and marketed as such. Lobster tails are not quite as tender and succulent as Maine lobsters, but they make a good substitute in Chinese lobster recipes.

Lobster meat, cooked and refrigerated or frozen, can sometimes be found in inland supermarkets or fish stores. The meat comes closest to that of cooked live lobsters, even though some natural juices are lost. Lobster meat is understandably expensive, since you get all meat, sans shells. It's an excellent substitute for live lobster in Chinese cooking.

Lobster Storage

We all know that the fresher a lobster is, the better it is. I prefer to keep my lobsters alive until the moment of cooking and had always thought this had to be done invariably. Life is so full of exceptions that each time I take an immovable stance I am clobbered by inescapable facts. In the case of storing lobster I am happy to tell you that I was wrong—and had been for years. This is good news, not so much for me, because I am not at all hesitant and have the experience and means to cut up a live lobster easily. However, for most housewives this is a hard and unpleasant chore on two counts. First, the idea of cutting something up that is alive and kicking is abhorrent to most people; and, second, it is a messy and tough job. I learned about storing cut-up lobster on a visit to a Chinese chef while he was working. I found him busily cutting up several dozen lobsters and arranging them on platters. I observed that he must be preparing for a big dinner party, and was surprised to learn that this was an accepted daily practice and that those cut-up lobsters are used throughout the day's business. He assured me, and his skill and reputation are very high, that there is no loss of flavor, texture, or quality if lobsters are cut up and refrigerated and used within the same day.

What it means to you is that when you buy a lobster for Chinese cooking—as for the Lobster Cantonese recipe that follows—you can have the fish dealer kill and cut up the lobster for you. Specify that you want it split, and each half cut into 3 or 4 sections. You also want the food sac and antennae removed. Fish stores usually have containers with covers, such as are used to hold shelled oysters. Have your lobster stored in that for transporting home, and store it in the refrigerator until ready for use. This little hint can make lobster cooking à la Chinoise much simpler.

Lobster Cantonese 炒龍蝦唐裝

CHOW LUNG HA, TONG JONG

Broiled lobster cannot be surpassed; neither can lobster Cantonese! This little contradiction is explainable because lobsters cooked these two different ways change qualitatively, and any argument about which is best is partisan and can never be proven.

I had a favorite Chinese restaurant where I took friends, and a *must* dish was Lobster Cantonese. Some of those non-Chinese friends enjoyed the dish so much that they would go back by themselves, and were invariably disappointed. Then they would complain to me about favoritism. I did a little investigation by keeping my eyes and ears open in Chinese restaurants. To my great amusement, the waiters have appointed themselves as censors of this dish; they signal the chefs how to cook it three different ways. If the customers are non-Chinese they will call to the cook, "Chow lung ha"—which means "Lobster Cantonese." Out will come a bland concoction which can only be *legally* identified as the item in question. Supposing those same customers say to the waiter, "The last time I came here with a Chinese friend, and it was much better! I want it that way." The waiter calls into the kitchen, "Chow lung ha, tong jong." Translation: "Lobster Cantonese, Chinese style." The cook will season the dish a bit more strongly by adding a little garlic. (Now they are getting pretty close!) The perceptive customers are still not completely satisfied, so the next time they bring their Chinese friend again and he orders. He says to the waiter "Chow lung ha," the exact same phrase which produced the anemic concoction before. But this time the waiter calls, "Chow lung ha, tong jong, tong yan hek" loud and clear. Out comes the dish in all its tantalizing glory! What are the magic words? He said, "Lobster Cantonese, Chinese style—eaten by Chinese."

If you really want Lobster Cantonese cooked the way it should be in a restaurant, there are now lifelike rubber masks of different nationalities and you— Nah! Just insist on your rights by telling the waiter you are onto his tricks and tell him to give the chef the last signal. Don't get mad at the misguided waiter. He is trying to do you a favor, because his experience has taught him that non-Chinese have to learn gradually to accept some Chinese seasonings. How could he tell that you are precocious? Better still, make it at home! It's simpler.

I	1	*live lobster, cut up (see page 217)†*
	¼	*pound pork*
	2	*eggs*
II	3	*scallions, cut into 1½-inch lengths, including green ends*
	2	*slices ginger, shredded*
	1	*clove garlic, minced*
III	1	*teaspoon sugar*
	2	*teaspoons cornstarch*
	1	*teaspoon salted cured soybeans, washed and crushed*
	1	*teaspoon monosodium glutamate*
	1	*tablespoon dark soy sauce*
	½	*cup stock or water*
IV	2	*tablespoons vegetable oil*
	2	*tablespoons sherry*
		Chinese parsley sprigs for garnish (optional)

Select one lively chicken lobster (1 to 1¼ pound) and have the fish dealer kill it, cut it up, and put it into a container. Refrigerate until ready to cook.

Chop or coarse-grind the pork. Crack eggs into a bowl and just break yolks with fork (don't beat well).

Mix together ingredients in Group III and put aside. Have all the other ingredients cut and ready. Heat wok or pan hot and dry. Put in the oil, then the ginger and garlic to brown. Add the pork and stir-fry for 2 minutes. Add the scallions. Put in the lobster pieces and fry 2 minutes more. Pour the sherry over and cover at once. Cook 1 minute more covered. Lift cover and stir in the sauce mixture in Group III. Cook until gravy slightly thickens. Pour the eggs evenly over the lobster (don't stir). Cover the pan and turn off heat. Allow eggs to get slightly firm (about 2 minutes). Scoop into serving dish, top with Chinese parsley and serve with plain boiled rice.

SUBSTITUTIONS AND VARIATIONS

Another favorite Chinese dish is "Shrimp with Lobster Sauce," in which no lobster is used. It got its name from the sauce used in the Lobster Cantonese recipe. All the steps and the ingredients for Shrimp with Lobster Sauce are exactly the same, except for the use of shrimp in place of lobster. Substitute 1 pound medium-size shrimp, shelled and deveined, for the lobster.

The long dissertation on lobsters may seem unwarranted because only a few recipes for lobsters are given here. Actually, Chinese chefs use lobsters for a great variety of dishes in combination with all sorts of ingredients. Here is another recipe, a variation of Lobster Cantonese. This variation is called "Yeung Lung Ha," and it is a steamed dish in contrast to its stir-fried cousin.

This will be the barest outline of a recipe; I hope that since you've gotten this far into the book, you will no longer need me to hold your hand (much as I may want to!) and give you minute instructions on everything. Let this recipe be a test of the skill you've acquired, and I hope as an affirmation of my original

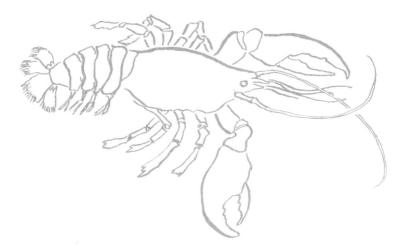

purpose in writing this book, i.e., to teach you how to cook the Chinese *way*, and not merely to give you a bunch of recipes. For the sake of us both, I hope you graduate magna cum laude!

Steamed Lobster 釀龍蝦

YEUNG LUNG HA

Have your fish dealer split a fresh lobster in half and remove the food sac and intestinal tract.

Refer to the recipe for Lobster Cantonese for all the ingredients you will need; they are exactly the same, including the way they are cut.

Place the lobster in a rimmed platter (about 1 to 1½ inches deep) large enough to accommodate the split lobster opened. Mix all ingredients together, except the eggs and water. (Do not use water in this recipe. The steam will condense and give the dish enough juices.) Spread the mixed ingredients evenly over the lobster. Crack the 2 eggs into a bowl and beat very slightly. Pour the eggs over the lobster. Place the platter with the prepared lobster in a steamer (see page 9 for steaming instructions). It will take about 35 minutes of steaming for the lobster to cook.

Lobster with Phoenix Livers 龍蝦鳳肝

LUNG HA FUNG GON

The marriage of the celestial dragon and the beautiful eternal phoenix is celebrated in poems, paintings—and naturally food, in the Chinese scheme of things. Since we can hardly find dragons or phoenixes around any more, we substitute lobsters and chickens for the real thing. If this dish is done with a master's touch, I doubt if even the gods would object to the substitutions!

The lobster should be cooked first, then the meat removed from the shell before slicing (see page 215). Cut the chicken livers into about ½-inch-thick slices, then blanch. See page 175 for blanching instructions.

I   1   *cooked lobster, shelled and sliced about ¼-inch thick†*
    ½   *pound fresh chicken livers, sliced and blanched*
    ¾   *pound fresh snow peas, or 1 package frozen†*

II   ½   *cup sliced bamboo shoots*
     3   *or 4 dried Chinese mushrooms, presoaked, then sliced*
     ½   *cup water chestnuts, sliced (optional)*
     1   *clove garlic, minced*
     1   *slice ginger, shredded*

III   1   *teaspoon sugar*
      1   *teaspoon monosodium glutamate*
      1   *tablespoon cornstarch*
      ¼   *cup oyster sauce*
      1   *or 2 tablespoons light soy sauce*
      ¾   *cup chicken broth*

IV   ¼   *cup vegetable oil*
     ⅛   *teaspoon salt*
     2   *tablespoons sherry*
         Sprigs of Chinese parsley (optional)

Mix together ingredients in Group III and put aside.

Heat wok or pan hot and dry. Put in ½ the oil. Add the salt. Add the garlic and ginger and fry till golden brown. Add the chicken livers and stir-fry 1 minute. Turn heat down, remove chicken livers from pan, and put with the lobster meat. Add remainder of vegetable oil and turn heat up to high until oil is hot (about ½ minute). Add all the vegetables except snow peas and stir-fry 1 minute. Add the sherry and cover at once. Cook 1 minute covered. Put in the snow peas, chicken livers, and lobster meat. Mix thoroughly, then add the sauce mixture from Group III while stir-frying. Cook only long enough for the gravy to thicken. Remove from pan into serving dish. Top with Chinese parsley (optional) and serve at once.

SUBSTITUTIONS AND VARIATIONS

Fresh or frozen green beans, cut French style (shredded) may be substituted for the snow peas.

A package of frozen king crab meat may be used in place of lobster.

No change in cooking time is needed.

Lobster in Jade and Pearls 玉珠龍蝦

YUK, JEE LUNG HA

It is a constant source of wonderment to me that mankind should value the same things throughout history. Why should the same gems and metals be precious to the Egyptians, the Romans, the Chinese, and the Incas of Peru, when their societies were so separated by space and time?

The Chinese love for jade and pearls was so great that they attributed magical properties to them. It was believed that if children wore such stones in a necklace or bracelet no harm could befall them. It is small wonder then that these two gems should wind up (by proxy) at the dinner table with the celestial dragon, represented by the lobster. In this recipe, the jade green of the peas, the glossy warmth of the button mushrooms, the ruby red of the pimentos and the pinkish white of the lobster meat does suggest a bowlful of treasures. One is tempted to call this a gem of a dish!

Use great care in choosing and cutting the ingredients, as though you were a jeweler, matching the size and color. Let this dish be a feast for the eyes as well as the stomach.

The lobster should be cooked and shelled before dicing (see page 215). Some supermarkets sell fresh-boiled lobsters in the shell. By all means use them if they are available.

I	1	*cooked lobster, shelled and diced†*
II	1	*small can whole button mushrooms, drained, liquid saved*
	½	*cup diced bamboo shoots*
	1	*small can pimentos, drained and diced*
	1	*package frozen peas, thawed†*
	1	*clove garlic, minced*
	1	*slice ginger, minced*
III	1	*teaspoon sugar*
	1	*teaspoon monosodium glutamate*
	1	*tablespoon cornstarch*
	¼	*cup oyster sauce*
	¼	*cup chicken stock plus liquid from mushrooms*
IV	2	*tablespoons vegetable oil*
	⅛	*teaspoon salt*
	2	*tablespoons sherry or 1 tablespoon gin*
		Chinese parsley sprigs or 3 scallions, chopped, for garnish (optional)

Mix together ingredients in Group III and put aside.

Heat wok or pan hot and dry over high heat. Add the oil. Add the salt. Turn heat down to medium, put in the ginger and garlic and fry till golden brown. Turn heat to high again and add all the remaining ingredients from Group II. Stir-fry for 1 minute. Add the sherry or gin and cover immediately. Cook for 1 minute more. Add the diced lobster meat. Stir to mix thoroughly. Slowly pour in the Group III sauce mixture while stirring food in the pan. Stir-fry until the gravy has thickened. Remove to serving dish and top with Chinese parsley or chopped scallions. Serve with plain white rice.

SUBSTITUTIONS AND VARIATIONS

Essentially the same dish can be made with the substitution of frozen king crabmeat for the lobster. One package of crabmeat will be more than enough. Dice the crabmeat after it has thawed.

Snow peas are wonderful in place of the frozen peas. Use 2 cups of fresh snow peas, or 1 package of the frozen.

SHRIMP

Buying Shrimp

Thanks to the technological marvel of quick-freezing, we have at our disposal a wide variety of shrimp from which to choose. I've gotten frozen shrimp from India that were shelled and cleaned and so tiny that each was no longer than about ¼ of an inch. Then, I've gotten, and often used, shrimp that are so large that they will weigh almost ¼ pound each. They are as

big as a small lobster tail. You can also buy shrimp in a variety of forms. They may be shelled, cleaned, with or without heads, partly cooked, fully cooked, or breaded. They have become a very popular food indeed in the United States, and deservedly so. Shrimp can be bought fresh or frozen, but since the taste difference between the two is imperceptible, I prefer the frozen, because there is a wide range of sizes from which to choose for different cooking needs. Frozen shrimp will keep without loss of quality up to 6 months at zero degrees or lower.

The classification of shrimp is by color, size, and country of origin. The great shrimp beds in the Western Hemisphere are in the Caribbean Sea, the Gulf of Mexico, and the Pacific Ocean. Some of the best shrimp come from Panama and Ecuador. These are frozen and come in 5-pound boxes. As to the color of shrimp, that's only a matter of personal preference. Both the pink and white are equally good. Following is a chart to serve as a guide in shrimp buying. This information is usually listed on the bottom of the box, and the particular shrimp in the box would be designated by checks (√).

WHITE	PINK	TITI	P.M.	TIGER	FANTAIL	INDIAN	FROZEN
	10/15	(10 to 15 shrimp to a pound)					
	16/20	(16 to 20 " " " ")					
	21/25	(21 to 25 " " " ")					
	26/30	(26 to 30 " " " ")					
	31/35	(31 to 35 " " " ")					
	36/40	(36 to 40 " " " ")					
	41/45	(41 to 45 " " " ")					
	46/50	(46 to 50 " " " ")					
	51/55	(51 to 55 " " " ")					
	56/60	(56 to 60 " " " ")					
	60/70	(60 to 70 " " " ")					
	70/u	(70 shrimp and up " " ")					
	U/10	(Under 10 shrimp to a pound. These are the largest available)					

Of the thirteen sizes listed in the above chart, we need concern ourselves with only about five. Although all the sizes listed are available at the wholesale level, chances are you will not have such a wide choice from your fish dealer. He may even have to order specially for you from his supplier.

The most popular sizes of shrimp and what each size is best suited for are briefly covered below:

Under 10's: These are used chiefly for deep frying as in the Puff Shrimp recipe (page 230). You can also split and broil them as you would lobster tails. Some Japanese, Philippine, and Korean restaurants stuff these large shrimp with ground pork or beef, season and bread them, then deep fry them.

10/15's: These are more available than the under 10's. They can be used for any recipe that the larger ones are used for. In addition, this size is ideal for the Butterfly Shrimp recipe on page 233. In non-Chinese cooking,· this is the size used for shrimp cocktails in a very high-class, expensive restaurant.

21/25's: This is the most popular size sold, and will be suitable for any general Chinese recipes in this book. These shrimp have the virtue of being just right in size, texture, and taste. They are easier to shell and devein than the smaller ones. They are also ideal for shrimp cocktails.

31/35's: Most of the fresh shrimp sold are this size. They can be used for all general cooking, American as well as Chinese. Fresh shrimp are shipped direct from the source with heads removed and packed in cracked ice. They have not been frozen. As I've mentioned before, there really is no advantage in insisting on fresh shrimp, since the frozen ones are as good.

70/and up: These are the smallest shrimp available, and can only be bought frozen. They may run up to 100 or more per pound. Only countries like India, Pakistan, and poor Middle

East countries, where wages are low, bother to catch and process these small shrimp. They are shelled and cleaned before being frozen, so they are absolutely no trouble to use. These shrimp have limited function in Chinese cooking, but they are most useful in certain recipes where larger shrimp would have to be cut up anyway. These recipes include the ones in which a shrimp filling is needed, as in won tons. Or they can be ground up and made into shrimp balls for stir-fried dishes or soups. These shrimp will make excellent shrimp salads in American cooking.

The prices of shrimp have skyrocketed, just as have those of other shellfish, and for the same reasons. There is more and more demand for them as the American palate becomes more adventurous. As of this writing, the largest shrimp sell for about $1.75-$2.00 per pound. Then, for each step down the ladder in size, the price decreases 5 to 10 cents per pound. Paradoxically, the smallest shrimp, which require the most labor to catch, clean, process, and ship from long distances, are the cheapest. The size 70 and up costs about half the price of the larger shrimp.

Most frozen-food counters in supermarkets now carry frozen, shelled, and deveined shrimp. They vary in price according to size. The average size (21/25's) costs about $2.50-$3.00 per pound. The convenience of this type of shrimp is undeniable, but you will pay quite a bit more. What is even more of a drawback, they do not have the flavor and succulence of the shrimp with the shells. Something was lost in the process. So, whenever possible, shell your own shrimp.

How to Shell and Devein Shrimp

Frozen shrimp will have to be thawed before the shells and veins can be removed. Some frozen shrimp come in 5-pound boxes. You will find that the shrimp are stuck together in a solid block. You can remove only as many as you need without defrosting the whole box in one of two ways: One way is to break up the encasing ice by hitting the unopened box with a rolling pin or a wooden mallet. Strike hard blows against all areas of the box, and the ice will break up, but the shrimp will be intact. Open box and remove as many as you may need. Replace remainder in the freezer before they thaw.

The other way is to remove the solid block of shrimp and place it in a sinkful of cool water. Let it stand until the outer layer of shrimp can be peeled off. After removing the amount of shrimp needed, replace the still frozen block in the box and put back in the freezer at once. Shrimp should not be thawed and refrozen.

After the shrimp have thawed, the shells can be easily removed by peeling from the underside of each. Leave on the tail section of the shell if the shrimp is to be picked up with the fingers and eaten as in the deep-fried recipes.

After the shells have been removed, rinse the shrimp in cold water to remove bits of shell and the slippery coating that may sometimes be present. To devein the shrimp, use a small sharp knife, such as the boning knife described on page 19. Grasp each shrimp by the middle with the back facing up. With the knife, make a shallow slit lengthwise from front to back. If the shrimp is to be deep fried, make the lengthwise cut almost all the way to the underside, so the shrimp will be in two halves attached only by the skin of the underside. Be sure to rinse the knife frequently to remove the sticky fluid from the shrimp so the knife can glide freely into the shrimp.

After all the shrimp have been split, rinse each one individually under running water to remove the dark vein that may be present. Some shrimp don't have a visible vein because the shrimp may not have eaten before being caught (the vein is in reality its intestinal tract). Drain dry after rinsing and put aside until ready to use. The cleaning may be done the night before and the shrimp refrigerated.

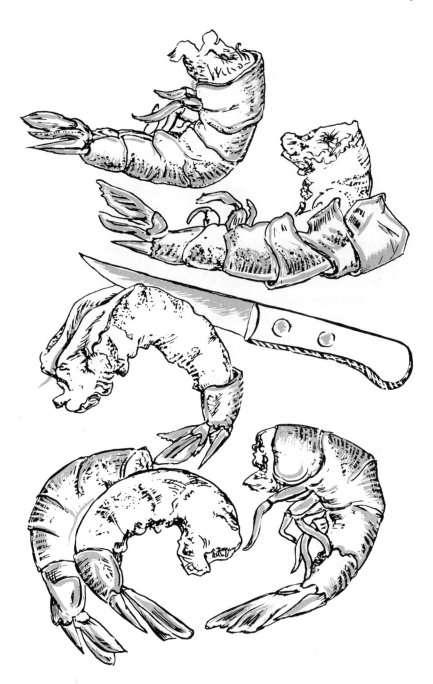

Precooking of Shrimp

There are times in Chinese cooking when partially cooked
shrimp are used for recipes such as Shrimp Lo Mein (shrimp
with soft noodles) or Shrimp Chow Mein. Very little time is required to cook the bean sprouts and shredded vegetables in such
recipes. If raw shrimp were used, the vegetables would be overcooked by the time the shrimp were done, so it is wise to precook the shrimp in such cases.

To precook shrimp, first shell and devein. Bring a pot of water
to a boil. Use only enough water to cover amount of shrimp to
be cooked. Add a little salt to the water. Add the shrimp and
stir to separate them. As soon as the shrimp turn to pinkish
white in color, drain off water and rinse shrimp with cold water
until they feel cool. This quenching in the cold water seals in the
shrimp goodness and prevents them from being overcooked by
any heat which may remain after they have boiled. Drain shrimp
and they are ready for use.

Puff Shrimp   浮炸蝦

FAU JAH HA

These wonderful, easy-to-make shrimp can be found only in
a very few Chinese restaurants, possibly because only a very
few non-Chinese know about them. In some Chinese "teahouses"
where special luncheon pastries and dumplings are served, puff
shrimp occupy a highly honored place in the menu.

The principal difference between puff shrimp and just plain
breaded fried shrimp is in the batter. This batter is identical to
that used for Fluff Chicken (page 152). Use the largest shrimp
available.

PREPARATION OF SHRIMP

I   12 *large shrimp (about 1½ lbs)*

II   ½   *teaspoon garlic juice (extract from fresh garlic with a garlic press or buy bottled garlic juice from super-market)*

III   ¼   *teaspoon salt*
       ½   *teaspoon monosodium glutamate*

IV   *Oil for deep frying (2-3 quarts)*
           Chinese parsley, watercress, lettuce leaves, for garnish (optional)

Remove shells from the shrimp except for the last tail section. With a sharp knife, cut the shrimp from the under side *almost* through to the back. Be careful not to sever the halves completely. Remove black veins and rinse the shrimp well. Place on paper towels and pat dry. Arrange shrimp on a plate or platter, with split side up. Rub a little garlic juice on each. Sprinkle a touch of salt and monosodium glutamate on each. Put aside.

BATTER

1½   *cups white flour (Do not use unbleached flour—it turns gray instead of golden brown)*
1   *tablespoon baking powder*
½   *teaspoon salt*
½   *cup vegetable oil*
1   *cup cold water*

Place flour, baking powder, and salt in a mixing bowl. Mix thoroughly. Add oil, a little at a time, while stirring with a wooden fork or spoon until all the ingredients form a ball and the sides of the bowl are clean. Add water a little at a time while stirring, until the dough becomes the consistency of pancake batter. (The thicker the batter, the thicker the crust will be on the cooked shrimp.)

Place the shrimp and the batter conveniently near your cooking utensil.

Heat the oil in a wok, or a deep-frying utensil, to 350°-360° F. You can also test the temperature of the oil by putting a drop of batter in it. If the batter sizzles, puffs up, and floats, the oil is ready.

Take each shrimp by the tail, and dip it into the batter. Put shrimp directly into the hot oil one at a time. As each turns a golden brown, remove from oil with tongs and place on paper towels to drain. Arrange on serving plate and garnish with parsley or watercress. (A few leaves of lettuce under the shrimps help to make the dish look fuller and prettier, and this allows any excess oil to drain.)

Puff shrimp need not be served at once, because the breading will not turn limp and soggy. Keep them in a preheated 180° oven and the shrimp will still be hot and crisp for half an hour or longer.

No dip or gravy is required.

Shrimp with Hoi Sin Sauce 海鮮蝦

HOI SIN HA

The shrimp used for this recipe may or may not be shelled, as you wish. The Chinese usually cook this dish with the shrimp unshelled, but again it is a matter of choice for an American table. If you cook them with shells on, the shelling and deveining are done by the diner as in the Dry Cooked Shrimp recipe on page 236. The sweet bean sauce (or hoi sin deung, see page 34) is a dark sweet sauce which is particularly well suited for sea-food. It masks fishy smells without affecting the seafood flavor.

I   2   *pounds shrimp, medium size (26-30)*
     6   *scallions, cut into 1½-inch lengths*

II 2   *slices ginger, shredded*
     1   *clove garlic, minced*

III   2   *teaspoons cornstarch in ½ cup water*
        ⅓   *cup sweet bean sauce (hoi sin deung)†*
        2   *tablespoons oyster sauce or light soy sauce*

IV   ¼   *cup vegetable oil*
        ⅛   *teaspoon salt*
        ¼   *cup whiskey or gin†*

Mix together all ingredients in Group III and put aside.

Wash the shrimp, with or without shells, and dry with paper towels. Heat wok or pan hot and dry. Add the oil, then the salt. Turn heat down to medium, then add the ginger and garlic. As soon as garlic and ginger have turned light brown, add all the shrimp at once and stir gently until they change to pink color (about 4 minutes). Put in scallions and stir well. Add the sauce mixture from Group III. Mix with shrimp and cover to cook 2 minutes longer. Stir in the whiskey or gin just before serving. Serves 4.

SUBSTITUTIONS AND VARIATIONS

The whiskey or gin gives a more distinctive alcohol flavor than sherry. The hoi sin sauce is already sweet, so the sweetness of the sherry is not required to modify the sauce. However, if you prefer sherry, which is less likely to get your guests roaring drunk, go ahead!

If sweet bean sauce is not available, a good substitute is ½ cup ketchup. But you must expect a horse—or a shrimp—of a different color.

Butterfly Shrimp

WOO TIP HA

Butterfly shrimp are a favorite among Chinese and Westerners alike. They are shrimp cooked with a slice of crisp bacon attached to each, and served with a separate sauce which you may or may not dip the shrimp into. It is a very expensive dish in a restaurant, and I have never quite understood the reason, since it is relatively moderate in cost when prepared at home.

There are several seemingly unimportant procedures that must be carefully followed if you hope to achieve success. The thing that disturbs beginning cooks most about this dish is that they cannot make the bacon stick to the shrimp. Follow these three rules, and the rest is simple:

1. The shrimp must be split almost in half, but the two halves should still be attached so that when opened up they look like butterfly wings. What's even more important is that the shrimp must be split from the *underside,* or else the natural curl of the shrimp will force the bacon off when fried.

2. Coat each shrimp with beaten egg before putting bacon on

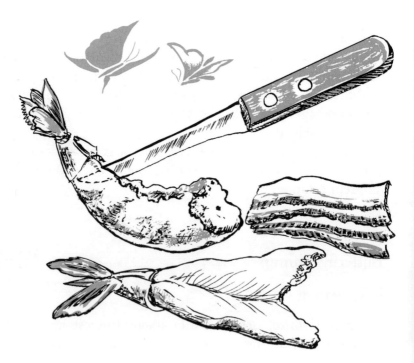

the shrimp. The egg mixture is what glues the bacon to the shrimp.

3. Fry with low heat, with the bacon on the bottom. The low heat prevents fast shrinkage of the bacon, and gives the egg coating a chance to bond the bacon and shrimp together.

I   12-16 *large shrimp, cleaned, split, dried with paper towels*
2   *eggs*
⅛   *teaspoon salt*
12-16 *half slices of lean bacon, uncooked*
½   *head of lettuce, shredded and placed in serving dish*

II 3   *tablespoons vegetable oil*
¼   *cup sherry*

Prepare shrimp as explained above. Beat up eggs with salt added. Place opened shrimp on platter with split sides up. Brush liberally with egg mixture. Place a half slice of bacon on each shrimp.

Heat wok or pan hot and dry. Add the oil. Turn heat down immediately to low. Take shrimp one at a time and put into wok or pan with bacon in contact with bottom until all have been put in. Cook slowly until bacon has turned slightly brown and crisp, and the egg has bonded the bacon to the shrimp. (Use 2 frying pans if one is not large enough to accommodate all the shrimp. Use ½ of the sherry for each pan.)

Turn each shrimp over carefully and fry the other side about 3 minutes. Quickly pour in the sherry. Cover and cook 1 minute more. Place shrimp on top of lettuce in platter and serve, with or without sauce.

Sauce for Butterfly Shrimp

The serving of a dipping sauce is traditional with butterfly shrimp. Following are recipes for two types of sauces usually associated with this dish; these sauces may also be used for any other seafood dishes you care to make.

Some people like these sauces very hot. The curry sauce is the hotter of the two. Adjust the sauce to suit your own taste, and the taste of your guests. The addition of a few drops of Tabasco will make the sauce hotter.

RED SAUCE — WITH KETCHUP

I   ½   *large Bermuda onion, chopped*

II   1   *teaspoon monosodium glutamate*
       1   *tablespoon cornstarch*
      ½   *cup ketchup*
       1   *dash Tabasco†*
       1   *cup chicken broth*

III   3   *tablespoons vegetable oil*
      ⅛   *teaspoon salt*

Mix together all ingredients in Group II and put aside.

Heat wok or pan hot and dry. Add the oil. Add the salt. Turn heat to medium. Add the onion and fry until golden yellow. Stir in the Group II mixture until thickened. Put into a bowl or gravy boat and let diner dip shrimp into it while eating. This sauce is also very nice to use over plain rice.

CURRY SAUCE

Make sauce exactly as above, except substitute 2 tablespoons curry powder in place of the ketchup.

Dry-Cooked Shrimp 乾煎蝦

GON DEEN HA

Frequently in Chinese cooking, shrimp are cooked in the shell. It may seem messy and inconvenient to shell your own shrimp as you eat, but some connoisseurs of seafood think that cooking within the shell retains more flavor of the shrimp. I believe this is true, but other factors do enter into our decisions about anything. The food habits and manners of people are an important part of people's food enjoyment. For some, the extra ritual of shelling their own shrimp may add to their pleasure, whereas others will find that extra little bit of flavor not worth the chore. Try it and decide.

The shrimp may be just washed and drained. No other preparation is required before cooking. The diner deveins the shrimp after he removes the shell. Most frequently, shrimp don't have any veins to be removed. The vein may be removed by peeling the outer layer of the skin from the back of the shrimp, which will expose it. Then just pick off the dark vein (if any) with fingernails or a fork.

These dry-cooked shrimp are wonderful for a regular meal, or as a snack or appetizer. The Chinese, who usually drink only if there is food around to go with the whiskey, often use this shrimp dish, hot or cold, for all-night festivities, such as bachelor dinners. It may be a good idea for your next poker or bridge party.

I 2 *pounds shrimp, medium size (26-30 to a pound)*

II 2 *slices ginger, shredded*
    2 *scallions, cut into 1½-inch lengths*

III ¼ *cup oil*
    1 *teaspoon salt*
    ½ *cup sherry*

Wash shrimp; leave shells on. Dry in towels. Heat wok or pan hot and dry. Add oil; add the salt. Turn heat down to medium low. Add the shrimp gently 1 at a time until all have been put in. Cover and cook for 2 minutes. Turn shrimp over to cook the other side. Sprinkle the ginger and scallions on top. Cover and cook 2 minutes more. Turn heat to high, stir to mix. Pour in the sherry. Cover again and turn off heat at once. Wait 1 more minute before serving to let the sherry flavor the shrimp. Serve hot or cold.

CRAB

Crabmeat rivals Maine lobster in flavor, texture, and general deliciousness. It certainly surpasses lobster tails, in my opinion. For people who are lucky enough to live near supplies of live crabs, along the Atlantic, Pacific, and Gulf coasts, crabs occupy a place of honor on gourmet tables. There is no finer eating than crabmeat, if one has the patience to pick the meat from a crab's complicated shell structure.

There are thousands of species of crabs, whose sizes vary from barely visible to over 18 inches across. Crabs are highly prized the world over. Chinese gourmets and cooks value crabs so much that they catch them, pen them in cages, and place them in rivers and harbors to be fattened like domestic fowls and animals. Some of the floating restaurants in China feature such crabs as their specialty. Several years ago a restaurant opened in New York City which served nothing but crabs.

We need only concern ourselves with a few species of crabs in the United States. The most abundant and best eating are the blue crabs, sometimes also called "blue-claw crabs," of the Atlantic coast. These crabs really have beautiful cobalt blue claws, from which they got their name. They are not very big. The really big ones (the males are larger than the females) may measure up to 8 inches across.

The Chesapeake Bay area is famous for crabs and crab dishes. Crab cakes can be bought there as easily as hot dogs in other areas. It is from this region that lump crabmeat (meat from cooked hardshell blue crabs) comes to market. This crabmeat has been refrigerated, but not frozen. Freezing seems to toughen the fibers in the crabmeat. I've frozen cooked crabs in the shell for varying periods. If crab is frozen for only a few days, there is only a slight loss in quality; but over longer periods the meat becomes stringy and tough, and loses its velvety smoothness.

The Dungeness crabs of the Pacific coast are equally famous. It is this species of crabs you may be able to find in inland markets, because lately I've noticed that they now are being cooked and frozen as soon as they are caught (as are Alaskan king crabs) and they are sold by the pound, whole. These crabs are much bigger than the blue-claws, weighing up to 3 or 4 pounds each. They also are delicious and easier to eat because they are larger. In flavor and texture, they must take second place to the blue-claws. This applies to the frozen Dungeness crabs only, because I've never eaten a fresh-cooked one. I suspect that the fresh-cooked ones are much better than the frozen.

The third variety of crabs, and the most available, are Alaskan king crabs. The name "Alaskan" reflects our national pride, because these crabs thrive in the cold waters near Japan too. There they are called "Japanese king crabs." King crabs are only available frozen. Only the legs and claws (shelled and unshelled) can be bought. The bodies do not yield enough meat for the processors, so are discarded. The flavor of king crabs is wonderful, but in other qualities, such as texture and tenderness, they place third to the other two species. However, their availability and convenience make them a great favorite. Use the cooked, shelled, and frozen meat for cooking in any Chinese recipe calling for crabmeat. Buy the legs or claws with the shell for plain snacking or dining. Use the same sauce recipe below for all three types of crabs.

Soft-shell crabs are blue-claw crabs of various sizes which have shed their hard shells and whose new shells are still soft from the molting process. Crabs change shells several times in a lifetime, to accommodate the growth of their bodies. The Chinese do not use soft-shell crabs much, but, when seasoned the "Chinese way" before deep frying, they are delicious. A recipe for them is given below. Soft-shell crabs are very difficult to find, even though they are available all year around. You may have to order them specially from your fish dealer—if they can be had at all.

The canned crabmeats are familiar to most cooks. They usually come from Japan or India. The meat may be used in Chinese recipes, but it is not as good as the fresh or frozen. The meat is very flaky and falls apart easily, so care must be used to keep the lumps together, as that is a desirable quality.

Steamed Blue-Claw Crabs 蒸生蟹

CHING SAANG HAAI

Live crabs can survive for several hours when kept cool and moist after you've taken them home from the fish dealer. Wet a few paper towels and place over them in the bag, then refrigerate. (Careful—lively crabs may pinch you with their claws if you come within reach.) Do not put them in water until you are ready to clean and cook them, since they may not survive more than ½ hour in water from your tap.

6   *large live blue-claw crabs (or 12 small ones)*
2   *slices ginger*
2   *cloves garlic, crushed*
½   *cup vinegar*
2   *cups water*
1   *tablespoon salt*

Place the live crabs in a sinkful of cold water, and allow them to clean themselves of sand or mud (about ½ hour). In a large pot, big enough to hold all the crabs with room to spare, place all the ingredients except the crabs and bring to a boil. Let simmer for 15 minutes to extract the flavor from the ginger and garlic.

Take the pot to the sink. Use long barbecue tongs to pick up the crabs one by one and put into the pot. Return pot to stove, cover, and turn heat to high. When a large volume of steam escapes from the pot, turn heat to medium. Cook 10 minutes. Remove crabs and allow them to cool (the crab shells will have turned bright red). When cooled, place in refrigerator until they are cold before serving with the sauce.

After the crabs have been cooked, they may be refrigerated for 2 to 3 days without loss of flavor if you do not wish to eat them right away. Serves 2 to 3.

SAUCE FOR CRABMEAT

⅓ cup dark soy sauce
⅓ cup vinegar
⅓ cup vegetable oil
½ teaspoon garlic juice (extracted with garlic press or bottled)
⅛ teaspoon Tabasco
½ teaspoon monosodium glutamate

Place the above ingredients in a jar with cover. Shake vigorously to mix. Pour 2 or 3 tablespoons into individual condiment dishes or bowls. Use this as a dip for the meat of all varieties of crab. Add more sauce to dish as needed. Be sure to shake the sauce mixture each time before pouring from jar. Oil rises to the top and must be mixed in, else only the oil comes out.

SHELLING STEAMED CRABS

This applies to blue claws and Dungeness crabs. The meat in king crab legs and claws can be easily removed after the shell is cracked with lobster or nut crackers.

Turn crab upside down and remove the long narrow cartilage (if male) or oval cartilage (in females) from the under side. With one hand grasp the shell by the pointed ends (be careful! there are sharp thorns on the shell and claws), and with the other hand firmly take the legs of the crab. Pull the shell from the body. The body has two meat-filled ends with a hollow in the middle. On the two ends are long, soft, pointed fibers, which are the gills. Pick those off with fingers and discard. Rinse the crab to remove any sand which may be present.

Place shelled crabs on plate and serve. The diner will have to break away the white hard shell which surrounds the succulent meat. Use nutcrackers to break claw shells. Dip the crabmeat into sauce according to individual preference.

Steamed crabs cannot be eaten in a hurry. One can buy cooked crabmeat, but it does not taste as good as steamed crabs when the eater removes the meat himself. Don't even make steamed crabs unless you know your guest has the patience and love of good eating to go through the trouble.

Crabmeat in Scrambled Eggs   蟹肉炒蛋

HAAI YUK CHOW DAAN

Few would deny that ham and eggs are a good combination. I think that crabmeat and eggs are an even better combination, especially scrambled together. Both eggs and crabmeat are so delicate and gentle in themselves that together they make a most happy marriage.

Do not cook this combination over high heat. Medium-low heat takes a little longer, but the smoothness and delicacy will be maintained.

I 6 *to 8 eggs, depending on size*
   ½ *pound fresh lump crabmeat†*

II 3 *scallions, chopped*

III   1   *teaspoon sugar*
      1   *teaspoon monosodium glutamate*
      ⅛   *teaspoon ground white pepper*
      2-3 *drops sesame oil*

IV   ¼   *cup vegetable oil*
      ⅛   *teaspoon salt*
        Light soy sauce or oyster sauce (optional)

Place crabmeat in a mixing bowl. Break up the larger lumps with a fork. Crack the eggs into the bowl. Put in all the other ingredients in Groups II and III. Take 1 teaspoon of the vegetable oil and add to mixture also (the oil helps to give the dish even greater smoothness). Break up the egg yolks and mix gently so the crabmeat is not too finely separated.

Heat wok or frying pan hot and dry. (This is particularly important in cooking eggs. The hot, dry frying pan will prevent eggs from sticking.) Add the remainder of the oil, then the salt. Turn heat down to medium low and pour in the mixture. Let it cook for about a minute or less, until the eggs start to firm. Then gently stir the mixture until the uncooked portions come in contact with the bottom of the wok or pan. Repeat process until the whole mixture has been scrambled and firmed. Serve while still hot.

Some people like to sprinkle a little soy sauce or oyster sauce on top of the scrambled eggs and crabmeat at the table. This is strictly optional. Let the eaters decide for themselves.

SUBSTITUTIONS AND VARIATIONS

Most large fish stores or departments in supermarkets now carry fresh crabmeat. This is not frozen, as is the case with king crabmeat. If fresh crabmeat cannot be found, a package of frozen king crab meat will do nicely. Be sure to cut and break up the king crab meat after it has thawed before combining into the mixture.

One large or 2 small cans of crabmeat can also be used in this recipe.

Fried Soft-Shell Crabs   炸蟹

JAH HAAI

When buying soft-shell crabs make sure that they are still alive. Their movements may be almost imperceptible, because at the soft-shell state a crab is very weak. If you are squeamish, have the fish dealer kill them for you. If you refrigerate them at once on returning home, no loss of quality will result if you use the crabs within 6-8 hours.

4   *live soft-shell crabs (6 if very small)*
1   *teaspoon garlic juice*
¼   *teaspoon salt*
½   *teaspoon monosodium glutamate*
⅛   *teaspoon ground white pepper*

Rinse crabs. Lift the ends of shell and pick off the fibrous gills and discard (see illustration for hard-shell crabs; they are the same crabs). With scissors, remove the mouth and eyes. Cut off loose cartilage from the underside. Dry crabs with paper towels. Lift shell ends again and rub garlic juice inside. Mix the salt, monosodium glutamate, and ground pepper together. Take a pinch of this mixture and sprinkle under and over each crab.

BATTER FOR SOFT-SHELL CRABS

Use recipe on page 231. Have batter ready and conveniently near before frying.

DEEP-FRYING SOFT-SHELL CRABS

Heat 2 quarts vegetable oil in a deep fryer or wok to medium temperature (350°-365° F.). Dip crab into batter. Allow excess batter to drain off. Gently drop crabs into hot oil, one at a time. (Oil may spatter. Stand back after each crab is added.) As each crab turns golden brown, remove with long tongs or long-handled strainer onto paper towels to drain dry. Serve with mayonnaise or tartar sauce.† Serves 2.

SUBSTITUTIONS AND VARIATIONS

If you desire a different, more "Chinese" taste to the crabs, use the Sauce for Crabmeat on page 241 in place of mayonnaise or tartar sauce.

Stir-Fried Clams with Red Sauce   茄汁炒蜆

KE'CHUP CHOW HEEN

This simple dish is a double gift. It is so easy to make and has a wonderful clam flavor. The Chinese call a dish like this one a "flavor dish," because the quantity of meat from the clams is very small in ratio to its great flavor. The gravy containing the clam juice is so full-bodied that even if the clam meat were to be removed it would still be a clam dish. The gravy mixed with rice is superb.

Buy the smaller clams such as littlenecks. The larger chowder clams or cherrystones may be used, but they may be chewier. Each clam has two tough, fibrous hinges with which it opens and closes its shell. Tell your eaters to remove these round muscles when they remove the clams from the shells and the meat will be tender and succulent.

I 2 *dozen small live clams*

II 2 *cloves garlic, minced*

III 1 *teaspoon sugar*
1 *tablespoon cornstarch*
1 *teaspoon monosodium glutamate*
¼ *teaspoon Tabasco†*
¼ *cup ketchup†*
Juice from clams

IV ½ *cup stock or cold water*
2 *tablespoons peanut oil*
½ *teaspoon salt*
2 *tablespoons sherry*
3 *scallions, chopped fine, for garnish*

Scrub and wash clam shells with brush to remove sand. Discard any clam whose shell is not closed tight. (Such clams are not alive.) Put clams in a saucepan. Add the ½ cup of stock or water. Cover and bring to a boil. Cook until the clam shells are slightly opened. Turn off heat. Remove clams with shells onto a plate. Allow the clam broth to cool slightly. Carefully pour almost all the broth into a mixing bowl (discard the little broth remaining in the saucepan, as there may be sand in it). Add all the ingredients from Group III to clam broth and mix well. Put aside.

Heat wok or pan hot and dry. Add the oil, then the salt. Put in the garlic to brown. Add the clams (with their shells) and stir-fry 1 minute. Add the sherry and cook covered 2 minutes more. Add the Group III mixture and stir-fry gently until the gravy thickens. Shut off heat and sprinkle in the chopped scallions. Serve with rice with the gravy over it.

SUBSTITUTIONS AND VARIATIONS

You can make this into another dish by using oyster sauce or soy sauce instead of ketchup. Then it would be called "Ho Yau Heen" or "Shi Yau Heen" respectively. Use ½ cup oyster sauce or ¼ cup dark soy sauce in place of the ketchup. Everything else stays the same.

Some people like this dish seasoned very hot. If you do, just increase the amount of Tabasco.

Periwinkles (Sea Snails) in Garlic Sauce   炒石螺

CHOW SHEK LOH

Periwinkles, or sea snails, are one of my favorite foods. However, preparing and eating this delicacy call for perseverance and skill.

The most time-consuming problem in preparing this dish is to nip the tip off the snail shell. The tip has to be removed because unless that is done you cannot get the meat out of the spiral of the shell. Breaking the tip of the shell also breaks the vacuum, so that the eater, with a little practice, can suck out the morsel from the front of the shell in one coordinated action. This can be quite an art. Just take a snail by your fingers, pucker your lips as for a kiss, and with one quick suck draw the meat into your mouth. You can also use a nut pick or a toothpick to pry the meat out, but it is not as much fun. (One of my friends claims that eating snails has made him the best kisser on the block!)

I've spoken to many chefs about the best ways to remove the tip from the snail shells. I've tried them all with varying success.

One method is to use a sharpened nail set. Nail sets come

in different sizes and they are used for driving the heads of finishing nails into the wood so that the nailheads won't show on the finished woodwork. Pick the smallest nail set, and have the point ground down to a sharp tip. Then, with the snail held against a cutting board, use the sharpened nail set and a small

hammer and drive a hole in the snail shell near the tip (see illustration). This method is fairly successful, although sometimes the snails will slip and scatter over the kitchen floor.

The best method I've found is an improvement over a method commonly used. That is to take a pair of special pliers (see illustration), that are used for cutting nailheads or heavy wires,

and just nip off the snail-shell tips. I've discovered a "special" special plier (called a "tile nipper"—be sure to specify "carbide tipped"), used by tile setters and mosaic workers to cut ceramic tiles, which works wonderfully. It is shaped very much like the other pliers in this group of tools, but the cutting edges are carbide tipped, and slightly ajar to allow room for the snail tip to be pushed against the cutters. Carbide is a very tough material, so will not be dulled easily by the not-as-hard shells.

Removing the tip is a very easy job with this tool. As is often the case, if the right tools can be found, any job becomes pleasanter and easier.

Periwinkles can be bought only in larger cities along both seacoasts. Most Chinese grocery stores that sell seafood carry periwinkles, which are called "shek loh," or "rock snails." There is no particular season for them, but they are available irregularly even in New York City, where large amounts of them are consumed.

If you should live near a rocky coast, at low tide these periwinkles can be found clinging to the rocks, and free for the picking.

You may have gathered by now that I love this dish—to go to all this trouble. I do. Before *you* go to all this trouble, I suggest you wait until you can get to a Chinese restaurant that serves this dish and order it to see if you like it. If you do, here is the recipe:

I   1½-2   *pounds periwinkles (sea snails)*

II   3   *slices ginger, shredded*
      3   *cloves garlic, minced*
      4   *scallions, chopped*
      2   *chili peppers, shredded (very hot peppers, sometimes called "pepper pods")*
      ½   *leek stalk, chopped (optional)*

III   1   *teaspoon sugar*
      1   *tablespoon cornstarch*
      1½   *tablespoons salted soybeans, washed and crushed*
      1   *teaspoon monosodium glutamate*
      2   *tablespoons soy sauce*
             Tabasco to taste
      2   *tablespoons hoi sin sauce*
      1   *cup chicken broth*
IV   ¼   *cup vegetable oil*
      ¼   *teaspoon sesame oil*
      ¼   *cup sherry*

Soak snails for an hour in clean, cold water. Scrub shells by putting snails in a sinkful of cool water and rubbing them together with both hands. Change water two or three times until water is clear. Nip off tips of each snail as described above, then rinse once more and drain.

Make sure that each snail is alive by smelling it. If a snail is dead, it will have a smell of decay. Drain snails in colander until ready to use.

Mix together ingredients in Group III and put aside.

Heat wok or pan hot and dry. Add both oils. Put in all the items in Group II and brown. Put in snails and stir to mix well with seasoning. Stir in sauce mixture from Group III. Cover and cook for 6 minutes. Lift cover and add the sherry. Cover and cook 1 minute more. Serve with plain rice.

12

Soups in the Chinese Manner

ONE glance at a Chinese menu will tell the most casual observer that the Chinese people love soup. There may be 20 to 30 different kinds of soups listed, made with every ingredient imaginable. But the Chinese people do not believe in making a soup which has many ingredients in it and then cooking them until they merge into one. Each item adds to the flavor, texture, and design of the whole, but remains true to itself, easily identifiable and retaining its own characteristics. Our concept of cooking in general is that different ingredients should work harmoniously together for the common good (dish), but none should lose its own identity in the process. This is a basic Chinese philosophy, and some mistaken Westerners who think of the Chinese as a "faceless horde" whenever any three of us get together should realize that we are the most individualistic "horde" imaginable!

Let's get back to the horde of soups. In order to enjoy your soup or soups with a meal, you must understand the function and style of service during a Chinese meal. We do not think of soup as a first course. Rather soup is left on the table throughout a meal. Our soups take the place of both wine and water, and are used for the same reasons: to wash down the food and to refresh our taste buds so we can better taste the different flavors.

Soup is so important to the Chinese people that it is not considered as only an adjunct to a meal. Frequently it becomes a meal in itself. There is but a thin line in some cases between a soup and a non-soup dish. Let's take the dish Young Jewel Woh Mein (on page 295) as an example. In ratio, there are more solid ingredients used than soup stock here. Where does this dish really belong when you try to categorize it? Is it a soup or a noodle dish? Another example is congee or "jook" (see page 283). Its main ingredient is rice, but it must be eaten with a spoon. In sum, then, these soups or dishes are meals in themselves, and need no classification except perhaps under "D"—for delicious!

There is a constant-seeming incongruity in Chinese thought. Perhaps incongruousness is the true state of man, and a society which accepts that lasts longer, is more pleasant to live in, and makes better food. If one soup can be a whole meal, then why do the Chinese sometimes serve 4 or 5 different soups at a banquet, in addition to dozens of other dishes? Perhaps the best way I can explain it is to remind you that several different wines may be served at a fancy Western banquet.

"High" and "Low" Soup Stocks (*Seung, Ha Tong*) 上，下湯

The designation of "high" and "low" as a measurement of quality is used by many peoples. The Chinese use those two words to describe anything from soup to morality. Actually only "high" soup stock is used for soups. The "low" soup stock is like the French court bouillon, used to boil seafood, or other food, then discarded. Who discovered this use first is not important, but in the eighteenth and nineteenth centuries there was a great wave of appreciation for the Chinese culture in France, and the resulting exchange of ideas and admiration may have influenced each country's cuisine.

The stock for Chinese soups can be had as easily as opening

a can, or be as elaborate as you wish to make it. In the first instance, canned chicken broth is a good stock and nothing can be more convenient. In the latter case, you can slave over it and use good-quality soup chickens, fresh ham bones, dried shrimp, and a myriad of other flavoring ingredients, as they do in restaurants. All this trouble is usually not justified in the home, because you do not need this much soup stock. If you make a whole batch of the stock at one time, and plan to freeze or refrigerate it for later use, you will find that the stock will take up a lot of room, and does not store well.

High Soup Stock

SEUNG TONG 上湯

There is a happy middle course to follow in making a good soup stock. Assuming that you are starting from scratch, the following will make 1½ quarts of good stock for Chinese soups:

1   quart cold water
1   can clear chicken broth
½   teaspoon salt
2   teaspoons monosodium glutamate
1   teaspoon light soy sauce
2   lean pork chops
3-4 drops sesame oil (for soups containing seafood)

Trim off most of the fat from the pork chops. Separate the bones from the meat. Slice the meat into thin slices and put aside.

Place cold water and chicken broth in pot and add the salt, monosodium glutamate, and soy sauce. Bring water to a boil. Add the pork-chop bones. Turn heat down to simmer for 15 to 20 minutes. Remove bones and eat the meat that clings to them as a snack, or discard. Bring water to a boil again. Add the sliced pork and boil uncovered for 5 minutes. Remove pork; save to be added back into the soup just before serving. This last instruction is to prevent the pork from being overcooked when you are boiling whatever other items you have for a particular soup.

The sesame oil is to be added only when you are making a soup which has seafood in it. The sesame oil subtly masks any fishy taste or smell.

This will be enough stock to make soup for 4 to 6 persons.

Low Soup Stock

下湯

HA TONG

When blanching some foods, a bit of the food's flavor is lost into the water in which they were blanched. To minimize this loss, the water should have some flavor in it, so that it puts some flavor back into the food. Therefore, the use of a low-grade soup is used instead of just plain water. After use, this liquid is discarded, unless there is more than one thing to be blanched. In that case, the "low" stock is self-perpetuating, as it will get richer and more flavorful each time it is used. Some flavor is added from each item in a reciprocal action.

We are so rich in this country that each household can afford to throw away more food than perhaps several families in a poor country have to eat each day. It is not necessary to "think poor," but waste should be avoided. In this connection, many items we completely discard can help us make a good "low" stock for blanching. Any bones of fowl, pork, or veal, when boiled in water for an hour or so, will yield a nice stock. Add to the bones the shavings and ends from carrots, celery, scallions, or onions which may be ordinarily discarded. A teaspoon of salt in the liquid completes the stock.

A few words of caution: While beef or lamb bones may yield a rich broth, their own character is too insistent for the purpose of low soup stock. Fish bones and heads and shrimp also make a good stock, but its use should be limited to seafood.

Watercress Soup   西洋菜湯

SAI YEUNG CHOY TONG

This is probably one of the easiest and most delicious soups in Chinese cooking. In essence, it takes into account all the elements necessary for a good soup. These elements may be described as "body," "purity," and "flavor," if I may borrow an advertiser's slogan. You must have a good soup stock to begin with; then the fresh, crisp taste of watercress makes this a superior soup. The eggs lend a lot of body and nutrition, but they may be left out to make a less filling soup if you wish.

When cutting the watercress, cut while it is still in a bunch before rinsing. This saves time, since if the watercress is rinsed first, the ends will be helter-skelter and will take longer to straighten and cut.

If you made the soup stock with pork slices (as on page 253), add them back to the watercress just before serving.

4 *cups high soup stock or chicken broth*
4 *eggs*
2 *bunches watercress, cut into 1-inch lengths, including stems*
1 *teaspoon light soy sauce*

Bring soup stock to a boil. Add the soy sauce, adjusting amount to taste if necessary. Lower heat so stock just simmers and gently crack the eggs, one at a time, into the soup stock. Let poach until the egg whites have turned firm, but the yolks are still soft as in soft poached eggs (about 3 minutes). Remove eggs gently, including the white that may have separated, with a slotted spoon or strainer, and put aside. The stock should remain clear. Bring stock to a vigorous boil and add the watercress. Stir until stock boils again. Remove from heat at once. Dish out into individual soup plates and top each with an egg. Serve at once. Serves 4.

Lettuce-Fish Soup   生菜魚片湯

SHAANG CHOY YEE P'IN TONG

This soup is so easy to make and so delicious that I am tempted to jazz it up by making it complicated! It is with the greatest restraint that I give it to you as follows:

1½ *quarts good soup stock*
1½ *cups pike fillets, sliced thin (about ½ pound)*
1 *head iceberg lettuce, cored and quartered†*
3-4 *drops sesame oil*

Boil the soup stock and adjust seasoning if necessary. Add the sesame oil. Add the lettuce. Stir to separate leaves. When stock boils again, add fish slices and shut off heat *immediately*. The stock must not boil again once the fish has been put in, else it will be overcooked. If you are using an electric stove, remove the soup pan from the burner, since the electric element in the stove retains heat and may overcook the fish. Leave covered for 2 minutes and serve. Serves 4.

SUBSTITUTIONS AND VARIATIONS

Another soup the Chinese like is called "Sour-Green Fish Soup" (Seun Choy Yee Tong). It is made exactly the same way except for the substitution of pickled Chinese mustard greens (seun gai choy) in place of the fresh lettuce. Also add 2 tablespoons sugar to the stock. Rinse the pickled mustard greens. Separate the leaves and shred them before adding to the soup stock. One and a half cups of this vegetable are needed (about ½ pound). If you enjoy sweet and sour dishes, I feel certain you will find this a nice change in soup taste.

Egg-Drop Soup

DAAN YUNG TONG

Egg-drop soups are runaway favorites with many Americans who eat in Chinese restaurants. Most Chinese restaurants have egg-drop as standard *soupe du jour*. It happens to be one of the easiest and fastest soups to make, and most households will have all the ingredients necessary for its production. The secret of good soup is naturally good soup stock. To keep the egg flakes afloat, the soup must be thickened with cornstarch *first* before the beaten eggs are stirred in.

1½ *quarts chicken broth or clear soup stock*
2   *tablespoons cornstarch, mixed in ¼ cup cold water*
2   *eggs, slightly beaten with a fork*
2   *scallions, chopped, including green ends*

Bring soup stock to a boil. Slowly pour in the cornstarch mixture while stirring the stock, until the stock thickens. Reduce heat so stock just simmers. Pour in the eggs slowly while stirring the soup. As soon as the last bit of egg is in, shut off heat at once. Serve with chopped scallions on top. Serves 4.

SUBSTITUTIONS AND VARIATIONS

Tomato Egg-Drop Soup is just a variation of plain egg-drop soup. The added tartness of tomatoes gives this soup an extra "zing" and helps to pick up sagging appetites. The addition of 1 medium-size can stewed tomatoes is all that is needed. A slight change in cooking procedure is also necessary:

Bring stock to a boil. Add the tomatoes. (Mash the tomatoes if the pieces are too large.) When soup boils again, add the cornstarch mixture as before. Add the eggs while stirring. Shut off heat at once and serve topped with the chopped scallions.

Winter Melon Soup

冬瓜湯

TUNG KWA TONG

I do not know to what family of gourds or melons this distinctive Chinese vegetable belongs, but it is aptly named. Winter melon (tung kwa) invokes the winter season, as does frost on the pumpkin. It is shaped like a pumpkin without the flutes.

Its color is a deep green, with white patches on it that look like frost. Its skin is very tough and inedible, so must be removed with a sharp knife or cleaver. A pound of winter melon will be only a small wedge from the whole melon, since some winter melons weigh 20 to 30 pounds. To pare, lay the wedge on its side on a cutting board and press down with the knife or cleaver just inside the green skin a bit at a time until all of it has been removed. Then the meat of the melon can be sliced easily into domino shapes about ¼ inch thick for this soup.

On very festive occasions, a whole winter melon may be used to make a great soup. The selection of the melon then becomes an important matter. It must be a small but mature melon for two good reasons: A large melon will not fit into an average household pot or wok to be steamed. The melon is not peeled but left intact so that the shell becomes a container for the soup *within* the other pot. Only a mature melon with a tough skin can stand the long process of steaming and not crumble. This whole-melon soup is only mentioned here as a sidelight, since you are not likely to make such a large soup dish.

Winter melons are available only in Chinese or Japanese stores, but there is a substitute. (See Substitutions and Variations.)

I   1½   *quarts soup stock or chicken broth*

     1   *pound winter melon, pared and sliced into domino shapes ¼ inch thick†*
         Cooked pork slices (if soup stock was made with pork)

II   4-6   *dried Chinese mushrooms, presoaked ½ hour or longer*

     ½   *cup sliced bamboo shoots (sliced crosswise, ⅛ inch thick)*

III   1   *teaspoon monosodium glutamate*

     ⅛   *teaspoon ground white pepper*

     2   *teaspoons light soy sauce*

Bring stock to a boil. Add the sliced winter melon, mushrooms, and bamboo shoots. Cook until the melon becomes translucent (about 20 minutes). Add everything in Group III and simmer for 5 minutes more. Put back the pork if it was used to make the soup stock (see page 253). Serves 4.

SUBSTITUTIONS AND VARIATIONS

There is a substitute for winter melon: watermelon rind (the white part) is quite similar in taste and texture to winter melon. Use that and try this recipe. Peel off the skin, remove any red meat (if some still clings to it after the red part has been eaten), and slice the watermelon just as instructed for winter melon. Complete the recipe as outlined.

Chop Suey Soup

DAAP SUI TONG

Some Americans know this as "Chop Suey" soup. The closer phonetic translation is "Daap Sui," which means loosely "various items" or "odd assortment." Whenever you run across Daap Sui recipes, you almost have carte blanche to do as you wish. The recipe below should be taken only as a guide, not as gospel:

I   1½   *quarts good soup stock*
      ½   *cup thinly sliced pork*
      8   *shrimp, medium size, shelled, cleaned, and split*

II   4-6 *Chinese mushrooms, presoaked*
      ½   *cup sliced bamboo shoots*
      ½   *cup sliced water chestnuts*

III   2   *teaspoons light soy sauce*
     3-4 *drops sesame oil*

Bring the soup stock to a boil. Add the soy sauce and sesame oil. Adjust flavoring to taste. Add the pork and cook for 3 minutes. Add the shrimp and cook 1 minute more. Remove both pork and shrimp from stock and put aside.

Add all the ingredients of Group II and simmer for 5 minutes. Put back pork and shrimp. Turn off heat and serve. Serves 4 people.

Chinese Mustard Greens Soup

芥菜湯

GAI CHOY TONG

Gai choy and mustard greens are very close in taste, but look quite different from each other. Mustard greens may have been Chinese gai choy transmuted by the American soil. The Chinese variety of mustard greens is a very handsome-looking vegetable. It has broad leaves and wide stems and looks somewhat like a large celery. Its color is a jade green. The leaves should be separated before soaking in water to remove the soil that may cling to the base of each leaf. Rinse well after soaking. Slice across the leafy tops at about 1-inch intervals. Cut the stems diagonally across into ¾- to 1-inch slices. Gai choy can be bought in Chinese or Japanese stores all year round. Since the American variety of mustard greens is so similar to gai choy, don't hesitate to use it as a substitute.

1½   *quarts soup stock or chicken broth*
1   *cup sliced lean pork*
3   *slices fresh ginger*
3   *cups (about 1 pound) sliced gai choy or mustard greens†*

Bring stock to a boil. Add the ginger slices. Put in sliced pork. Simmer for 3 minutes. Remove pork and ginger. Put aside. While soup stock is boiling, add gai choy or mustard greens. Cook for 2 minutes more after stock reboils. Put back the pork and ginger, mix, and serve. (If you make the soup stock with pork slices before, use those slices here.) Makes 4 generous servings.

SUBSTITUTIONS AND VARIATIONS

Two other vegetables, baak choy and Chinese cabbage (also called celery cabbage), make excellent soups. If they are used, follow the recipe exactly as for the gai choy dish.

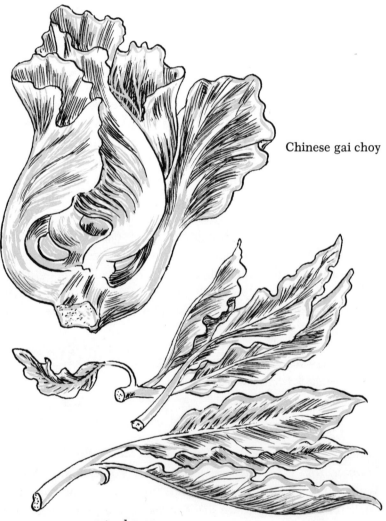

Chinese gai choy

mustard greens

Velvet Chicken Cucumber Soup 滑鷄黃瓜湯

VOT GAI WONG KWA TONG

The subtle flavor of cucumber and chicken can best be appreciated in this soup. Both ingredients are smooth and velvety in texture. Since the flavor of cucumbers and chicken are so delicate, the educated palate can truly appreciate this happy harmony of tastes.

Cut the chicken meat in slices (p'in, page 44) and precook according to instructions for making velvet chicken.

1 *cup velvet chicken, precooked (see page 167)*
1 *pint chicken broth or soup stock*
2 *cucumbers, peeled†*

Cut cucumbers into 1½-2-inch lengths, halve the lengths, then cut into domino shape about ¼ inch thick.

Bring chicken broth or soup stock to a boil. Add the cucumbers. When stock boils again, turn heat to medium. Cook cucumbers for 3 minutes more. Turn off heat. Put in the velvet chicken. Let stand, covered, 2 minutes to heat through. Adjust seasoning to taste and serve.

SUBSTITUTIONS AND VARIATIONS

Any bland vegetables may be substituted for the cucumbers. Fresh iceberg lettuce makes a happy variation. If lettuce is used, shred 1 small head, discarding the core (which is slightly bitter when cooked). Lettuce requires less cooking time. When broth reboils, turn heat off at once and add the chicken and lettuce.

Chinese cabbage also makes an excellent substitute here.

Frequently, when you may wish for a light, simple, but tasty meal, Chinese soups will fill your wish very well. Add more meat (2 cups instead of 1) to make the soup more filling.

Subgum Soup

什錦湯

SHAP GAAM TONG

The name "shap gaam" (or more popularly written as "sub-gum") literally means "miscellaneous garnishes." A truer translation would be "Precious-Item Soup." These precious items are highly personal, so again you have a freedom of choice. The possible combinations are so numerous that no two chefs make this soup exactly alike. However, the spirit of this soup should be kept. The ingredients used are all diced into small cubes. The color of the items should be considered more than usual, to make the soup as eye appealing and festive as possible, and the stock is slightly thickened to give it more body.

I   1½   *quarts good soup stock*
     ½   *cup diced cooked shrimp*
     1   *whole breast of chicken, cooked, boned, and diced*
     ½   *cup diced green peppers*
     ¼   *cup diced celery hearts*
     ¼   *cup diced canned pimentos*
     ¼   *cup frozen green peas*

II   1   *small can whole button mushrooms, including liquid*

III 1   *teaspoon sugar*
     2   *teaspoons light soy sauce*
     3-4 *drops sesame oil*
     2   *tablespoons cornstarch, mixed with ¼ cup cold water*

Bring soup stock to a boil. Add all the items in Group III except the cornstarch. Turn heat down so soup just simmers and slowly add the cornstarch mixture, while stirring, to thicken the stock.

Add all the ingredients in Groups I and II. Bring to a gentle boil. Turn heat down and let simmer for 3 or 4 minutes to blend the flavors. Serves 6.

Three Sea-Fresh Treasures Soup   三鮮湯

SAAM SIN TONG

This is a seafood soup. I am struck by how much the French bouillabaisse closely resembles some of the Chinese seafood soups. The three sea-fresh treasures usually refer to shrimps, lobsters, and abalone. However, any other combinations of seafood may be used.

It may be of passing interest to you to know that the Chinese character 鮮 , meaning fresh, is sometimes replaced by the character 仙 , which means fairies or spirits. Both characters are pronounced exactly the same way ("sin"), and when the fairy character is used in describing foods it has a more magical, colorful connotation. In Chinese mythology there are eight 仙 or benevolent spirits, and this soup may have up to eight "sea-fresh treasures."

It will take one average 1-pound lobster in the shell to produce ¾ cup cooked lobster meat. If the lobster happens to be very plump and yields more than that, think of it as a bonus, and put in all the meat. See page 215 on how to cook and shell a lobster. About ⅓ pound raw shrimp will yield 1 cup of cooked, diced shrimp.

I	1½	*quarts soup stock or chicken broth*
	¾	*cup diced cooked lobster meat†*
	1	*cup diced cooked shrimp†*
II	3-5	*dried Chinese mushrooms, soaked and diced†*
	½	*cup finely diced canned abalone*
III	1	*teaspoon light soy sauce*
	¼	*teaspoon sesame oil*
IV	3	*scallions, chopped, including green ends (for topping)*
	1	*tablespoon cornstarch, dissolved in ¼ cup cold water*

Cook, shell, and dice the lobster meat and shrimp. Put aside.

Bring soup stock to a boil. Add all the ingredients in Groups II and III. Let simmer for 3-4 minutes. Adjust seasoning if necessary. Slowly stir in the cornstarch mixture until the stock thickens slightly. Add the shrimp and lobster meat and turn heat off at once. Serve with chopped scallions sprinkled on top of soup. Serves 4 to 6.

SUBSTITUTIONS AND VARIATIONS

Cooked lobsters in their shells are often available in high-class seafood stores. They may also have cooked lobster meat, which is refrigerated but not frozen after cooking. Frozen king crabmeat may be substituted for the lobster meat.

The other seafood items which may be used for this soup are: sliced fish fillets, oysters, clams, sea cucumbers (*bêche-de-mer*), squid, fish balls, and shark's maw. (No—not the shark's mother! It's a specially prepared delicacy of shark stomach.)

13

Rice and Rice Dishes

RICE is the mainstay of a Chinese meal, and most Chinese will eat at least one large, heaping bowl of it with each meal—if they can get it. Americans, on the other hand, hardly touch the rice that accompanies a Chinese meal, and then complain about being hungry again a little later.

When I was a boy in China many did not even have rice to eat. I will never forget the wandering beggars (usually entire families) who stopped in our village and went from house to house to beg for a handful of rice on which to live for one more day.

Because my father was able to send us money from America, where he was working in a laundry, we were among the more affluent families in the village. We kept two earthen crocks of rice. The larger one held the family supply of polished white rice. The other held the coarser, unpolished rice for wandering beggars. (It is ironic that modern nutritionists say the beggars' rice held more food value than our own. But then the beggars had only rice to eat if anything at all, while our meals were supplemented by vegetables and fish and sometimes even meat.) As the youngest in the household, I was given the privilege of giving out the usual handful of raw rice to each member of a beggar family. This was the custom in our village, and it was a practical one. Not only did a child learn compassion and gratitude for his own good fortune, but his hands were small.

I told you about a great-uncle I had who was a farmer, who would sometimes share his meager repast with me. Usually there would be only a pot of rice and perhaps a tiny bit of salted fish or a saucerful of ground salted shrimp paste. Twice a year he had meat, on his birthday and on New Year's Day. During the rice-planting season, my uncle and his wife worked from dawn to dusk, planting rice in knee-deep water. I would sit on the narrow borders that separated the fields and watch them. When they finally got out of the water to eat their noonday meal of a bowl of rice, I was given the job of removing the long slimy bloodsuckers that had feasted on their work-worn legs. It doesn't conjure up a happy childhood picture, but my life was influenced unalterably in some respects by these haunting memories. To this day it hurts me to throw away even a tiny bit of leftover rice. After a dinner party when Isabella and I scrape the dishes, the hardest thing for me to put into the garbage bag is the rice, and not the other leftover food that cost a good deal more in time, money, and labor.

I cannot expect you to have the same reverence for rice that I have because our experiences are different and because we live in an affluent society. But since rice is so important to the Chinese, we've learned to extract every possible use out of this versatile grain, and not a grain is wasted.

In a typical home, rice is boiled, and when ready it is served for dinner. Usually more rice is made than the family can eat, and as the family's consumption grows the quantity of rice is automatically increased—so that there will still be leftover rice. One never knows who may want an extra bowl, nor when a visitor may come and sit down with you for dinner. Then, leftover rice is so good cold! When the children come home from school, just add a little soy sauce and peanut oil to it. Instantly it becomes the Chinese equivalent of a peanut-butter sandwich!

If by some chance there is still some rice left, simply add it to the top of the next pot of rice, about ten minutes before the fresh rice is ready (after the water has been absorbed), and let it steam, and it is as good as new.

Sometimes a crust is formed on the bottom of the pot in which rice has been cooked. This crust can be used in two ways; it can be just boiled with a little water and eaten with meals. This rice is called "Faan Deul" and is highly prized by many Chinese for its nutty flavor and *al dente* texture. The other use for this rice crust is in the famous Sizzling Rice dishes which will be dealt with in detail in the recipes that follow. In an American home, another dimension can be added to the leftover rice: rice pudding. The recipe for that is not included here.

The most gracious phrase in Chinese hospitality is 同我食飯 ("Tung ngoh shik faan"), "Come and eat rice with me!"

Plain Boiled Rice

保飯

BOH FAAN

It is with wonderment that I encounter so many Americans who do not know how to cook plain rice well.

It seems to me that many American cooks beat the rice to death. I've seen recipes that call for bringing water to a boil, putting in the rice, draining and rinsing in cold water, then steaming in a double boiler. The rice comes out terrible! Too much care in cooking often is as bad as not enough. This goes for children too. But this topic is better left to Dr. Spock.

PROCEDURE

Buy long-grain rice when possible. This strain of rice is firmer and less likely to become mushy when cooked. Allow 1 cup uncooked rice for every 2 people in your dinner plan. One cup of uncooked rice will make almost 2 cups of cooked rice.

Place the dry rice in a heavy saucepan which has a well-fitting cover. The pan should be large enough so that the dry rice will not fill more than half the pan, since its volume increases so much.

Cover rice with cold water and rub between your hands. The water will become milky with loose starch. Drain off this water and fill pan again with clean water. Repeat this washing process until the water is clear. Usually 4 to 6 changes of water will be enough.

After the final washing and draining, cover the rice with enough water so that when your index finger is placed on top of the rice, the water will come just below the first joint of your index finger. This of course excludes long fingernails in the measurement, since some ladies' fingernails rival the former Chinese mandarins' in length! The depth of water, if measured with a ruler, will be between ¾ and 1 inch above the rice. The natural question arises, shouldn't the depth of the water vary with the quantity of rice? Because of some physical phenomenon called "displacement," which I don't understand, no matter how much rice you cook or whatever pot you use, this practical rule seems to work. Rice does vary in the amount of water it will absorb according to types and brands, but you can count on this system for most of the rice that is available in the American market.

If you insist on an exact ratio (oh, you purist!) of uncooked rice to water, it should be 1:1 (1 cup of rice to 1 cup of cold water). This makes for a cooked rice with a dry, toothy texture, preferred by most Chinese. If you prefer your rice softer, add a little more water; if you like it firm, use a little less.

After the rice has been washed and the correct amount of water put in, place the covered pot of rice on the stove and turn heat up high. When rice comes to a vigorous boil, turn heat down to low immediately. Let cook at this heat for 5 minutes longer and turn heat down to very low. Don't lift cover to peek because it is the steam that is under the cover which continues the cooking process. After heat has been turned down to very low, another 10 minutes will give you perfectly cooked rice.

Here are a few extra tips on cooking rice:

Rice may be washed, then the right amount of cooking water placed in the pot, and the rice left uncooked for hours or overnight until you are ready to prepare your meal. This advance preparation can save time and lessen the pressure of doing everything at once in making a Chinese meal.

The rice can be cooked an hour or more before the meal and kept warm on an unneeded burner, with the heat turned down to very low. As long as the rice does not scorch on your burner, no change in taste or texture can be found in keeping the rice warm over an extended period of time.

How can you tell when the rice comes to a vigorous boil if the cover is on? Look at the pot and cover. Steam will come billowing out, and sometimes the lid may even summon you by its clatter as the steam lifts and lowers it.

Rice can scorch and be ruined, as well as leave a tough-to-clean burnt bottom on the pot, if you forget to turn the heat down after the water has been absorbed in boiling. If you should forget (it happens to the best of cooks), as soon as you detect the smell of burning rice, rush to the stove and remove the pot from the burner. Fill the sink with about an inch of water and set the bottom of the pot in it to stop the cooking quickly. Remove the lid to allow the burnt smell to escape. Scoop the unburnt rice into another pot, sprinkle about ½ cup of cold water over the rice and put back onto the stove. Cover the pot, turn heat to medium. This time *stay by the stove* until steam rises from the pot again. Turn heat to low immediately and let rice cook for 5 minutes. Turn heat to very low and continue cooking for another 10 minutes. If you've caught it before the rice was burnt to the point of no return, your rice has been saved.

Fried Rice with Choice of Flavors   炒飯

CHOW FAAN

There are more ways to make fried rice than I would care to count. Which is more authentically Chinese? Well, it is like the fable of the blind men who felt an elephant and each described it as being like whatever part of the elephant he happened to touch.

Young Jewel Fried Rice is one version of a regional treatment of the subject. Wherever people gather, fried rice will be varied and reinvented, so wherever you may be, we may have such names as "Detroit Fried Rice," or "Paris Fried Rice," or "Tel Aviv Fried Rice." Do not hesitate to change and substitute on this dish. It is the variety of the ingredients and the inventiveness of the cook that lift it from the ordinary.

I   4   *cups cooked rice*
     4   *scallions, chopped, including green ends*

      2   *cups diced cooked pork, ham, chicken, shrimp, or what you will†*

II   1   *slice ginger, minced*
      1   *clove garlic, minced*
      ¼   *cup sliced button mushrooms, drained (optional)*

III   2   *eggs*
      1   *teaspoon monosodium glutamate*
      ⅛   *teaspoon ground white pepper*
      ¼   *cup soy sauce*

IV   ¼   *cup vegetable oil*

Put all the Group III ingredients in a mixing bowl and stir slightly; the eggs should not be well beaten.

Heat wok or pan hot and dry. Add the oil. Brown the garlic and ginger slightly, then add the rice. Cook for 2-3 minutes. If cold cooked rice is used, cook a little longer to heat rice through, stirring to break up lumps and coat evenly with oil. Add all the rest of the ingredients except the egg mixture. Fry and stir constantly until thoroughly mixed. Add the egg mixture while stirring the rice so it will cover as much of the ingredients in the pan as possible. Stir constantly while cooking until the egg mixture begins to firm up—in about 2 minutes. Remove and serve while hot.

SUBSTITUTIONS AND VARIATIONS

Fried rice, Chinese style, can be varied infinitely by following a basic recipe and just changing the main ingredients used in conjunction with the rice. Roast pork, ham, chicken, or any type of seafood or preserved meats may be used. Fried rice can be a great help in menu planning because it can utilize any leftover bits and pieces.

An alternate method of utilizing the eggs is to make them into an omelet, then cut the omelet into small pieces and add to the fried rice. This makes for a drier fried rice if that is your preference.

Cold Rice Snack

Have you ever retasted something you were fond of as a child, only to be disappointed? I understand that some scientific studies prove that our taste buds actually change as we grow older, so that what tasted so wonderful to us in our youth will do so no longer even if the food is exactly the same as it was before.

But this simple dish, being so unassuming, has retained all its virtues for me. I don't remember how I came across it, but I do remember how I enjoyed it during my grade-school days.

I would come home after school with a ravenous appetite, which had to be satisfied in quick order. Dinner would still be hours away, and in my house there were no snacks like the thousand and one items children have today. The old rice pot is where I looked. If I was lucky (and I usually was) there would be some leftover rice from the night before. It was really room temperature rather than cold as it would be in today's refrigerator. (By the way, rice does not have to be kept in the refrigerator, where it takes up room. If you plan to use it within a day or so, even in the summer no refrigeration is necessary.)

After spotting the cooked rice, I would scoop some into a large bowl, pour some peanut oil on it at random, then sprinkle some dark soy sauce on it and mix it well and have a feast! If they were available, and my hunger could wait, I chopped some scallions and sprinkled them on the rice. It needed nothing more.

I wondered how my American friends would take to this simple fare but could not test it since one would not serve this at a dinner party. But I did once describe it to a friend in a fit of nostalgia. To my surprise, one day I saw her eating this dish and, forgetting I had told her about it, asked her where she had gotten the recipe. She told me that she had been eating rice this way often since the time, many years ago, I had told her about it. She works in a restaurant and could have her choice of foods, but she often craves only this humble dish and can hardly wait to get home to make it. This is only a test panel of one, but she has a nice sense about food and I was tempted into making it again when I returned home. It was every bit as good as I remembered!

1   *bowl of cooked, cooled rice*
2   *tablespoons peanut oil*
1½ *tablespoons dark soy sauce*
2   *scallions, finely chopped (optional)*

Add the oil to the rice and mix thoroughly. Then add soy sauce and mix again. The oil must be put in and mixed first so that each grain is coated, otherwise the soy sauce will soak into the rice spottily. A good soy sauce should be used, since its flavor will determine the success of this dish.

Rice with Chinese Sausages

蒸臘腸

CHING LAAP CHEUNG

One of the simplest hot meals you can make is Chinese sausages cooked with the rice. If you are eating alone, or just with your spouse, sausages and rice without anything else makes a delightful, filling meal. This is only true if you like rice as much as the Chinese do. The aroma of the sausages permeates the rice and gives it a fragrant, delicious flavor. It can also be served as a company dish, but other dishes should accompany it. In that case, allowing one sausage link to a guest is enough. For yourself, and/or your spouse, two or even three links are needed, depending on your appetite.

Chinese sausages are unique, and can be bought only in Chinese groceries, either in person or by mail (see back of book for mail-order purchases). These sausages are well seasoned with soy sauce, Chinese spices, and alcohol. There are two major types of Chinese sausages. Both are made with pork, but one is all pork, while the other is pork and duck livers mixed in about equal portions. They are air-dried and not subjected to any cooking process, so must be cooked before eating. However, only a short cooking period is needed. These sausages should be stored in the refrigerator, and will keep for months. In China, where there was no refrigeration, they were kept in the rice crock. A pound will yield about 8 links of sausages.

1½ *cups raw rice*
4   *links Chinese sausage, rinsed†*

In a saucepan wide enough to accommodate the lengths of sausages, wash and prepare the rice for boiling (see page 270). Bring rice to a vigorous boil and cook for 2 minutes. Lift cover and insert the sausages *into* the rice, so that the sausages are completely, or almost completely, covered by the rice. Replace cover and turn heat down to medium. Cook for 5 minutes and turn heat down to low. Allow another 15 minutes for rice and sausages to cook.

When they are done, remove the sausages from the rice. Either slice them diagonally across into ⅛-inch slices before serving, or place them on a plate and cover with rice (to keep them hot) for the diner to cut at the table. Be sure to supply a sharp knife (such as a boning knife) because the sausages will be mangled by a dull knife.

Serve only with the rice in which they were cooked; it's part of the recipe! Add a little soy sauce if desired. (The rice will already have some of the soy sauce and sausage flavor in it from the cooking process.)

SUBSTITUTIONS AND VARIATIONS

There is a preserved duck the Chinese use for the same purpose. The duck has been pressed flat as a kite and cured with soy sauce, spices, and alcohol. In addition, some (not all) of these ducks are further preserved in oil, so that they can be shipped in cans. In Chinese groceries, it is possible to buy preserved ducks by the quarter. Use exactly the same technique and timing for preserved ducks as for the sausage in the above recipe. Allow one quarter duck to a person.

Young Jewel Fried Rice

揚州炒飯

YEUNG CHAU CHOW FAAN

The Chinese system of transliteration tries not only to make Chinese words phonetically accurate in English but also to give words a pleasant meaning and spirit. "Young Jewel" is a fit description for this fried-rice dish, but actually Yeung Chau was the name of a province in ancient China famous for its noodles, won ton and fried-rice dishes. Usually each of these dishes is a meal in itself, because so many tasty items go into it. Another nice thing about Young Jewel dishes is that they give a cook the widest possible leeway to exercise his own ingenuity and preference as to what will go into the dish. I've never had a Young Jewel dish made exactly alike by different chefs, but the spirit of the dish is always there.

The rice should be hot before it is put in, so it can cook quickly; otherwise the vegetables may get overcooked. If you use leftover rice, preheat it in a double boiler before use.

This is a good dish to make with leftover roasts, ham, chicken, etc. Most leftover dishes are looked down upon by people, which I think is a mistake. In this case you start with the idea of *making* leftovers, if you don't have any!

Add, subtract, substitute to your heart's content. Have fun!

I 4 *cups hot cooked rice*
   1 *cup diced roast pork*
   1 *cup diced cooked shrimp*
   1 *cup diced cooked chicken*
   2 *cups fresh bean sprouts†*
   2 *scallions, chopped, including green ends*
   1 *cup shredded lettuce*

II 2 *eggs, slightly stirred*

III ¼ *teaspoon ground pepper*
    1 *teaspoon monosodium glutamate*
    ¼ *cup soy sauce*

IV ¼ *cup vegetable oil*

Mix together ingredients in Group III and put aside.

Heat wok or frying pan hot and dry. Add one half of the vegetable oil. Turn heat to medium. Add the eggs, and stir lightly so the whites and yolks are mixed slightly. Remove from pan while still a little soft, and put aside.

Turn up heat; add remainder of oil and all the items in Group I, *except* the rice and shredded lettuce. Stir-fry for 2 minutes. Add the hot rice. Pour in the mixture from Group III and mix sauce with all ingredients thoroughly. Put back the scrambled eggs. Turn off heat and add the lettuce. Stir and serve.

SUBSTITUTIONS AND VARIATIONS

The fresh bean sprouts may not be obtainable in your area. You may leave them out of the recipe and increase the amount of shredded lettuce to 2 cups. A small green pepper, halved and finely diced, is also a good substitute for the bean sprouts, and will add a bright green color to your dish.

The Legend of the "Singing Rice"

By now, I hope that you are aware that a good Chinese cook does not let anything go to waste, let alone rice, the mainstay of the Chinese diet. But a good cook needs to be more than frugal, or else all misers would be great cooks. The legend of the "Singing Rice" covers the above points well because all the elements are present that legends are made of.

One of the gourmet emperors of China was on a long journey, alone and in disguise. He had traveled far, and the hour was late, when he stopped for the night at the provincial inn. He was very hungry and asked for food, but it was after the dinner hour, and the innkeeper, who was also the cook, had planned the day well so that all the food he had anticipated he would need had indeed been sold. While the innkeeper did not know that he was serving a mighty ruler, being his usual gracious self he treated this unknown guest as a king!

Gracious hospitality must include good food when the guest is hungry. But there was no food left, except a crust of rice that was left at the bottom of the rice pot, and a bowlful of soup, which by this time was very concentrated, at the bottom of the soup kettle. The innkeeper served his emperor the only two things he had left, but he added the most important thing in his kitchen—his own inventiveness.

While neither the rice crust nor the concentrated soup was fit to be eaten alone, he reasoned that they might be good together. But how to carry it off so that this very humble fare would take on a new and tempting guise? Our innkeeper was equal to the task because he was also a good showman; he knew that appearance, smell, and taste are indispensable ingredients to good dining. He added a fourth dimension: sound!

He took the golden-brown rice crust, heated it very hot, put it in his best soup bowl and placed the bowl in front of his guest. There, before the eyes of the emperor, he poured the soup on top of the hot rice. What ensued was a pleasant singing sound as the hot rice crust absorbed the soup. Thus Singing (or Sizzling, if you prefer) Rice was born.

The emperor was delighted. The food was delicious. When he finished eating, he revealed his true identity and invited the cook to his palace and made him the royal chef. There the innkeeper perfected many dishes with the rice-crust base, to the delight of the emperor and us.

I love legends like this, which reveal mankind's nobler attributes. It shows what a fine man this innkeeper was, as good cooks should be. He treated high and low with equal respect, and produced each meal as though it was for a king. It shows how inventive a good cook must be under trying circumstances, and how valuable a calm temperament and a logical mind are. He also knew his craft so well that he recalled hearing the "singing" noises made by liquid when poured into a hot pan, and used that experience in a different context. He was well organized— in this case he didn't have any food when he shouldn't have. And how frugal! You and I might have thrown away that rice crust, and it would have taken future generations to make this discovery. Then, there is such a happy ending, in which skill, goodness, and industry triumphed!

Someday I would love to write a children's book based on this legend; it might make all children want to learn to be good cooks like this ancient Chinese innkeeper. How delightful it might be if we could turn our younger generation into all chefs and no Indians!

Rice Crust for Singing Rice Dishes

The heart of any Singing Rice dish is, of course, the rice crust. Fortunately, it is easy to make since it is the by-product of the regular boiled rice made daily for Chinese meals. It takes a little alteration in the boiled rice recipe for everyday use (page 270), as I usually try to make rice with the least amount of crust. But, if you want to make a Singing Rice dish, you would want to produce the *most* crust from your pot of rice.

To produce this crust, follow the recipe for rice on page 270, but when the rice boils turn the temperature of your stove to medium, instead of low, and keep it at that level for 5 minutes. Then turn the temperature to medium low and allow it to stay there for 30 minutes. By altering the heat in these two steps you should get a thick golden crust on the bottom, after the white, soft rice has been removed for its regular purposes.

Observe these two precautions:

1. A pot with a thick bottom is better for making rice. It will distribute the heat more evenly and lessen the possibility of burning.

2. Smell the vapor coming from the pot frequently during the 5 minutes when it is at medium heat. If you detect the slightest burnt smell, turn the temperature down immediately.

With a little foresight, it is possible to have rice crust on hand at all times to suit your whim for Singing Rice dishes. Rice crust can be stored indefinitely, since it is a cereal. Once I was on a Singing Rice kick and for days I made the thick crust as outlined above each time I cooked rice. I broke up the whole crusts into manageable pieces and stored them in air-tight plastic containers and kept them in my cupboard. Thereafter, I had the "crust" to invite anyone any time to enjoy a Singing Rice dish with me! I compared a rice crust made and stored 10 months earlier with one made the day before in an identical recipe and could not tell the difference in any respect.

This is how you can dry and store the rice crust after you've made it according to directions:

1. While the rice is still hot, scoop out all the soft rice that it is possible to remove. Use this rice for your regular meals. If there is leftover rice, do not return it to the pot with the rice crust in it.

2. Leave pot with the rice crust in it uncovered to dry overnight. The crust will then dry, contract, and separate itself from the pot. This makes it possible to remove the whole crust effortlessly. If by chance part of the crust is still stuck to the bottom of the pan, it can be easily pried loose with a spatula or pancake turner.

3. Break the crust into smaller segments, about 2 inches in diameter. The crust may now be used right away or stored for future use.

Singing Rice Recipes

Once the rice crust is made, a whole range of recipes is open to you, either for soups or regular Chinese dishes. In either case, this method must be followed, since to achieve the "singing" sound a step-by-step procedure is necessary:

Have soup or regular dish prepared and ready. If a regular recipe is used, increase the amount of gravy by adding soup stock, water or chicken broth. The extra gravy is essential, because the "singing" noises are created by the absorption of liquid into the rice crust. Double the amount of water or chicken broth called for in Group III of a recipe. Of course if you are making Singing Rice soups, the liquid is already present, and the only adjustment needed, if any at all, may be to increase the seasoning slightly to allow for the unseasoned rice crust.

Heat deep-frying oil to medium temperature, about 350°-365° F. Drop in chunks of rice crust and fry till golden brown on both sides. Scoop from oil with strainer, drain on absorbent paper, and place in preheated plates or soup bowls enough fried rice crust to cover bottom of dish. Bring to the table the dishes and the food or soup separately, but immediately. Ladle the food or soup onto the rice crust at the table to a hushed audience and let the rice sing for your supper!

Use the following information only as a guide as to what recipes can be used in connection with the Singing Rice crust. I picked the recipes below as being particularly suitable, but almost any dish made with extra gravy may be used, as you will discover. Also, any rich soup (they don't even have to be Chinese) can be used in Singing Rice dishes.

Diced Pork with Vegetables, page 106
Beef with Tomatoes and Green Peppers, page 123
Chicken with Almonds, page 163
Chop Suey Soup, page 260

Congee (Jook)

If there is anything Chinese that is the equivalent of the typically American hot-dog stand, perhaps the "jook" stand comes closest. It serves the same purpose of serving a fast inexpensive meal. And each is distinctive; we may go miles to a particular stand for either the hot dog or the jook because we claim an undisputed superiority for "our" stand. In China, during market days in the rural areas, men actually have pushcarts with umbrellas over them like itinerant hot-dog sellers here. Instead of the choice of "with or without mustard, sauerkraut, chili sauce, or onions" that we have here, you can choose to have your jook plain or "with" a variety of meats, special foods, seafood, or roast meats. This is only possible because the jook base is the same for all and can be kept in one bubbling caldron; it can accommodate the tastes of hundreds of gourmets by the addition of the different ingredients. In large American cities where there is a big Chinese population there will be many little two-by-four luncheonettes which cater to the jook lovers.

Jook or congee is nothing more than rice cooked in much more liquid than usual. In the United States, we use "meat extenders" when we want to economize. In the poor Chinese society, jook is the magic extender of everything. It extends the rice! The Chinese character 粥 for congee "jook" is most revealing. The component 弓 on the left and right is "kung," the symbol for "bow" or "bowman." In between is 米 ("mai," or "rice"). The implication is quite clear; jook is one serving of rice which can be made to feed two robust warriors.

Making congee is so easy that it also extends my time (and yours) to muse: Why can't we have a "congee Klatch" instead of a coffee one? It certainly is more delicious and warming than a cup of coffee. What about serving jook as a late supper after an evening of card playing? It can be that last "one for the road." It is so safe that I can statistically prove no one ever got into a serious accident under the influence of jook.

To make the jook, use raw rice rather than leftover cooked rice. Raw rice can absorb more liquid than cooked rice, and each grain will swell up to become light and fluffy. This produces a better over-all consistency and a velvety smoothness. The

amount of liquid to rice is variable, since different strains of rice vary in thirst. The general ratio should be about 1 cup rice to 6 or 8 pints liquid. Some of the liquid will evaporate as steam. Congee should be the consistency of a thin porridge. Check the pot every half hour or so to see if there is enough liquid. Add water from time to time to maintain the consistency you want, if necessary.

The following recipe is for the basic congee or jook, and then it is converted into beef congee with the addition of sliced marinated steak.

Basic Congee 粥

JOOK

1 *cup raw rice, washed and drained*
3 *quarts soup stock or chicken broth*

Use a large, thick-bottomed saucepan with cover. Put in the soup stock or chicken broth and bring to a vigorous boil. Add the rice. Keep liquid boiling vigorously for 30 minutes with cover off. Lift pot and place asbestos pad on burner to keep rice from burning. Replace pot and turn heat down to a simmer. Cover and cook until the grains of rice disintegrate. This will take 2 to 3 hours.

This recipe will make enough congee to serve 6 to 8. Excess congee may be frozen and kept for months.

Beef Congee

NGAU YUK JOOK

This recipe reduces jook to its absolute fundamentals. From this point on, it can only become more elaborate, since it cannot be further simplified.

Any other meats, *except raw pork,* can be sliced, marinated, and used the same way. Roast pork is delicious in jooks. All seafood, such as shrimp, oysters, fish fillets, can be prepared and used the same way as the beef mentioned below.

Jook, because of its consistency, will be above the boiling point of water, and will remain hot much longer. It is this higher, longer-staying heat which cooks the food in the soup bowls. By the same token, be very careful not to spill any jook on you because it is *hot!*

I	2	*cups thinly sliced lean steak (about ¾ pound)*
II	2	*scallions, chopped (for garnish)*
III	1	*teaspoon monosodium glutamate*
	3	*tablespoons soy sauce*
	2	*tablespoons vegetable oil*
	1	*teaspoon sugar*
	⅛	*teaspoon ground white pepper*

Make a marinade of all the Group III ingredients in a mixing bowl. Add the steak slices and marinate for 1 hour before use.

TO SERVE: Divide the marinated steak into 6 portions and place at bottom of soup bowls. When jook base is ready, bring it to a vigorous boil again. Ladle it on top of the steak and fill soup bowls almost full. Let stand for 5 minutes, stir jook gently, top with the chopped scallions, and serve. The heat of the jook will cook the beef.

14

Noodles and Noodle Dishes

THE name of the inventor of noodles has been lost to history, which is a pity, for he deserves to be immortalized. Perhaps my nationalism is showing, but I like to think that he was a Chinese. It *is* a fact that Italy's glorious pastas originated in China; it is one of the many things Marco Polo brought back to the West. Today, it is fun to try to trace Italian dishes back to their Chinese ancestors: ravioli to won ton, spaghetti to noodles, cannelloni, perhaps, to egg rolls. But, in the manner of all good cooks, the Italians brought their own individuality to bear, and have over the years invented and elaborated on their borrowed basic theme to produce unique dishes.

Noodles have become part of the cuisine of many countries and peoples, and while it may seem heretical to say so, any good homemade noodle, regardless of national origin, can be used in Chinese cooking. It may offend some purists, but even store-bought egg noodles may be used for Chinese noodle dishes, although there will be a slight difference in taste—as mass-produced products seldom are as good as homemade. Actually, the noodle is but the canvas for you to paint your masterpiece on. It's the content and skill you bring to it that make a work of art.

I have, however, included a simple recipe for making Chinese egg noodles, which can also be used for won ton wraps.

Since noodles have been enjoyed by so many people for so long, legends have grown up around them. Here's one I just made up: A Chinese man and his wife were having a meal of noodles together around 450 B.C. As the man picked up a chopstickful of noodles, he gazed at it contemplatively and said to his wife, "You know, life is like a bowl of noodles." A quizzical expression crossed her face and she asked, "Honorable husband, why is life like a bowl of noodles?" "How should I know?" he replied. "Am I Confucius?" Of course this is a direct steal from Sholem Aleichem, the great Jewish writer. But who can prove now that he didn't convert the "bowl of noodles" into "a glass of tea" when he wrote his story? There really is a philosophical concept in the Chinese mystique regarding noodles. They are a symbol of longevity and served as such to celebrate birthdays.

Noodles are great meat extenders. The proportion of noodles to meat is so great that it is like the proverbial soup that one adds water to if unexpected company arrives!

Noodle dishes are meals in themselves. There are actually Chinese restaurants in this country, as in China, which specialize in noodle dishes. In those places you can get 20 or 30 different dishes, made with a variety of noodles. We shall confine ourselves to only a few typical noodle dishes here. Once you've mastered these recipes, there are infinite variations you can make up for yourself.

The Chinese noodles used for the recipes which follow are fresh-made and still soft. They can be bought only in large cities where there are Chinese stores, or by mail. This type of noodles has to be refrigerated. I've experimented very successfully with freezing them. They will keep indefinitely in the freezer. You may buy them in 1- to 5-pound packages, wrapped in wax paper. The won ton and egg roll skins or wrappings are sold in packages in the same stores. Mail-order places where these items may be bought are listed in the back of this book.

If you prefer the convenience of dried noodles, which are easily available everywhere, use thin egg noodles, or spaghettini, and cook according to directions on the package. The recipes do not have to be altered in order to use this type of noodles. Of course, won tons cannot be made without the soft noodle wrappings. Either order these, or make your own according to the recipe on page 314.

THE FOUR BASIC METHODS

The noodles used in these four basic ways are the same soft egg noodles described in the preceding paragraphs and for which a recipe can be found on page 314. It is the different *ways* in which the noodles are cooked that transform them, so that they become four separate and distinct personalities. But, before the transformation can take place, the noodles must be precooked as follows:

Bring a large pot of water to a rolling boil. Immerse the noodles in the boiling water while stirring constantly. When the noodles are done, in 10 minutes or less, they are drained in a colander and rinsed with cold water to remove any loose starch that may still be present. After draining, they are ready for use as a base for noodle soup dishes. This method of cooking makes the noodles very smooth and soft.

Chow Mein

Chow mein means "fried noodles." Since raw noodles cannot be fried directly without turning black, the noodles must be precooked, as described above. The cooked noodles are then made into a nestlike cake. About ½ to ¾ inch of vegetable oil is placed in a frying pan and heated to medium temperature. The nest of noodles is lowered into the oil to brown gently on one side, then the other. When browned, the nest is removed from the pan onto absorbent paper to drain off excess oil. The result is a crunchy crust but a still-soft interior, not unlike a pie with a good crust. Do not confuse this type of noodle with the deep-fried crunchy noodles you get in some Americanized dishes also called "Chow Mein." This kind of deep-fried noodle is seldom used in authentic Chinese cooking.

Lo Mein

The Chinese word "lo" translates into "making a profit." Any food which comes into contact with noodles made this way profits from it indeed! The raw noodle is again precooked. Then, the cooked soft noodle is stir-fried with the different ingredients called for in a recipe. The result is a noodle that is *al dente*, smoothly coated with oil and seasoning, and in harmony with the other ingredients associated with it.

In frying the noodles for these types of dishes, care must be exercised so that a crust is not formed, or the noodles become hard. There should be no gravy or juice apparent in good Lo Mein dishes.

Voy Mein and Woh Mein

Voy mein can best be described as double-boiled noodles. They are first precooked, rinsed, and drained. They are then boiled again in a concentrated high soup stock so the noodles absorb the stock's flavor. The soup stock is then drained off, and not used in the final voy mein recipe. Now, these deliciously flavored soft drained noodles are used as a base to receive the other separately cooked ingredients, which are poured on *top* of it, and not mixed into it, to complete the dish.

Woh mein is basically voy mein with the stock retained. It is really a soup, but it fits comfortably into this section on noodle dishes. For it, the noodles are also precooked, and then reboiled in a high soup stock. The addition of ingredients to the noodles and stock completes the dish.

Yee Foo Mein

The legendary noble Yee created this method of cooking noodles, which still bears his name. Basically, the idea is to deep fry the precooked noodles until they are golden and crunchy, then to soften them again in salted boiling water. All this effort is not wasted. The noodles, having gone through this double process, are qualitatively different from either boiled noodles or fried noodles. If you can imagine such a thing, they are un-crunchy crisp noodles. The Chinese prize this dish so highly that they specify it as a noodle base for any number of noodle dishes at the extra cost of a dollar or more in restaurants. The directions for cooking the noodles will be found in the recipe for Yee Foo Mein (page 308).

QUANTITIES FOR PRECOOKING

The amount of noodles you will need for a given number of people varies with recipes and appetites and whether the noodles are to be used for a meal in themselves. As a guide, 1 pound of raw soft (or homemade) egg noodles will produce about 3 to 4 cups cooked noodles. If you use dried noodles, the ratio is about 1 pound to about 5 cups cooked noodles. The exact amount of noodles needed will be given for each recipe. Both dried and soft noodles must be precooked before use with any recipe here. To do so, bring a large pot of water to a vigorous boil. Allow 3 to 4 quarts of water for each pound of dried noodles, or every 4 or 5 cups of fresh noodles. The same amount of water can be used for 1 pound of store-bought soft Chinese egg noodles. Add 1 tablespoon salt. Shake noodles so that they are not matted into a ball before immersing in the water. If you use dried noodles, add a little at a time to the boiling water. Stir to keep from sticking. Test noodles for doneness by lifting one from the pot and squeezing with fingers or tasting it to make sure there is no hard center or starchy taste left. When they are done (10 to 15 minutes), drain and rinse noodles in cold water to remove any loose starch. Be sure to stir the noodles so that all parts cool evenly in the rinse water. Drain the noodles dry in a colander or strainer and they are ready for Chinese cooking.

Noodles with Pork and Tomatoes   番茄會麵

FAAN KE VOY MEIN

I think this dish must be copied from the Italian way of using tomatoes in their spaghetti, since tomatoes were relative late comers into Chinese cuisine, at least to the district from which my family came. If my hunch is correct, that the Chinese adapted this recipe from the Italians, then it is a fair and happy exchange between our two peoples.

I   4   *cups cooked noodles, rinsed and drained (above)†*
     1½   *cups chicken broth or high soup stock*
     ⅛   *teaspoon salt*

	2	*cups shredded lean fresh pork (about ¾ pounds)†*
II	2	*medium-size tomatoes, red but firm, cut into ¼-inch cubes*
	1	*cup shredded celery hearts*
	1	*cup shredded fresh asparagus or green beans*
	3	*scallions, 2-inch lengths, shredded, including green ends*
III	3	*tablespoons oyster sauce or 2 tablespoons dark soy sauce*
	1	*tablespoon cornstarch*
IV	3	*tablespoons vegetable oil*
		Sprigs of Chinese parsley or chopped scallions, for garnish (optional)

Place the chicken broth and salt in a saucepan. Bring to a boil. Add the precooked noodles and heat in broth for 2-3 minutes. Drain off chicken broth and save. Keep noodles warm in pan. Add the ingredients in Group III to the chicken broth and put aside.

Heat wok or frying pan hot and dry. Add the oil. Add the shredded pork and stir-fry 2 minutes (shredded pork cooks quickly because it's so thin). Add all the items from Group II and fry for 2 minutes. Cover and cook 1 minute more. Lift cover and add the chicken broth mixture. Stir until gravy has thickened. Turn off heat.

Place noodles in deep serving dish. Pour vegetables, meat, and gravy over the noodles. Top with chopped scallions or parsley and serve.

SUBSTITUTIONS AND VARIATIONS

This dish is very similar to Chow Mein. You can also use Yee Foo Mein noodles (page 308) instead of the boiled noodles.

Beef, ham, abalone, or other shellfish may be used in place of the pork.

Abalone and Roast Pork Woh Mein

HOI MEI CHA SUI WOH MEIN   海味叉燒窩麵

This is a wonderful dish for after theater or a late evening snack. It is so delicious and so simple to make. The noodles can be cooked beforehand, and all the remaining ingredients cut up in advance and refrigerated. Chinese often eat this dish at night because it has all the required elements for a complete meal in itself without being heavy or too rich for comfortable slumber later.

Abalone is a particularly happy ingredient in combination with roast pork in this dish. It is not fishy and its flavor is sweet and subtle. The texture of abalone is smooth and firm, but not tough or rubbery—unless it is overcooked. Canned abalone has already been thoroughly cooked, so all you need to do to it is warm it up *without* boiling. Abalone comes in cans of several sizes. The smaller cans are preferable because you can use it up for one recipe so that there is no leftover problem. The Japanese variety of abalone is best, if available. Be sure to use the liquid in which it is canned for broths or gravies, since it is filled with flavor. Abalone can be bought in most fancy groceries, and of course in all Chinese and Japanese grocery stores. Have a few cans on hand. You will find it a friendly, useful aid to your Chinese cooking.

The soup stock must really be of "high" quality for this dish. Since the rest of the recipe is so easy, it is worthwhile to concentrate your effort on the soup stock. You will find a basic recipe on page 253 for making high soup stock. The addition of a few dried Chinese mushrooms while making the stock will give it even more flavor.

4   *cups cooked noodles, rinsed and drained page (292)*
1   *small can of abalone sliced thin, roughly ⅛ by 1 by 2 inches in size*

1 *cup thin-sliced roast pork*
⅛ *teaspoon sesame oil*
6 *cups high soup stock*
2 *scallions, diced fine*

Bring soup stock to a boil. Add the sesame oil. Add the noodles and bring stock to a boil again. Turn the heat down to low. Remove the noodles and divide equally into soup bowls. Put the roast pork and abalone slices in the broth to warm up for 3 to 4 minutes. (Don't let stock boil.) Arrange slices of the roast pork and abalone on top of noodles. Pour the hot broth over the meats and noodles. Top with the diced scallions and serve. Serves 4 to 6.

SUBSTITUTIONS AND VARIATIONS

This is a good dish to use up certain leftovers in your refrigerator. If there are a few cooked shrimps from shrimp cocktails, a bit of roast beef or cooked chicken, or a few shredded string beans or carrots, do add them to this dish. They will give it variety and color.

Young Jewel Woh Mein

YEUNG CHAU WOH MEIN

This noodle soup dish is a glorified version of Roast Pork Woh Mein. By the very nature of its glorification, it is transformed into a party dish, and can be served at any meal. It is particularly attractive for a late-evening snack for 6 to 8 people. It is even more fun if you serve it Chinese style, with chopsticks, an empty bowl, and a porcelain spoon for each guest. Bring the dish out in a large tureen in all its glory. Place it in the center of the table and let your guests help themselves with their chopsticks. Be sure to provide a soup ladle so the diners can easily and quickly transfer the broth into their bowls.

Woh Mein dishes should not be completely made beforehand and then just reheated. The separate ingredients should not be allowed to swim together for any length of time or they will lose their individual character (familiarity breeds contempt?). However, all the preparations, including the blanching of the chicken livers and shrimps may be done, and all ingredients held in readiness for the final assembly. Then you will truly have a symphony, where each instrument plays its part.

This dish must have a very good soup stock or chicken broth, perfectly adjusted and seasoned to your taste, to be at its best.

I	4	*cups cooked noodles, rinsed and drained (page 292)*
	8	*medium-size shrimps, shelled and deveined*
	2	*chicken livers, cut into quarters*
	1	*small can abalone, sliced (add liquid to broth)*†
	1	*cup thin-sliced roast pork*
	1	*cup thin-sliced cooked chicken breasts*

II	4	*to 6 Chinese mushrooms, presoaked and sliced (add liquid to broth)*
	1	*box French-style frozen green beans, thawed*†
	½	*cup thin-sliced bamboo shoots (about ¾ to 1-inch in diameter)*
	3	*scallions, finely diced, including green ends*

III	1½	*quarts high soup stock or chicken broth, seasoned to taste*

In a small saucepan place 1 cup water and 1 teaspoon salt. Bring to a boil and add the raw chicken livers and shrimps to blanch. Bring to a boil again for 1 minute. Remove shrimps and livers. Discard liquid. In a large saucepan bring soup stock to a boil. Add the mushrooms, green beans, and noodles. Bring to a boil again and add everything else except scallions. Let simmer for 2 minutes. Ladle into large soup tureen, top with scallions, and serve. Serves 6 to 8.

SUBSTITUTIONS AND VARIATIONS

This dish can be a complete meal in itself for 2 people, or used as a soup for 6 to 8 at a dinner party. Since so many ingredients are used, many substitutions can be made. Instead of abalone, if it is not available, a can of crabmeat or a package of frozen king crab meat is a wonderful change. If you have a package of frozen snow peas, use it in place of the string beans. It is even better and more "Chinesey." Be sure to thaw beforehand. Naturally fresh snow peas cannot be surpassed. Use a cup of them, ends removed, washed, and added to the broth just before serving.

No two chefs I know make this dish exactly alike. The ingredients seem to say to you, "Make us into a masterpiece!" This is both a pleasure and a challenge, since it offers you almost complete creative freedom.

Spiced Beef Chow Mein   牛肉炒麵

NGAU YUK CHOW MEIN

If you've never had *real* Chinese Chow Mein, this recipe will be a good introduction. It is representative of Cantonese Chow Mein dishes and once you've tasted it cooked this way it is doubtful if you will ever go back to the rather doubtful Americanized version, made with brittle deep-fried noodles.

The distinctive feature of Cantonese Chow Mein is that a "nest" of cooked noodles is fried until a crunchy crust is formed on the outside, leaving it still soft and smooth in the middle. The other ingredients are ladled over the noodles but not combined with them. This is more like the Chinese way of eating rice, in which the rice is eaten from a separate bowl and the other foods are picked up with chopsticks a bit at a time and placed in the mouth. In this fashion, the diner can taste the separate flavors of each ingredient rather than having all the flavors become blurred by being mixed with the rice.

The beef has to be marinated ahead of time. You may adjust the hotness of the dish by controlling the amount of Tabasco used. The amount listed in the recipe makes a mildly hot gravy. More gravy is needed than usual, since the noodles will absorb quite a bit of it.

I   4   *cups cooked noodles, rinsed and drained (page 292)*
     2   *cups shredded steak (about ¾ pound) (shreds about ⅛ inch thick, 2 inches long)†*
     2   *cups fresh bean sprouts†*
     1   *cup shredded snow peas†*

II   1   *small can sliced button mushrooms*
     2   *scallions, cut into 2-inch lengths and shredded, including green ends*
     2   *slices fresh ginger, shredded*
     1   *clove garlic, minced*

III 1   *teaspoon sugar*
     1   *tablespoon cornstarch*
     1   *teaspoon monosodium glutamate*
     3   *tablespoons oyster sauce, or 2 tablespoons light soy sauce*
     2   *cups soup stock or chicken broth*

IV   1½   *cups vegetable oil*
     ⅛   *teaspoon salt*
     2   *tablespoons sherry*

MARINADE FOR BEEF

1   *tablespoon dark soy sauce*
½   *teaspoon monosodium glutamate*
1   *tablespoon vegetable oil*
¼   *teaspoon Tabasco*

Mix together marinade in a bowl and put in shredded beef to marinate for 1 hour. Drain before cooking.

Preheat oven to 200° F.

Mix together ingredients in Group III and put aside.

Use a medium-size frying pan. Heat hot and dry. Add the oil in IV. Heat oil to medium temperature (350°-365° F.). Put the noodles into the oil and push them into the middle of the pan with a turner so they form a round nestlike mass. Fry until a golden-brown crust is formed on the bottom (about 5 to 7 minutes; check by slightly lifting the "nest" to see). Gently turn the noodles over to fry the other side. When done, remove the nest of noodles onto absorbent paper to drain. Place in preheated oven to keep warm while draining.

Heat wok or another frying pan hot and dry. Scoop from first frying pan about 2 tablespoons oil used to fry the noodles and place in the pan that is now being used. Add the salt, then the ginger and garlic, then the shredded beef.

Fry while rapidly stirring for ½ minute. Turn down heat, remove the beef into a bowl and put aside.

Turn heat up again. Put in bean sprouts, mushrooms, and scallions. Stir-fry for 2 minutes. Add the sherry and quickly cover the wok or pan. Cook 1 minute more. Stir in the sauce mixture in Group III until the gravy thickens. Put back the beef; and the shredded snow peas. Mix well and turn off heat.

Take the nest of noodles from the oven and place on serving platter. Ladle the meat, vegetables, and gravy on top of the noodles and serve. Serves 2 (if this is the only dish).

SUBSTITUTIONS AND VARIATIONS

Shredded tender celery hearts make a good substitute for bean sprouts, and finely shredded green peppers may substitute for snow peas if these items are not available.

Cooked shrimps, lobster meat, or fillet of pike in the same quantity may be substituted for the beef. Then it will become a

Seafood Chow Mein. Lobster meat and shrimps need not be marinated, but the slices of pike should be for about 15 minutes before cooking.

King Crab Lo Mein 蟹肉撈麵

HAAI YUK LO MEIN

The great cuisines of the world are like highly talented people. They are sophisticated, temperamental, and full of contradictions. You just cannot make rules for them and confine them to a narrow mold. We have just had a recipe for Cantonese Chow Mein in which the aim is *not to mix* the noodles with the other ingredients, and, lo and behold, we have this Lo Mein recipe in which the aim is to *mix* the ingredients with the noodles.

Perhaps it is such elusiveness and contradiction that give Chinese food its magic. Science has immutable laws, but art cannot be chained. Instead of considering these contradictions as flaws, let's see them as enchanting inconsistency. More love matches may be broken up by predictable behavior than by the mystery of uncertainty!

The quality to seek in Lo Mein is a glossy light tan color; the noodles must be firm and dry, but not browned or crisp.

King crab is so widely available in frozen form that I have chosen it over the softer and more flaky lump crabmeat, which may not be found in your locality. Be sure to remove the hard cartilage embedded in the meat of the king crab legs. You can shred the meat by pulling it apart with your fingers.

I
4 *cups cooked noodles, rinsed and drained (page 292)*
1 *package (12 ounces) frozen king crabmeat, defrosted and shredded†*
1 *package frozen French-style green beans, thawed*
2 *cups fresh bean sprouts*

3 *scallions, cut into 2-inch lengths, shredded*
3 *or 4 medium Chinese mushrooms, presoaked and shredded*

II   1 *slice ginger, shredded*
     1 *clove garlic, minced*

III 1 *teaspoon monosodium glutamate*
     1 *teaspoon sugar*
     ¼ *cup soy sauce*

IV   ¾ *cup vegetable oil*
     ⅛ *teaspoon salt*
     ¼ *teaspoon sesame oil*
     2 *tablespoons sherry*
     3 *or 4 sprigs of Chinese parsley, for garnish (optional)*

Mix together ingredients in Group III and put aside.

Heat wok or pan hot and dry. Add 3 tablespoons of the oil. Add the salt and the sesame oil. Put in ginger and garlic to brown first, then all the other vegetables. Stir and cook for 1 minute over high heat. Add the sherry. Cover and cook 1 minute longer. Turn off heat. Remove vegetables, and drain off and discard any juice from wok or pan. Put aside.

Heat wok or pan hot and dry again. Put in remainder of the oil. Turn heat to medium. Add the noodles and stir constantly to heat through and to coat the noodles with oil for 2-3 minutes. Add the crabmeat and cooked vegetables and mix thoroughly. Add the Group III sauce mixture and stir until noodles become one even color. Shut off heat. Place on serving platter and top with parsley and serve. Serves 2 (if this is the only dish).

SUBSTITUTIONS AND VARIATIONS

This is a basic Lo Mein dish. By substituting the same quantity of cooked shrimp, it becomes Shrimp Lo Mein. It is also possible to use roast pork, chicken, fish fillets, clams, or whatever you care to combine with the noodles and vegetables, as long as they're used with the Group III sauce to give them flavor. (Sometimes I am too rash and make too inclusive statements. I've never made a Banana Lo Mein! I dare you!)

Velvet Chicken Stir-Fried Noodles   滑鷄撈麵

VOT GAI LO MEIN

This recipe is easy to make and delicious. The shredded smooth chicken is made beforehand as outlined in the instructions on page 167. It can even be made the day before at your leisure, and refrigerated. This applies to cooking the noodles, too. Many working Chinese women (and men) often partially prepare their meals a day or two ahead, during spare moments. On their return from a hard day's work, tired and hungry, the effort and time needed to cook dinner are thereby happily reduced.

The shreds of smooth chicken blend almost invisibly with the shape and color of the noodles and bean sprouts. Yet, when it is eaten, its texture and flavor come as a pleasant surprise to the taste buds.

I   2   *cups shredded cooked velvet chicken (see page 167)*
     4   *cups cooked noodles, rinsed and drained (see page 292)*
     2   *cups fresh bean sprouts*
     3   *scallions, cut into 2-inch lengths and shredded*
     1   *cup shredded snow peas (fresh or frozen)*

II   1   *small can sliced mushrooms, drained*
     1   *slice ginger, shredded*
     1   *clove garlic, minced*

III 1   *teaspoon monosodium glutamate*
     1   *teaspoon sugar*
     ¼   *cup soy sauce or oyster sauce*

¼ *cup chicken broth or water*

3 *or 4 sprigs Chinese parsley, for garnish (optional)*

I V   ¾ *cup vegetable oil*

Mix together ingredients in Group III and put aside.

Heat wok or pan hot and dry. Add 3 tablespoons of the oil. Put in the ginger and garlic to brown, then quickly add all the other vegetables. Stir and cook for 1 minute over high heat. Cover and cook for 1 minute longer. Turn off heat. Remove all the cooked vegetables from wok or pan. Drain and discard liquid from the vegetables and put vegetables aside.

Heat wok or pan hot and dry again. Put in remainder of the oil. Turn heat down to medium. Add the noodles while stirring constantly to heat and coat them with oil, for 2-3 minutes. Add the shredded chicken and the cooked vegetables and mix thoroughly with the noodles. Add the Group III sauce mixture and stir until the noodles become one even color. Shut off heat. Place on serving platter, top with parsley and serve.

Won Ton Soup　　　　雲吞湯

WAN T'AN TONG

Won tons are really international in their many guises. The Jewish people have one version called "kreplach" and the Italian people have theirs, called "ravioli." Other nations have their versions of meat-filled dumplings which are akin to the Chinese won tons. Basically, all the above items are alike in that they are small dough-wrapped meat balls.

Won ton soup is a meal in itself, and no other dishes need to be served with it. Won tons are served in the broth in which they are cooked, topped with a generous serving of cooked meats, plus other ingredients. Thus, a dish is called "Roast Pork Won Ton" if it is garnished with pork; it would become "Roast Duck

Won Ton" if it were topped with roast duck. The won ton itself is made with the same ingredients in each case. Won tons are interchangeable with noodles in soup dishes. Thus, you can get Young Jewel Won Ton instead of Young Jewel Woh Mein (page 295) just by substituting won tons for the noodles.

One very nice variation is to deep-fry the raw won tons before adding to the soup. It's more trouble, but there is a qualitative change, which may be worth the extra trouble to you. The rationale for frying, then softening the won tons is the same as for the noodles in Yee Foo Chow Mein (page 310).

Won tons are very easy to make at home if you can get the "skin" or dough wrappings from a Chinese store or noodle manufacturer. They come in 1-pound packages. It is a lot more trouble to make the dough yourself, but if you have the inclination and time, or if you cannot readily buy the dough sheets, you can use the recipe for homemade egg noodles on page 314, or your own favorite recipe for egg noodles. After rolling out the noodle dough as thin as possible, cut it into 3- or 4-inch squares. Allow from 8 to 10 won tons to a diner.

The filling for the won tons is made as follows (enough to serve 4-6 people with 6 to 10 won tons each). The filling for each won ton will be bigger than you'll find in restaurant won tons. This is a better ratio of meat to dough, which restaurants find too expensive.

½ *pound lean pork*
¼ *pound shrimp, shelled and deveined*
½ *cup water chestnuts*
3 *scallions*
½ *teaspoon salt*
1 *teaspoon monosodium glutamate*
1 *teaspoon cornstarch*
⅛ *teaspoon white pepper*

Chop or grind all the above ingredients together. Mix thoroughly after chopping or grinding.

WRAPPING THE WON TONS

Have your won ton skins ready, whether they are bought or homemade.

Beat 2 egg whites well, and place in a small bowl. This is used for sealing the dough around the filling.

Place a teaspoonful of meat filling in the middle of a piece of dough skin. Fold the dough diagonally from one corner to

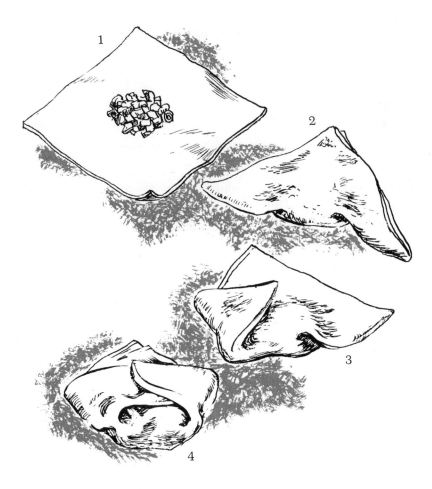

the other to form a triangle. Moisten the two contact surfaces of the triangle with egg white and press together to seal (see illustration page 305).

The raw won tons are now ready for cooking. They should be parboiled in a pot of boiling water for about 3-4 minutes before they are transferred to the broth and served.

I've given you the basic information of how to make the won ton first because they must be ready to cook before you start to assemble a recipe using them. Following is a complete recipe for a popular won ton soup. A good broth is an absolute essential to this dish.

Roast Pork Won Ton　　　　　　义燒雲吞

CHA SUI WAN T'AN

This recipe is for a meal-in-itself dish. No other dishes need be made to supplement it. If it is to be served as a first course, cut the recipe in half—or call in more people!

I　40　*won tons, ready to cook*
　　1　*pound Chinese roast pork, sliced thin†*
　　2　*quarts high soup stock or rich chicken broth*

II　1　*cup thin-sliced bamboo shoots (about 1 by 2 inches)*
　　1　*small can sliced mushrooms, including the liquid*

III　2　*teaspoons light soy sauce*
　　⅛　*teaspoon ground white pepper*

IV　⅛　*teaspoon sesame oil*
　　3　*quarts water, 1 tablespoon salt (for boiling won tons)*
　　½　*cup chopped scallions including green ends, for garnish*

Bring soup stock or chicken broth to a boil in a large saucepan. Add the bamboo shoots, mushrooms and liquid, soy sauce, pepper, and sesame oil. Taste broth and adjust seasoning if necessary. Turn heat to low to keep hot.

In another pot, boil the water and salt. When boiling vigorously, add the won tons a few at a time. As the dough turns translucent and the won tons float, remove from water with slotted spoon and transfer to the pot with the broth. Repeat until all the won tons have been cooked.

Bring the broth to a boil and cook 2 minutes. Turn off heat immediately. Ladle the won tons and vegetables into a large tureen. Scatter the slices of roast pork on top of the broth, then scatter the scallions on top as a garnish. (The hot soup will warm the slices of roast pork, but will not rob them of their flavor, because they are put in at the last minute.)

Take tureen to table and serve soup in individual bowls. Provide light soy sauce at table and small condiment dishes for it so the diners may dip the won tons into the soy sauce if they wish. Serves 4 to 6 people.

SUBSTITUTIONS AND VARIATIONS

Fresh pork may be used instead of roast pork. Use 2 cups lean pork and slice thin. Bring the soup stock or chicken broth to a boil. Add the sliced fresh pork and simmer for 3 minutes before adding the vegetables and turning heat down to low.

Shrimp, lobster, or crabmeat in addition to the pork will upgrade the dish.

If you wish to fry the won tons before putting into the broth, heat deep-frying oil to medium hot (350°-365° F.). Drop the won tons in one at a time. As soon as the won tons turn golden brown, remove from oil and place in prepared soup stock and serve. They need no further cooking.

Favorite Noodles of Noble Yee 伊府麵

YEE FOO MEIN

In the old days in China, the wealthy masters and mistresses may never have ventured near a kitchen, yet some were considered great cooks. Yee Foo was a noble in the emperor's court. He was a noodle nut, and much of his time was spent in concocting new noodle dishes. His fame has endured through the centuries because of this preoccupation.

Although Noble Yee never cooked in his life, still he was truly a gourmet, and he left no stone unturned, and no sweat unsweated (by his cooks), to make the perfect noodle dish. He deserved the acclaim for his inventiveness, but I think his unsung cooks should have gotten some credit too! Once I was invited to a cookout by a "Sunday chef." The food was delicious, and the chef showed great skill, but I knew from experience that his wife did all the shopping, preparing, and seasoning (as well as the cleaning up). I said to him, "From now on, I am going to call you Noble Yee. He was a great Chinese gourmet!" My friend was very pleased.

YEE FOO NOODLE BASE

The instructions here are only for cooking the noodles, which are the *base* for various noodle dishes. The noodles used must be the Chinese soft egg noodles. You can buy them in a Chinese grocery or make them at home (see recipe on page 314).

4 *cups cooked noodles, rinsed and drained*
  Oil for deep frying (about 2 quarts)
1 *tablespoon salt*
3 *quarts boiling water*

Preheat oven to 200° F. After the noodles have been pre-cooked, rinsed, and drained, put them in a colander or wire strainer to let air-dry for at least 1 hour. Lift the noodles occasionally to expose the noodles in the middle so they can dry too.

Heat deep-frying oil to medium (350°-365° F.). Lower all the noodles as a cluster gently into the oil. (A Chinese bamboo-handled strainer is very helpful.) Deep fry until one side is golden brown. Gently turn noodles over to brown the other side. (The noodle cluster will float, so only one side gets done at a time.)

Remove noodles from oil onto absorbent paper to drain. Add the salt to the boiling water in a saucepan. Gently lower the fried noodles into the boiling water for 1 minute. Remove noodles from pot and drain dry. Keep warm in preheated oven until ready to use.

The justification for this extra work is that the noodles really taste different and better. Noodles made this way seem to combine the nice characteristics of boiling and frying. The frying process gives the noodles a nutty flavor, while boiling them again makes them soft without being sticky or soggy.

The noodles are now ready for whatever use you wish to make of them.

A recipe using this noodle base follows:

Yee Foo Noodle Chow Mein 伊府炒麵

YEE FOO CHOW MEIN

This noodle dish using clams is similar in spirit to the Italian white clam sauce used over spaghetti. Both the Chinese and Italian versions are delicious. Clams must not be cooked too long, or else they'll be tough and rubbery.

I	4	*cups cooked noodles, à la Yee Foo (above), kept warm in oven*
	2	*dozen cherrystone clams†*
	2	*cups fresh bean sprouts*
	1	*cup shredded onions*
	½	*cup shredded canned pimentos*
	1	*small can sliced mushrooms, drained*
	1	*cup shredded snow peas*
II	2	*cloves garlic, minced†*
III	½	*teaspoon ground white pepper*
	1	*teaspoon sugar*
	1	*tablespoon cornstarch*
	1	*teaspoon monosodium glutamate*
	2	*tablespoons light soy sauce*
	1½	*cups cooled clam broth (from the steamed clams)*
IV	¼	*cup vegetable oil*
	⅛	*teaspoon sesame oil*

⅛   *teaspoon salt*
2   *tablespoons sherry*
     Chinese parsley or chopped scallions, for garnish

Scrub and rinse the clams clean and place in a saucepan with ½ cup water. Cover and bring to a boil for 5 minutes. Lift cover to check if clam shells have opened (when a clam will open varies). As soon as the clams are partially open, turn off heat at once. Remove clams from shells into a bowl to cool. Save the clam broth. Slice clams into thin strips.

Have all the vegetables cut and ready. Mix the sauce in Group III.

Heat wok or pan hot and dry. Add the vegetable oil and sesame oil. Add the salt. Put in the garlic and stir-fry quickly until browned. Add all the vegetables in Group I, except the snow peas. Stir-fry for 2 minutes. Add the sherry and cover quickly. Cook 1 minute longer. Stir in Group III sauce mixture and cook until gravy thickens. Add the clams and snow peas. Mix well and turn heat off at once.

Remove the noodles from oven and place on serving platter. Ladle the clam and vegetable mixture on top of the noodles. Top with Chinese parsley or chopped scallions. Serves 2 (if this is the only dish).

SUBSTITUTIONS AND VARIATIONS

Using more garlic makes this dish closer in taste to the Italian clam sauce.

A red sauce can be made by the addition of ¼ cup tomato paste.

Fish fillets, shrimp, lobster meat can be substituted for the clams. Canned clams are acceptable, but the dish will not be as good. Use 1 can of clams for this recipe. Make sure the clams have not been preserved in vinegar. If so, they cannot be used for this recipe because the vinegar will overpower the delicate flavors.

Vermicelli 粉絲

FON SZ

The Chinese do not consider vermicelli, or cellophane noodles, as noodles. However, fon sz are so much in the noodle spirit that I want to discuss them here. What distinguishes the fon sz from noodles is that they are not made from flour but from bean paste. They are white, translucent, very slender noodles, sold in cellophane bags or boxes. They look not unlike white yarn, since they have been wound around a special spinning wheel during their manufacture. "Fon sz" literally means "silken threads made of powder." They are dry and brittle, but will become soft and pliable when soaked in cold water for 15-20 minutes before cooking. Unlike noodles, which are left long and uncut for cooking, fon sz should be cut into 2-inch lengths by knife or scissors before cooking.

Like all specialties, fon sz is made by specialists, who pass the knowledge on from father to son. The best fon sz makers are said to be a Chinese minority group called "Haak Ga." (It was not until recently that I realized that there are minority groups in China. We all look so Chinese!)

Fon sz recipes are varied by the change of major ingredients with which they are associated in cooking. You can use your own ingenuity and make a host of other fon sz dishes—by using your noodle! The following fon sz dish is just to get you started. Other possible combinations are mentioned in Substitutions and Variations.

312

Vermicelli with Dried Shrimps 粉絲蝦米

FON SZ HA MAI

This recipe will not only introduce you to vermicelli cooked the Chinese way, but it is intended to acquaint you with dried shrimp. The Chinese for centuries have used dehydration as a way of preserving food. In a typical Chinese grocery store you will find hundreds of dried items on sale. The most common seafoods used in this form are dried shrimp, scallops, and oysters. It is good to have a pound of dried shrimp in your larder. Choose the medium-large size of shelled dry shrimp (they come shelled or with shells in several different sizes). They can be bought only from Chinese or Japanese grocery stores. Keep them in a tightly covered jar and they will stay good indefinitely. Dried shrimp must be soaked in water for at least an hour before use.

Besides being used for this recipe, dried shrimp are added to soups, congee, and steamed dishes to enhance their flavor.

I   4   cups vermicelli (fon sz)
    1   cup dried shrimp†
    2   eggs, slightly beaten
    3   scallions, cut into 2-inch lengths and shredded,
        including green ends
    2   cups lettuce, shredded

II 2   slices fresh ginger, shredded
    1   clove garlic, minced

III 1   teaspoon sugar
    1   teaspoon monosodium glutamate
    3   tablespoons light soy sauce
    2   tablespoons water

IV ¾   cup vegetable oil
        Pinch of salt

Rinse shrimp and soak for 1 hour in water. Drain and discard water.

Soak the vermicelli for 15-20 minutes in cold water. Drain dry and cut into 2-inch lengths.

Mix together ingredients in Group III and put aside.

Heat wok or pan hot and dry. Add 2 tablespoons of the oil. Add the pinch of salt. Turn heat to medium low, add the slightly beaten eggs, and scramble. Shred the eggs with the turner; remove from wok or pan and put aside.

Add 2 more tablespoons oil to wok and fry the ginger and garlic till browned. Add the drained shrimp and stir-fry 2 minutes. Turn heat to high and add the remainder of the oil and the fon sz and scallions and stir-fry for 3 minutes. Put back the eggs and add the shredded lettuce. Add the sauce mixture from Group III. Mix well and turn off heat at once.

There should be no gravy in this dish. The fon sz should be dry but soft. Serves 2 (if this is the only dish).

SUBSTITUTIONS AND VARIATIONS
Fresh shrimp may be used in place of the dried variety. Use 1 pound fresh shrimp, shelled, split in halves, and blanched before use. (See page 64 on how to blanch.)

The recipes for Spiced Beef Chow Mein, King Crab Lo Mein and the Yee Foo Noodle Chow Mein can be easily adapted for this fon sz dish.

Homemade Noodles and Won Ton Wraps　麵皮

MEIN PEI

The convenience of mass-produced products need not be emphasized here. Very few (if any) of us would want to grow our own wheat, harvest it, mill the flour, and then bake our own bread nowadays. This is true with Chinese egg noodles and the wrappings (skin) for won ton or dumplings. Chinese housewives buy these items from noodle manufacturers. But suppose you cannot buy them where you are? Dried American egg noodles are a very good substitute for the soft Chinese variety. But there is nothing I know of in the American market which can be used for won ton skins. Therefore, the all-purpose recipe is included below for both noodles and the won ton wrappings. They are easy to make and are better than the ones you can buy. Excess noodles may be kept refrigerated in airtight jars for a week, or may be frozen for months. This is also true of the ones you buy from Chinese grocery stores and noodle makers.

3   *eggs*
1   *teaspoon salt*
3   *tablespoons cold water*
2½   *cups sifted all-purpose flour*
     Extra flour for the rolling-out process

Crack the eggs into a mixing bowl. Add the salt and water and beat mixture lightly. Stir in the sifted flour with a wooden spoon and mix until a stiff dough forms. Knead with your hands if the dough is too stiff for the spoon. Divide the dough into 4 parts.

Cover a cutting board (or bread board) with a smooth cloth or linen dish towel. Sprinkle a little flour evenly on the cloth. Place a piece of dough on the cloth and sprinkle some flour on the dough. Roll out dough as thin as possible. Sprinkle more flour on dough from time to time to prevent it from sticking to rolling pin. Remove the noodle sheet and place on paper towels. Repeat until all 4 pieces of dough have been rolled out. Allow the sheets of noodle to dry to a semi-stiff state. (It will take an hour or more depending on weather conditions. The sheets should not be limp and stretchable, yet should not crack when folded.)

When the noodle sheets are dry enough, take one sheet at a time to a cutting board. If you are going to make them into noodles, sprinkle a little flour on top of the noodle sheet. Rub the flour evenly over it with the palm of your hand. Roll the sheet into a loose scroll. With a sharp knife or Chinese cleaver, cut across the scroll into very thin rings (about $\frac{1}{16}$ inch). Shake out the rings into long noodles.

If the noodle sheets are to be used for won ton or dumplings, trim the uneven edges of the sheets to form a square or rectangle. Sprinkle a little flour on top and spread with the palm of hand evenly. (This is to keep the sheets of noodles from sticking together when stacked.) Cut the trimmed sheets into about 3½-inch squares.

Follow directions in particular recipe for cooking the noodles or won tons. This recipe will make 5 to 6 cups of cooked noodles, or about 3 dozen won ton wrappings.

15

Jim's A-Shame-to-Throw-Away Pages

I N practically all households, there is a magical space called the "A-Shame-to-Throw-Away Drawer." You may know it by another name. This storage place is a veritable cornucopia of indispensable treasures for which one doesn't have an immediate use.

These are my A-Shame-to-Throw-Away Pages. They are not afterthoughts, because I wanted to include them from the beginning, but somehow they didn't quite fit in other pages. Each A-Shame-to-Throw-Away item is labeled, but they are dumped together haphazardly as such things should be. Rummage through them and you may find ingredients suitable for after-dinner rumination as well as for cooking.

Food, Art, and Man

In the history of man no single subject has occupied him more than the quest for food. But to prepare and truly enjoy food, man must have the peace and leisure required for an art.

Some of the most beautiful works of art created since the dawn of mankind are the cave paintings in the Lascaux caves in France. Beautifully drawn and colored, these cave paintings depict the animals which abounded in southern France twenty to forty millennia ago. The genius of the artists who decorated those rough cave walls is a permanent testament to man's greatness.

Man had come into existence long before the Lascaux man. Why did they not produce great works of art? Anthropologists conjecture that the answer may be food. Like his ancestors, the Lascaux man hunted for his food, but with one difference. Other hunter societies lived always in the shadow of hunger. If they made a kill, they had a feast; otherwise they went hungry. The Lascaux man, on the other hand, lived in a warm, pleasant climate, with no human enemies and an abundance of food. The animals he hunted were in such great supply that it was almost as if he had his own herd (though actually the domestication of animals did not occur until thousands of years later). Thus, all his energies were not consumed in the search for food, and he had the time and energy to spare for the creation of a work of art.

The world's great cuisines must have been born under similar circumstances. Only when man's energies are not all bent on a struggle for survival can art flourish, whether it be painting or cooking.

Chinese Stores—The Last Refuge from Supermarkets

If you are lucky enough to live in a city where there is a Chinatown, you have the added advantage of buying chicken already cooked in several styles. In some Chinese stores where barbecued pork, roast ducks, and other cooked delicacies are sold, they usually sell cooked chicken also. I don't know how the custom got started, but cooked chickens are sold by the pound, and roast ducks are sold by the duck, by halves or quarters. Possibly it was because the weight of a roast duck is pretty standard, but the size of a chicken can vary by several pounds. Squabs are also sold by the bird. They may also be bought cooked, but not every day. Sunday is the day when many more cooked items are prepared and sold, because that's when the Chinese people, many of whom work six days a week, come to Chinatown from near and far to do their shopping.

Do not hesitate to ask for and buy things in a Chinese grocery. The people who run them have not yet gotten so impersonal (like clerks in a supermarket) that they will not give you the time of day. So many grocery stores in Chinatown can survive because of the personal touch each store has, which attracts and holds a loyal clientele.

You'll like these Chinese grocery stores. I've briefly touched on them earlier, but you may be interested in a few more comments.

Most of these stores are employee or family owned, as many Chinese restaurants are. The workers in such stores form a loose corporation, with varying shares for whatever an employee may be able to afford or care to invest. Consequently, aside from the natural gregariousness of the Chinese, each man in the store has a stake in your goodwill. On that they stand or fall.

Many of these men are great cooks, by the way. All their meals are eaten at the store when they are working, and often a rotating system is used so no one is stuck with the job of being the one and only cook, as we housewives are. The system really has merit, because before the repertoire of one man runs out another man takes his place, as in a relay race. When his time comes around again, it may be another season, with different fresh vegetables available, and he has a whole new chance to prove his excellence again. I've often been asked to sit in on those grocery-store lunches and dinners. Out of politeness I usually refuse. But once in a while I succumb to mouth-watering temptation and eat with them. If you get to be a frequent customer in a Chinese grocery store, and if you show a genuine interest in Chinese cooking, the men may even give you their special Chinese recipes. I've gotten many good recipes that way.

Although the men take turns cooking, the one who cooks the meats for sale specializes in this job, and he is not rotated. It's his job, and he is good at it. He is not likely to give you his recipes—just as Macy's doesn't tell Gimbels. However, he will select the right piece of meat for you, the proper half or quarter of chicken or duck, and cut it into pieces to save you the chore. Since he made the cooked meats, he can select for you the leanest cut of roast pork, for example, because he knows that non-Chinese like their meat lean. The fattier pieces he'll save for a Chinese customer.

Don't be timid about asking for information in a Chinese grocery store. Of course you do need to use your common sense. If the store is crowded with customers, or if the man is about to wield his heavy Chinese cleaver (which can cut through a drumstick or a finger with equal ease), save your questions for a more appropriate time!

Party Dishes

At one point in writing this book, I intended to have a chapter on Chinese party dishes. Then I remembered the legend of the "Singing Rice." Whatever the dish you may make, if it is done perfectly, it is fit for kings—or your guests. I've gone to many Chinese banquets, and after the dazzle of the chef's tours-de-force has dimmed, I've concluded that many Chinese party dishes are everyday dishes dressed up for the occasion. In their dolled-up versions, they are transformed into something very special, and a new enjoyment and respect are given to the food, pretty much as a hard-working housewife is transformed into a butterfly in party finery! Start with the basic good dishes, dress them up with a pretty garnish, and take them to a party.

It also helps if you give a dish a party name when it goes to a party. Think of the time one spends choosing a proper name for a child. A dish you cook is also your creation and deserves a good name so that people will respect and remember it.

If a Chinese chef is equally good as a poet he may conjure up names for his creation that whet our imagination as well as our appetites. One frequently found ingredient in a Chinese menu is "Phoenix livers." I was puzzled by the use of the liver of this mythical bird, which is so beautifully written as a Chinese character 鳳 "fung." I was relearning Chinese writing at the time from a wonderful young man of eleven years, Herman Woo. To check if I'd recognized the word correctly, I showed him the item in a Chinese menu. He studied it a long moment and said to me very seriously, "Mr. Lee, this must be a very expensive dish because there are only a few phoenixes left in the world!" Of course, phoenix liver is just plain chicken liver, but doesn't the word "phoenix" conjure up a heavenly dish?

Chinese Desserts and Sweets

What do the Chinese have in the way of sweets? Not much. When we consider the wide variety of goodies available in the West, the traditional Chinese items that can be put into that category seem most limited.

Well, what are some Chinese confections? If you broaden the definition, there are endless varieties of items that the Chinese nibble on between meals, as we do candy or ice cream here. Most of them are based on preserved fruits with a licorice flavor. Others are just preserved with salt or sugar. In a Chinese grocery store there may be a dozen different kinds of preserved plums, olives, nuts, fruit skins, and ginger root which are sold as confections.

There is a paucity of desserts in the Chinese diet. This is due less to lack of invention than to philosophy. The Chinese believe that after a satisfying meal the memory of the foods themselves is the best of desserts. However, Chinese foods welcome almost any American dessert you care to serve with them.

Consistent Steps in Chinese Cooking

I asked my friend Lee Lum how he was trained as a chef and how he became so good at it. He smiled and said mischievously, "One doesn't have to be Chinese—but it helps!" Then he explained that he had learned the fundamentals—as many Chinese do—just by watching his mother cook. He also had the advantage of knowing what a certain dish should taste like when it was done well. But the most important thing he remembered from his training was that to cook well consistent and repeated practice is needed. The processes that are repeated in many recipes should be mastered so that they come automatically. Once learned, the repetitive actions become instinctive and free the cook for creative acts in front of the stove.

Whenever you are doing a chow or stir-fry dish, this sequence has to be consistently followed:

A. All the ingredients are cut, prepared, and ready to cook.
B. They are arranged in dishes or platters near the cooking pot, within convenient reach.
C. The sauces and seasoning should also be conveniently near.
D. Heat the wok or pan with the highest heat possible from your stove, until it is thoroughly dry and hot, then lower the heat to medium.
E. Add the oil, tip and turn the wok or pan until the oil has covered most of the cooking surface. This can also be done by using a scoop to spread the oil around.
F. Add the salt to the oil.
G. Add the garlic and ginger (if used) to the hot oil and stir quickly until they turn a golden brown. Watch carefully as the ginger and garlic burn very quickly.
(Some cooks prefer to scoop out the ginger and garlic, to be added again when the other ingredients are cooking.)
H. Raise the heat to high again and add the other ingredients.

This is the basic procedure. Follow it in order, because if the sequence is mixed up the food may stick to the pan or the flavor of the completed dish may not be at its peak.

Of course, once you've done all the steps up to the browning of the garlic and ginger, the process from then on will vary with the dish you are cooking. The items are added in sequence as outlined in each recipe.

I might add that these consistent steps are not limited only to the chow method of cooking. They are totally or partially applicable to all Chinese cooking. Once you've mastered these steps, you will know instinctively how to make variations.

Another good learning technique is to go into a restaurant for dinner and order your favorite dishes. Then do a scientific research job with pencil and paper to analyze how you think the dish was made. Discover what ingredients were put in it, in about what proportion. In short, take an "individual inventory" of the dish you are eating. Then, at the first opportunity, try it in your own kitchen. If the dish is worth it, repeat and adjust until you've really perfected the recipe. It may turn out to be better than you've ever had it before anywhere else, because you would have recreated this dish exactly to your taste.

How do the Chinese adjust the seasoning for individual tastes of a whole family? They don't. The cook seasons it to *his* taste and lets it go at that. But you may alter or change the seasoning as you wish. I recommend that you follow the recipes as written for the first try. Make mental notes when you eat the dish on how you should improve it next time. After dinner make penciled notes right in the book. The notes can be erased and new ideas or changes can be made until you've really perfected *your* recipe.

What to Do with Leftovers

Suppose you have seven trunkfuls of Chinese food left over. What could you do with it? Could it be frozen? Refrigerated? Reheated? To begin with, I doubt if you will ever be stuck with *that* much leftover food. A more likely situation is that your food is so good that you'll wish you had cooked more. But there will be times when you have cooked more than was eaten at one time, or you may even deliberately plan for leftovers. In

the latter case the leftovers should lend themselves to reheating without loss of flavor, or actually improve upon a second encounter. Briefly listed below are the categories of Chinese foods, with instructions for reheating:

Stir-Fried or "Chow" Dishes

This is the Humpty-Dumpty that all the king's horses and men cannot! Some dishes are meant to be eaten right away, like a soufflé, and therefore will never be as good again after that exact moment when they are at their best. Most stir-fried (chow) dishes fall into this classification. This is not to say that you cannot save and reheat leftover stir-fried Chinese food. It may still be very good—but never as good as it was. I have indicated such dishes by the injunction "serve at once" at the end of their recipes.

If you fry a chow dish again, the vegetables will all be overcooked and become mushy. The secret is to reheat at very low temperatures until it is hot again. It should not boil. Place the leftover food in a pan with cover. Turn heat to low. Stir occasionally to warm evenly. Serve when just hot enough.

325

Barbecued and Roast Meats and Fowls

This category of food presents no problem as leftovers, since they are as good cold as hot. I do not mean ice-cold; by cold I mean room temperature. Since all barbecued meats are made beforehand in Chinese restaurants, you cannot really get roast pork (page 93) or fire duck (page 185) "just as it comes from the oven." When such foods are served to the Chinese customers, the food is at room temperature. As a concession to American tastes, the chefs will pour a thin, hot gravy over the meat or fowl to make the food warm just before serving. In the case of barbecued spareribs (page 102) they may be separated into single ribs, placed on an oven-proof platter, with a few tablespoons of gravy or chicken stock poured on them to keep them from drying out, then placed under the broiler until the spareribs are piping hot. The "bone side" of the ribs should be up; otherwise the meat will shrink excessively and become too dry.

Leftover Meats and Fowls, Cooked Without Gravy

To reheat this type of food, whether it is Chinese (as soy sauce chicken, page 165) or American (such as roast fowls, ham, pork, or beef), the instructions below should be simple and foolproof. Always take the food out of the refrigerator beforehand so that the food will be at room temperature to speed the heating process.

Cut and arrange the meat or fowl on a serving platter. Take several layers of cheesecloth or use clean cloth napkins and soak them with chicken broth. Spread on top of meat on platter. Arrange broiler rack of the oven so that top of meat is at least 6 inches from the flame. Turn on broiler and heat for 5 to 10 minutes, depending on quantity and distance from heat. Check frequently. Ladle more chicken broth over cheesecloth or cloth napkins if they become too dry. The food should get piping hot in 10 minutes or less. Remove cloth or napkins. Garnish and serve.

An alternate method is to cover the meat with cheesecloth or napkins as in the method above. Heat in saucepan a can of chicken broth (or your own soup stock) to a vigorous boil. Pour boiling broth over the cloth-covered meat or fowl. Drain the cooled broth back into saucepan, heat to boiling again, and repeat process several times (3 or 4 times is usually enough). Remove covering, garnish and serve.

When pouring the broth back into the saucepan, spread your fingers over the cloth to prevent the food from slipping out and becoming disarranged. Don't pour too much broth onto the platter at a time, since most platters are shallow. Repeat the process more often if necessary.

Reheating Steamed Dishes

For steamed dishes, merely put back in pot and steam until hot again.

Leftovers, Unite!

I've heard several legends from the folklore of different nations in which a dying father called his sons together to give them an object lesson on why they should stick together. Usually the father handed each son an arrow and asked him to break it. This they did with ease. Then he took a quiverful of arrows and asked them to break them all at once, which they were not able to do. Moral: Make a delicious dish out of a handful of arrows?

I may have missed the point somewhere along in the story. However, there may be times when your leftovers are in such bits and pieces that they cannot stand alone. Put them together skillfully and you will have a delectable dish. Chinese cooking is eminently suited to use up leftovers, since ingredients are cut small, so that even scraps can look beautiful; and such a great variety of ingredients is used to cook many Chinese dishes that the small quantities of each left over can be an advantage.

Following are some suggestions on using up, singly or in combination, the leftovers that are not enough for a meal in themselves.

If you have a few slices of roast pork, chicken or a shrimp or two, dice them up and make the Egg Foo Yung recipe on page 99.

Or cook some rice and use the same leftover ingredients for the Young Jewel Fried Rice recipe on page 277.

Also, these few slices of leftover meats may be used as a topping for a Woh Mein dish (see pages 294 and 295).

I hope that these few suggestions will only indicate the endless possibilities of what can be done with leftovers. Your own experience and ingenuity will take over where my suggestions end.

And, Finally . . .

There is an old German proverb that says, "He who has choices has misery." I chose, then dropped, certain recipes as being too exotic for Western tastes. In the process I also dropped certain exotic seasonings and ingredients, because they would only be used in these recipes. There are, therefore, no recipes for jellyfish skins or sea slugs or sharks' fins in this book, all standard items in the Chinese cuisine, though not precisely everyday fare.

I cannot, either, pretend to have covered the entire range of Chinese cooking in this book. In self-defense, I must say that I doubt if anyone ever has, ever will, or ever can, so great is the variety of regional dishes, of ingredients, and of methods of cooking. But I have made a conscientious effort to include at least one or two recipes for every major category of Chinese cooking.

There may be other omissions in this book, intentional or unintended. If there are, I beg the reader's forgiveness. I can only say that I have done my best to make the recipes foolproof—or perhaps I should say novice-Chinese-cookproof.

"Hoh Sik! Joy Geen."—Eat well! Till we meet again.

好食再見

APPENDIX

Sources for Mail-Order Chinese Foodstuffs

If you live in or near a fairly large city, there may be one or more Chinese or Japanese stores where you can buy the special ingredients needed for Chinese cooking. Consult the classified pages of your telephone directory under "Groceries, Retail," if you live in the East. The remainder of the country, and Canada, lists these groceries under "Chinese Food."

Listed below are the names and addresses of groceries in some major cities. Many of them also carry a small line of cooking utensils.

See Sun Company
36 Harrison Avenue
Boston, Massachusetts

Wing Fat Company
33-35 Mott Street
New York, N.Y.

Mon Fong Wo Company
36 Pell Street
New York, N.Y.

Mee Wah Lung Company
608 H Street, N.W.
Washington, D.C.

Sam Wah Yick Kee
2146 Rockwell Avenue
Cleveland, Ohio

Min Sun Trading Company
2222 South LaSalle Street
Chicago, Illinois

Cheng Mee Company
712 Franklin Street
Houston, Texas

Wah Young Company
717 South King Street
Seattle, Washington

Gim Fat Company, Inc.   Kwong On Lung Co.
953 Grant Avenue   686 North Spring Street
San Francisco, California   Los Angeles, California 90012

The following stores will fill mail orders. When ordering Chinese foods by mail it is a good idea to copy or trace the Chinese characters for it in this book. While phonetic transcriptions vary widely, depending on the dialect, the written Chinese characters are universally understood by all Chinese, regardless of the differences in the spoken dialect.

The Gourmanderie
P.O. Box #5
New York, N.Y. 10034
   Chinese groceries and utensils.
   Catalogue on request

Kwong On Lung Co.
686 North Spring Street
Los Angeles, California 90012
   Chinese groceries and utensils.

INDEX

Abalone
    and Roast Pork Woh Mein, 294
    Three Sea-Fresh Treasures Soup, 265
    Young Jewel Woh Mein, 295
    see also Noodles with Pork and Tomatoes
Alcohol, used in cooking, 27
Almonds, Chicken with, 163
Amounts to cook, 6

Baak Choy
    Beef with Chinese Cabbage, 126
    Chicken Slices with Vegetables, 151
    Creamed, *see* Chinese cabbage, Creamed
    Diced Pork with Vegetables, 106
    hearts
        Bean Curd Chicken Soup, 175
        Stir-Fried Chicken and Vegetables, 176
        substitute for, 176
    Sirloin Steak Cubes, 135
    see also Chinese Cabbage; Chinese Mustard Greens Soup; Elegant Stir-Fried Vegetables
Ball-Shaped Cut (K'au), 42
Bamboo shoots, 36, 63
    Beef with String Beans, 124
    Foo Yung Eggs #2, 101
    pickled, 140
    Roast Pork Won Ton, 306
    substitute for, 173
Barbecue tongs, 15

Barbecue(d)
    Chicken, 156
    Chinese Roast Pork, 93
    Duck, Chinese, 185
    meats
        freezing, 93
        to reheat, 326
    Spareribs, 102
Barbecuing (Foh, Shiu, Guk), 11
    marinade for chicken, 157
    in oven, 94–96
    using charcoal grill or hibachi, 96–97
    using rotisserie, 96
Basic Congee, 285
Bass
    Sea, *see* Sea Bass
    striped, 195
Batter for deep-frying, 231
Bean curd, 36
    Chicken Soup, 175
    Sea Bass with, 209
    substitute for, 176
Bean sauce
    sweet (Hoi Sin Deung), 34–35
    yellow (Yuen Shaai She Deung), 35
Bean sprouts (nga choy), 60
    Beef with Fresh, 121
    Chicken Slices with Mushrooms, 154
    Foo Yung Eggs #1, 98
    how to grow, 60–62
    King Crab Lo Mein, 300
    Spiced Beef Chow Mein, 298
    Stir-Fried, 74

substitute for, 156, 278, 299
Velvet Chicken Stir-Fried
   Noodles, 302
Yee Foo Noodle Chow Mein, 310
Young Jewel Fried Rice, 277
Beans
   green, *see* Green beans
   string, see String beans
   see also Bean sprouts
Beef
   Beefsteak in Curry Sauce, 128
   with Chinese Cabbage, 126
   Chinese-Style Sirloin Steak, 119
   Chow Mein, Spiced, 297
   Congee, 285
   Five Fragrances, 141
   with Fresh Bean Sprouts, 121
   Ginger Steak with Peas, 133
   marinade for, 298–299
   Peking Style, Stewed Shin, 137
   with Pickled Bamboo, Steamed
      Chopped, 139
   to slice, 117–118, 120
   with Snow Peas, 129
   Steak with Oyster Sauce, 120
   with String Beans, 124
   Sirloin Steak Cubes, 135
   with Tomatoes and Green Pep-
      pers, 123
   with White Radish, 131
   see also Chicken Slices with
      Mushrooms; Noodles with
      Pork and Tomatoes; Pork
      with Bitter Melon; Pork and
      Pea Fluff, Roast; Pork with
      Pickled Greens or Sauer-
      kraut
Bitter melon, 63, 112
   Pork with, 111
Blanching, 64–65
   and low soup stock, 254–255
   stock for, 172
Bluefish, 195, 196
Boneless Pressed Duck, 189
Boning knife, 19
Broccoli
   Chinese, *see* Sweet Broccoli with
      Pork
   Jade-Green, 70
   in Oyster Sauce, Pork with, 88

with Pork, Sweet, 90
Broiling
   Pork Chops, Chinese Style, 88
Butterfish, 196, 200
Butterfly Shrimp, 233

Cabbage, Fried Sweet and Sour, 66
   see also Chinese cabbage
Cantonese Chow Mein, 297
Capon with Vegetable Stuffing,
   Roast, 169
Carp, 196
   with Chicken Fat, Live, 210
Carrots
   Pickled Sweet and Sour Vege-
      tables, 67
Carving knife, 19
Cashew Nuts, Chicken with, 165
Cauliflower
   Pickled Sweet and Sour Vege-
      tables, 67
Celery
   hearts
      Capon with Vegetable Stuffing,
         Roast, 169
   as substitute for
      baak choy, 107
      bean sprouts, 298
      Chinese vegetables, 156
Celery cabbage, 55, 58, 107, 176
   Bean Curd Chicken Soup, 175
   Beef with Chinese cabbage, 126
   Sirloin Steak Cubes, 135
   see also Baak Choy; Chinese Cab-
      bage; Diced Pork with Vege-
      tables; Elegant Stir-Fried
      Vegetables
Celestial Chicken, 158
Cha kwa, 35, 76
   Poached Sea Bass, 204
   substitute for, 122, 206
   see also Cucumber
Charcoal
   barbecuing with, 12, 96–97, 158
   grill
      Barbecued Spareribs on, 103
      duck roasted on, 185
Chicken
   with Almonds, 163
   Barbecued, 156

to bone, 147–148
broth, canned, 28
to buy, 144–146
Capon with Vegetable Stuffing, Roast, 169
Celestial, 158
  batter for deep-frying, 159
Chinese-Style Fried, 160
Deep-Fried Fluff, 152
defrosting frozen, 147
fat, to render, 65, 211
Fried Rice, 272
giblets, 171
  Bean Curd Chicken Soup, 175
hints for cutting, 174–175
leftover
  Chicken Slices with Vegetables, 151
livers
  Lobster with Phoenix Livers, 221
  and Scallops, 172
to poach, 151–152
Pure-Cut, 148
to refrigerate, 146–147
Slices with Mushrooms, 154
Slices with Vegetables, 151
Smooth, 167
soup
  Cucumber, Velvet, 263
  Subgum, 264
Soy-Sauce, 165
Sweet and Sour—Bones In, 178
and test for doneness, 157
Three Ways, 174
Triple Dragon, 114
Velvet, 167
  Stir-Fried Noodles, 302
and Vegetables, Stir-Fried, 176
Young Jewel Fried Rice, 277
Young Jewel Woh Mein, 295
see also King Crab Lo Mein; Pork with Bitter Melon; Pork with Pickled Greens or Sauerkraut; Roast Pork and Pea Fluff; Steamed Chopped Beef with Pickled Bamboo
Chili peppers, hot
  Pickled Sweet and Sour Vegetables, 67

Chinese
  Barbecued Duck, 185
  bitter melon, see Bitter melon
  broccoli, see Sweet Broccoli with Pork
  cabbage (baak choy), 58
    Beef with, 126
    Creamed, 77
    Diced Pork with Vegetables, 106
    Elegant Stir-Fried Vegetables, 80
    substitute for, 107, 156
    Triple Dragon, 114
    see also Baak Choy; Chinese Mustard Greens Soup; Velvet Chicken Cucumber Soup
  cleavers, 18–19
    chopping pork with, 86
  grocery stores, 319–320
  mushrooms, dried, 33
    see also Mushrooms
  Mustard Greens (Gai Choy), 59
    Pork with Pickled Greens, 91
    Soup, 261
    see also Lettuce-Fish Soup
  noodles, see Noodles (Chinese)
  parsley, 62–63
    as garnish, 107
    see also Diced Pork with Vegetables
  Roast (Barbecued) Pork, 93
  sausage(s)
    Rice with, 275
    substitutions for, 108
    see also Sausage
  white radishes, see White radishes
  winter melon, see Melon, winter
Chinese-Style Fried Chicken, 160
Chinese-Style Sirloin Steak, 119
Chon, wok, 15
Chop Suey Soup, 260
Chopping (p'eng), 45
Chopping block, 22
Chow (stir-frying), 7–8
  cooking
    to reheat, 325
    sequence of steps in, 323–324
  dishes, see Stir-Fried dishes

Chow Mein (Noodles), 289–290
  Spiced Beef, 297
Chunks
  cutting into (K'au), 42
  with Bones (Luk), 42–43
Clams
  with Red Sauce, Stir-Fried, 245
  Yee Foo Noodle Chow Mein, 310
  see also King Crab Lo Mein;
      Three Sea-Fresh Treasures
      Soup
Cleavers, Chinese, 18–19
Cod, 195, 196
Cold Rice Snack, 274
Congee (Jook), 283
  Basic, 285
  Beef, 285
Cooking
  Chinese
      methods of, 7–12
      sequence of steps in, 323–324
  oil, 24–25
  temperatures, judging, 16–17
  utensils, 12–22
  wine, 27
Coriander, 62, 63
Cornstarch, 29
Crab(s)
  Alaskan king, 239
  blue (blue-claw), 238–239
  Dungeness, 239
  Fried Soft-Shell, 244
  Lo Mein, King, 300
  shelling steamed, 241–242
  soft-shell, 240
  Steamed Blue-Claw, 240
Crabmeat
  Sauce for, 241
  see also Lobster in Jade and
      Pearls; Lobster with Phoenix
      Livers; Roast Pork Won Ton;
      Three Sea-Fresh Treasures
      Soup; Triple Dragon; Young
      Jewel Woh Mein
Creamed Chinese Cabbage, 77
Cucumber
  preserved (Chinese sweet), 35
  Soup, Velvet Chicken, 263
  see also Cha kwa

Curry Sauce
  Beefsteak with, 128
  for seafood, 236
Cut, harmony of, 38, 41, 154, 163
Cutting
  board, 22
  methods of, 38–45

Deep-fried dishes
  batter for, 153, 231
  Boneless Pressed Duck, 189
  Celestial Chicken, 158
  Chinese-Style Fried Chicken, 160
  Deep-Fried Fluff Chicken, 152
  Fish Balls and Fish Cakes, 207
  Puff Shrimp, 230
  Sea Bass with Garlic and Soy-
      bean Sauce, 198
  secret of crust, 152
  Soft-Shell Crabs, 244
  Sweet and Sour Fish, 201
  Won tons, 304, 308
Deep-frying (Jah Yau), 8
  batter for, 153, 231
  hazards of, 51
  judging temperature for, 16
  oil for, 25
  thermometer for, 15–16
Desserts
  Chinese, 322
  peaches, pickled, 69
Diced Fluff Duck or Squab, 188
Diced Pork with Vegetables, 106
Dicing (Ting), 43
Domino cut, 44
"Dop mah," 37–38
Dried Chinese mushrooms, 33
  see also Mushrooms
Dry-Cooked Shrimp, 236
Duck
  Boneless Pressed, 189
  to buy, 182
  Chinese Barbecued, 185
  Chinese Style, Roast, 182
  Diced Fluff, 188
  eggs, preserved, 108
  Fire, 185
  "Peking," 181
  preserved, *see* Rice with Chinese
      Sausages

to thaw frozen, 182
"duck sauce," *see* Plum sauce

Egg(s)
  Crabmeat in Scrambled, 242
  Foo Yung #1, 98
  Foo Yung #2, 101
  Fried Rice, 272
  with Pork and Sausages,
    Steamed, 107
  Soup
    Egg-Drop, 257
    Tomato Egg-Drop, 258
    Watercress, 255
  Young Jewel Fried Rice, 277
Electric stove, *see* Stove
Elegant Stir-Fried Vegetables, 80

Fat, to render chicken, 211
Fire Duck, 185
Fish
  balls, 206
    preparing, 207
    with White Radishes, 206
    see also Three Sea-Fresh Treas-
      ures Soup
  to buy, 195–197
  cakes, 206
    preparing, 207
  to clean, 197
  fillet(s), 195–196, 203
    to poach, 205
    see also Beef Congee; Pork
      with Pickled Greens or
      Sauerkraut; Three Sea-Fresh
      Treasures Soup; Yee Foo
      Noodle Chow Mein
  Poached Sea Bass, 204
  removing fishy taste and smell,
    194–195
  to serve steamed, 200–201
  Soup
    Lettuce-, 256
    Sour-Green, 257
  Steamed, 200
  Sweet and Sour, 201
  tests for doneness, 197–198,
    205
  see also King Crab Lo Mein *and*
    under names of fish
Five Fragrances Beef, 141

Flavors, five, 4, 23
Flounder, 196, 200
Flour, water-chestnut, 190, 191
"Fluff method" of cooking, 188
Fon Sz, 312
  see also Spiced Beef Chow Mein;
    King Crab Lo Mein; Yee Foo
    Noodle Chow Mein
Foo Yung Eggs
  #1, 98
  #2, 101
Food cooked in rice (Guk May),
  10–11
Food, how much to cook, 51
Fragrances, five, 4
  powder, 32, 162
  spices, 33
    Boneless Pressed Duck, 189
    Chinese-Style Fried Chicken,
      160
Freezer
  pork stored in, 85
  and shrimp, 225
French knife, 20
Fried
  Pork Chops, Chinese Style, 86
  Rice
    with Choice of Flavors, 272
    Young Jewel, 277
  Soft-Shell Crabs, 244
  Sweet and Sour Cabbage, 66

Gai choy, *see* Mustard Greens, Chi-
  nese
Game birds, *see* Chinese-Style Fried
  Chicken
Garlic, 26
  Sauce
    Periwinkles (Sea Snails) in,
      247
    Sea Bass with, and Soybean,
      198
    Spareribs with, 103
  to peel and mince, 27
Gas stove, *see* Stove
Gherkins, sweet, 76
  and cha kwa, 35, 122
Giblets, 171
  see also Chicken giblets; Chicken
    livers

Ginger root
  storing fresh, 30–32
  using, 133
Ginger Steak with Peas, 133
Gravy(ies)
  for Foo Yung Eggs #1, 100
  to thicken, 180
Green beans
  King Crab Lo Mein, 300
  see also Lobster with Phoenix
    Livers; String beans
Green pepper(s)
  Beef with Tomatoes and, 123
  Pickled Sweet and Sour Vegeta-
    bles, 67
Grill, outdoor, 12
  and chicken, 158
  duck roasted on, 185
Grocery stores, Chinese, 319–320

Halibut, 195, 196
Ham
  Celestial Chicken, 158
  fresh, 84–85
  Fried Rice, 273
  Smithfield, *see* Creamed Chinese
    Cabbage
  see also Noodles with Pork and
    Tomatoes; Roast Pork and
    Pea Fluff; Stewed Shin Beef,
    Peking Style; Stir-Fried
    String Beans
Hibachi stove, using, 96–97
"High chicken," 145
High Soup Stock, 253
Hok, wok, 15
Homemade Noodles and Won Ton
    Wraps, 314
Honing stones, 20–21

Jade-Green Broccoli, 70
Jook, *see* Congee

Kale, *see* Sautéed Spinach
King Crab Lo Mein, 300
King crab meat, *see* Crabmeat
Knives, 17–18
  care of, 20–21
  types of, 18–20

Leeks, substitute for, 167
Leftovers
  reheating, 325–327
  using, 324–325, 327–328
  see also Abalone and Roast Pork
    Woh Mein; Stewed Shin
    Beef, Peking Style
Lettuce
  -Fish Soup, 256
  Vermicelli with Dried Shrimps,
    313
  see also Velvet Chicken Cucum-
    ber Soup
Live Carp with Chicken Fat, 210
Lobster
  to buy, 213–215
  Cantonese, 217
  in Jade and Pearls, 222
  meat, frozen, 215–216
  with Phoenix Livers, 221
  removing from shell, 215
  Steamed, 220
  storing cut-up, 216
  substitute for, 222
  tails, frozen, 215–216
  Three Sea-Fresh Treasures Soup,
    265
  Triple Dragon, 114
  see also Roast Pork Won Ton;
    Spiced Beef Chow Mein; Yee
    Foo Noodle Chow Mein
Lo Mein (Noodles), 290
Low Soup Stock, 254

Marinade
  for Barbecued Spareribs, 102
  for barbecuing, 94, 157
  for beef, 119–120, 128, 132
  for Spiced Beef Chow Mein, 298
Marketing, 5
Meal planning, 4–6
  and organization, 37–38
Meat(s)
  to cut, 40–41, 117–118
  as garnish, 71
  hints for slicing, 148
  leftover, *see* Beef Congee; Young
    Jewel Fried Rice
  reheating, 326–327
  yield per pound, 118

see also Beef; Ham; Pork; Steak;
  Poultry
Melon
  Chinese bitter, *see* Bitter melon
  Chinese winter, *see* Winter
    melon
Monosodium glutamate, 25–26
Mushrooms
  Chicken Slices with, 154
  dried Chinese, 33
    Elegant Stir-Fried Vegetables,
      80
    substitute for, 107
Mustard greens, *see* Sautéed Spin-
    ach
Mustard Greens, Chinese (Gai
    Choy), 59
  pickled, 91
  Soup, 261
  see also Lettuce-Fish Soup

Noble Yee, Favorite Noodles of, 308
Noodle(s)
  Abalone and Roast Pork Woh
    Mein, 294
  Base, Yee Foo, 309
  Chow Mein, 289–290
    Yee Foo, 310
  to deep fry, 291, 299, 309
  double boiled, 291
  freezing, 288
  fried, 289–290, 291
  Homemade, 314
  King Crab Lo Mein, 310
  Lo Mein, 290
  with Pork and Tomatoes, 292
  to precook, 289
    quantities for, 291–292
  Spiced Beef Chow Mein, 297
  stir-fried, 290
  test for doneness, 292
  Velvet Chicken Stir-Fried, 302
  Voy Mein, 291
  Woh Mein, 291
  Yee Foo Mein, 291
  Young Jewel Woh Mein, 295

Oil
  deep-frying in, 51
  peanut, 25
  vegetable, 24

Omelets
  Foo Yung Eggs #1, 98
  Foo Yung Eggs #2, 101
  see also Fried Rice
Oyster(s), *see* Beef Congee; Three
    Sea-Fresh Treasures Soup
Oyster sauce, 32
  Pork with Broccoli in, 88
  Steak with, 120
  Triple Dragon, 114
  see also Jade-Green Broccoli;
    Roast Pork and Pea Fluff

Parsley, Chinese, *see* Chinese pars-
    ley
Party dishes, 321
Peaches, to pickle, 69
Peanut oil, 25
Peas
  Diced Fluff Duck, 188
  frozen petite
    Diced Pork with Vegetables,
      106
    Ginger Steak with, 133
    Lobster in Jade and Pearls, 222
    Roast Pork and Pea Fluff, 97
    snow, *see* Snow peas
"Peking Duck," 181
Periwinkles in Garlic Sauce, 247
Phoenix Emperor Chicken, *see*
    Celestial Chicken
Phoenix liver, 321
Pickerel, 195
  see also Yellow pike
Pickled
  Greens, Pork with, 91
  Sweet and Sour Vegetables, 67
  vegetables
    substitutes for, 180
    see also Sweet and Sour
      Chicken—Bones In
Pike, yellow, *see* Yellow pike
Pineapple, canned
  Sweet and Sour Sauce, 110
Plum sauce, 35
Poached Sea Bass, 204
Pompano, 196, 200
Porgy, 196, 200, 204
Pork, 83–84
  with Bitter Melon, 111

with Broccoli in Oyster Sauce, 88
Chinese Mustard Greens Soup, 261
Chinese Roast (Barbecued), 93
chopped, 86
Chops, 85
    Chinese Style, Fried, 86
Chop Suey Soup, 260
cuts to buy, 84–85
doneness, testing for, 96, 103
Foo Yung Eggs #1, 98
Foo Yung Eggs #2, 101
Fried Rice, 273
High Soup Stock, 253
loin, 85
and Pea Fluff, Roast, 97
with Pickled Greens or Sauer-kraut, 91
roast
    freezing, 93
    see also Beef Congee
and Sausages, Steamed Eggs with, 107
shoulder, 85
Spareribs
    Barbecued, 102
    with Garlic Sauce, 103
storing, 85
Sweet and Pungent, 109
Sweet and Sour, 109
Sweet Broccoli with, 90
and Tomatoes, Noodles with, 292
Triple Dragon, 114
with Vegetables, Diced, 106
Winter Melon Soup, 258
Woh Mein, Abalone and Roast, 294
Won Ton, Roast, 306
Won ton filling, 304
Young Jewel Fried Rice, 277
Young Jewel Woh Mein, 295
    see also Chicken Slices with Mushrooms; King Crab Lo Mein; Stir-Fried String Beans
Preparation, meal, 37–38
Preserved Cucumber, 35
    see also Cha kwa
Puff Shrimp, 230

Pure-Cut Chicken, 148

Radish(es), White
    Beef with, 131
    see also White radishes
Recipes
    grouping of ingredients, 49–51
    how to use, 51–52
Red Cooking (Tung Woh), 10
    Five Fragrances Beef, 141
    Stewed Shin Beef, Peking Style, 137
Red Sauce—with Ketchup, 236
    for Stir-Fried Clams, 245
Red Searing (Tung Shiu), 10
    Sweet and Sour Chicken—Bones In, 178
Red Snapper, 196
Reheating, *see* Leftovers, reheating
Rice
    amount to cook, 6, 24
    with Chinese Sausages, 275
    crust, 269
        for Singing Rice Dishes, 281–282
    as filler, 5–6
    food cooked in, 10–11
    Fried, with Choice of Flavors, 272
    to keep warm, 271
    leftover, 268–269
    Plain Boiled, 270
    to reheat, 269
    Snack, Cold, 274
    storing cooked, 274
    Young Jewel Fried, 277
    see also Congee
Roast
    Capon with Vegetable Stuffing, 169
    Duck, Chinese Style, 182
    Pork and Pea Fluff, 97
    Pork Won Ton, 306
    see also Roasting
Roasting (Foh, Shiu, Guk), 11
    Capon with Vegetable Stuffing, 169
    Fire Duck, 185
Rock Cornish hens, *see* Chinese-Style Fried Chicken

Rock sugar, 165–166
Rotisserie
  barbecuing on, 96, 103, 158
  duck roasted in, 184–185

Saccharin, using, 69
Salt, Spiced, 162
Salt Dip, for chicken, 150
Sauce(s)
  for Crabmeat, 241
  curry, 236
  Garlic
    Periwinkles (Sea Snails) in, 247
    and Soybean, for Sea Bass, 198
    Spareribs with, 103
  Red
    —with Ketchup (for seafood), 236
    for Stir-Fried Clams, 245
    see also Yee Foo Noodle Chow Mein
  Soy, 30, 246
  Sweet and Sour, 110
    for fish, 201
  to thicken, 180
Sauerkraut, Pork with, 91
Sausages
  Eggs with Pork and, Steamed, 107
  Rice with Chinese, 275
  see also Chinese Sausage
Sautéed (dishes)
  Sea Bass with Bean Curd, 209
  Spinach, 65
Sautéing (Poh Yau), 8
  temperature for, 17
Scallions, 28–29
  to cut, 76
Scallops, Chicken Livers and Sea, 172
Sea Bass, 195, 196
  with Bean Curd, 209
  with Garlic and Soybean Sauce, 198
  Poached, 204
  Sweet and Sour Fish, 201
Sea cucumbers, see Three Sea-Fresh Treasures Soup

Sea Scallops, Chicken Livers and, 172
Sea Snails in Garlic Sauce, 247
Seafood, 193–250, 299–300
  Fried Rice, 273
  Three Sea-Fresh Treasures Soup, 265
  see also Chicken Slices with Mushrooms; Pork with Bitter Melon; and under names of shellfish
Sesame oil, 34
  and fishy smell, 194
Shark's maw, see Three Sea-Fresh Treasures Soup
Shellfish, see Noodles with Pork and Tomatoes; Seafood
Sherry, 27
Shredding (Sz), 44
Shrimp(s)
  Butterfly, 233
  to buy, 224–227
  Dried, Vermicelli with, 313
  Dry-Cooked, 236
  in fish balls, 207
  Foo Yung Eggs #2, 101
  Fried Rice, 272
  with Hoi Sin Sauce, 232
  with Lobster Sauce, 219
  precooking, 230
  Puff, 230
  to shell and devein, 227–228
  sizes of, 226–227
  Soup
    Chop Suey, 260
    Subgum, 264
    Three Sea-Fresh Treasures, 265
  won ton filling, 304
  Young Jewel Fried Rice, 277
  Young Jewel Woh Mein, 295
  see also Abalone and Roast Pork Woh Mein; Beef Congee; Foo Yung Eggs #1; King Crab Lo Mein; Pork with Pickled Greens or Sauerkraut; Roast Pork Won Ton; Spiced Beef Chow Mein; Triple Dragon; Yee Foo Noodle Chow Mein

Simmered dishes
  Abalone and Roast Pork Woh Mein, 294
  Pure-Cut Chicken, 148
  Soy-Sauce Chicken, 165
Simmering (Loh May), 9
Singing Rice, *see* Beef with Tomatoes and Green Peppers; Chicken with Almonds; Chop Suey Soup; Diced Pork with Almonds
"Singing Rice," legend of, 279–281
Sirloin Steak Cubes, 135
Slicing (P'in), 44
Smithfield ham, *see* Creamed Chinese Cabbage
Smooth Chicken, 167
Snack, Cold Rice, 274
Snails in Garlic Sauce, Sea, 247
Snow peas, 59
  Beef with, 129
  Celestial Chicken, 158
  Chicken Livers and Scallops, 172
  Chicken Velvet Stir-Fried Noodles, 302
  Elegant Stir-Fried Vegetables, 80
  Lobster with Phoenix Livers, 221
  Sirloin Steak Cubes, 135
  Spiced Beef Chow Mein, 298
  substitute for, 160, 176, 222, 299
  Triple Dragon, 114
  see also Ginger Steak with Peas; Lobster in Jade and Pearls; Young Jewel Woh Mein
Soft-Shell Crabs, Fried, 244
Sole, 196
Soong dishes, 97, 106
  Diced Fluff Duck or Squab, 188
Soup(s)
  Bean Curd Chicken, 175
  Chop Suey, 260
  Egg-Drop, 257
  Lettuce-Fish, 256
  Sour-Green Fish, 257
  stock, *see* Soup stock
  Subgum, 264
  Three Sea-Fresh Treasures, 265
  Tomato Egg-Drop, 258
  Velvet Chicken Cucumber, 263
  Watercress, 255

Winter Melon, 258
  Won Ton, 303
Soup stock
  chicken broth, using canned, 253
  High, 252
  Low, 252
Soy sauce, 30, 246
Soy-Sauce Chicken, 165
Soybeans, salted cured, 34
Spiced Beef Chow Mein, 297
Spiced Salt, 162
Spices, five fragrances, 141
Spinach
  Celestial Chicken, 158
  Sautéed, 65
Squab, Diced Fluff, 188
Squash
  Tender-Fried Zucchini, 73
Squid, *see* Three Sea-Fresh Treasures Soup
Steak(s)
  Beef Congee, 285
  Beefsteak in Curry Sauce, 128
  Chinese-Style Sirloin, 119
  marinade for, 121
  with Oyster Sauce, 120
  with Peas, Ginger, 133
Steamed (dishes)
  Blue-Claw Crabs, 240
  Chopped Beef with Pickled Bamboo, 139
  Eggs with Pork and Sausages, 107
  Fish, 200
  Lobster, 220
Steamer, improvising, 9
Steaming (Ching Ngaau), 9–10
Stewed Shin Beef, Peking Style, 137
Stir-Fried (dishes)
  Bean Sprouts, 74
  and beef, 118–119
  Beef
    with Chinese Cabbage, 126
    Chow Mein, Spiced, 297
    with Fresh Bean Sprouts, 121
    with Snow Peas, 129
    with String Beans, 124

with Tomatoes and Green Peppers, 123
with White Radishes, 129
Beefsteak in Curry Sauce, 128
Broccoli
   Jade-Green, 70
   with Pork, Sweet, 90
Chicken
   with Almonds, 163
   Livers and Scallops, 172
   Slices with Mushrooms, 154
   Slices with Vegetables, 151
   and Vegetables, 176
Chinese Cabbage, Creamed, 77
Clams with Red Sauce, 245
Crabmeat in Scrambled Eggs, 242
Diced Fluff Duck or Squab, 188
Fish Balls with White Radishes, 206
Ginger Steak with Peas, 133
Lobster
   Cantonese, 217
   in Jade and Pearls, 222
   with Phoenix Livers, 221
King Crab Lo Mein, 300
Noodles
   Chicken Velvet, 302
   with Pork and Tomatoes, 292
Periwinkles (Sea Snails) in Garlic Sauce, 247
Pork
   with Bitter Melon, 111
   with Broccoli in Oyster Sauce, 88
   and Pea Fluff, Roast, 98
   with Pickled Greens or Sauerkraut, 91
   with Vegetables, Diced, 106
Shrimp with Hoi Sin Sauce, 232
Sirloin Steak Cubes, 135
Spinach, Sautéed, 65
Steak with Oyster Sauce, 120
String Beans, 72
Sweet and Sour Cabbage, Fried, 66
Tomatoes, 79
Triple Dragon, 114
Vegetables, Elegant, 80
Yee Foo Noodle Chow Mein, 310

Young Jewel Fried Rice, 277
Zucchini, Tender-Fried, 72
Stir-frying (Chow), 7–8, 38
   advantages of, 54
   on electric stoves, 11–12
   implements for, 13–15
   judging temperatures for, 16–17
Stock, Soup
   chicken broth, using canned, 253
   High, 252
   Low, 252
Stores, visiting Chinese, 319–320
Stove, and Chinese cooking, 11–12
   and blanching for, 64
String Beans
   Beef with, 124
   Chicken Livers and Scallops, 172
   Chicken Slices with Mushrooms, 154
   Foo Yung Eggs #2, 101
   Stir-Fried, 72
   see also Celestial Chicken; Green Beans
Stuffing, vegetable (for capon), 170–171
Subgum Soup, 264
Sugar, 27–28
   rock, 165–166
Sunfish, 200
Sweet and Sour
   Cabbage, Fried, 66
   Chicken—Bones In, 178
   Fish, 201
   Pork, 109
   Vegetables, Pickled, 67
Sweet bean sauce, 34
Sweet Broccoli with Pork, 90
Sweet gherkins, 76

Temperatures, how to judge in cooking, 16–17
Tender-Fried Zucchini, 73
Thermometer, deep-frying, 15–16
Three Sea-Fresh Treasures Soup, 265
Tomato(es)
   Egg-Drop Soup and, 258
   and Green Peppers, Beef with, 123

Noodles with Pork and, 292
Stir-Fried, 79
Triple Dragon, 114
Trout, 200
Turnips, *see* Beef with White Radish
Turnip greens, *see* Sautéed Spinach

Utensils, Chinese cooking, 12–22

Vegetable(s), 65–82
Chicken Slices with, 151
Diced Pork with, 106
Elegant Stir-Fried, 80
marinated, 110–111
methods of cooking, 54, 64–65
Pickled Sweet and Sour, 67
special Chinese, 55–63
Stir-Fried Chicken and, 176
storage of, 63–64
Stuffing, Roast Capon with, 169
see also Sweet and Sour Chicken
—Bones In *and under name of vegetable*
Vegetable oil, 24
Vegetarian dishes, 80
Velvet Chicken, 167
Cucumber Soup, 263
Stir-Fried Noodles, 302
Vermicelli, 312
with Dried Shrimps, 313
Vinegar, 28
Voy Mein (Noodles), 291

Walnuts, Chicken with, 165
Water chestnut(s), 36, 63
flour, 190, 191

Watercress Soup, 255
Watermelon rind, as substitute for winter melon, 59, 260
White radish(es)
Beef with, 131
Fish Balls with, 206
Pickled Sweet and Sour Vegetables 67
Wine, cooking, 27
Winter melon
Soup, 258
substitute for, 59, 260
Woh Mein (Noodles), 291
Wok, use of, 12, 13–15
Wok chon, 15
Won Ton(s)
to cook, 306
deep frying, 304, 308
filling for, 304
Soup, 303
wrapping, 305–306
Wraps, 314
to make, 314–316

Yee Foo Mein (Noodles), 291
Yee Foo Noodle Base, 309
Yee Foo Noodle Chow Mein, 310
Yellow pike, 195
fillets, 203
see also Spiced Beef Chow Mein
Fish Balls or Fish Cakes, 206
Lettuce-Fish Soup, 256
Young Jewel
Fried Rice, 277
Woh Mein, 295

Zucchini, Tender-Fried, 73